EXPERIMENT IN DEPTH

EXPERIMENT IN DEPTH

A Study of the Work
of Jung, Eliot and Toynbee

by

P. W. MARTIN

ROUTLEDGE & KEGAN PAUL
Boston, London and Henley

First published in 1955
and first published as a paperback 1976
Reprinted 1978
by Routledge & Kegan Paul Ltd
9 Park Street,
Boston, Mass. 02108, USA,
39 Store Street
London WC1E 7DD and
Reading Road,
Henley-on-Thames,
Oxon RG9 1EN
Printed and Bound in the USA by the Vail-Ballou Press

ISBN 0 7100 8393 9

FOREWORD

THE experiment in depth set out in the ensuing pages derives mainly from the work of three men: C. G. Jung, the psychologist; T. S. Eliot, the poet; and A. J. Toynbee, the historian. Each of them, in his own way, has employed what Eliot once termed the 'mythical method'—the exploration of those symbols, visions, *idées-forces* which, acting powerfully from the unconscious depths, enable men and communities to find new energies, new values and new aims. In the present age the mythical method has been used chiefly by the totalitarian ideologies, for purposes of domination and power. The question examined here is whether and how it can be used to better purpose.

Central to this question is what Toynbee, in *A Study of History*, calls the withdrawal-and-return. His hypothesis is that, when a civilization comes to a 'time of troubles', such as we are now in, individuals here and there turn from the outer world of political and social chaos to the inner world of the psyche; there come upon the vision of a new way of life; and, returning to the outer world, form the nucleus of a 'creative minority' through which that civilization may find renewal.

Toynbee derives this hypothesis from his reading of universal history. At the same time as he was assembling the comprehensive data on which it is based, Jung, in complete independence, was working out the psychological means by which the withdrawal-and-return can be made. And while Jung and Toynbee were thus approaching the problem from opposite ends—Jung from the depths of the individual psyche, Toynbee from a case-study of all the civilizations of which we have record—Eliot was personally making the experiment and expressing it in the greatest poetry of the age.

The point at which these three approaches meet is in the direct realization of what Toynbee calls a 'different spiritual dimension' interpenetrating life. The purpose here is, as far as possible, to

FOREWORD

communicate what it is these men have found; to describe the techniques worked out by Jung in this field; to devise methods for
making these techniques more generally available; and to consider
how they can be brought to bear upon the world situation at the
present time.

In seeking to do this I have had to cover far more specialist
territory than any one man can reasonably cope with. Anthropology,
religion, philosophy, history, psychology, politics are all inevitably
involved. I have done what I can with the means at my disposal,
but they are altogether inadequate to the task. Accordingly, I should
like, if I may, to make acknowledgement not only to those great
spirits and intellects whose work is here brought together, but also
to those into whose fields of competence I am driven, for their
charity and forbearance in trying to understand and re-phrase
correctly what I am attempting to say.

Acknowledgement is made to Mr. T. S. Eliot, O.M., and Messrs.
Faber & Faber, Ltd., for extracts from his poems; Messrs. J. M
Dent & Sons, Ltd., for an extract from W. H. Hudson's *Green
Mansions*; The Hogarth Press, Ltd., for an extract from the poems
of R. M. Rilke, translated by J. B. Leishman; Mrs. J. E. Flecker,
Messrs. William Heinemann, Ltd., and Messrs. A. A. Knopf, Inc.,
for an extract from J. E. Flecker's *Hassan*; John Farquharson, on
behalf of the Estate of the late William James, for an extract from
The Varieties of Religious Experience; Jonathan Cape, Ltd., and the
Trustees of the T. E. Lawrence Estate for an extract from *Seven
Pillars of Wisdom*.

P. W. M.

CONTENTS

Part One

THE APPROACH

I

THE LIVING MYTH

YTH' is a word in process of enlargement. The *Concise Oxford Dictionary* defines it as: 'A purely fictitious narrative usually involving supernatural persons, actions or events, and embodying some popular idea concerning natural or historical phenomena.' This coincides with ordinary usage. Jove hurling thunderbolts from Olympus, the lost continent of Atlantis, Father Christmas, the Great Sea Serpent, are all 'myths'. But, already, even in these random examples, there are undertones and overtones showing the direction in which the enlargement is taking place. Jove hurling thunderbolts has become wholly fabulous. He wakes no echoes in our souls. The lost continent of Atlantis is somewhat different. We look on it sceptically perhaps . . . but, if it were true, it would be very interesting. Father Christmas is pure invention, yet millions of people bring up their children on it; and, moreover, feel it so important that they will go to considerable trouble and expense to enact the myth themselves. Questioned on this strange behaviour they will say that in some way it represents the 'spirit of Christmas'. As for the Great Sea Serpent, it is of course a sailor's yarn; but nevertheless there are strange things in the sea. Five miles down, on the sea bottom, there may be extraordinary creatures totally unknown to man, a form of life unguessed at. And when a Loch Ness Monster rears its head, everyone is agog. Why? Because, as we would say, the imagination is moved. And when a hysterical little man with a comic moustache starts talking of blood and soil, of living space, of a mystical unity, *Ein Reich, ein Volk, ein Führer*, the imagination is again moved; and so moved as to change the whole course of history. The myth itself may be a 'purely fictitious narrative'. But the living myth is a force.

The present age is dominated by a particular kind of living myth the so-called ideologies. It is because of this that the word myth is

3

changing under our eyes. We are being compelled to recognize that certain symbols, certain ideas, certain images, have tremendous effect. As dictator after dictator has conclusively demonstrated, the secret of success is to have the right myth at the right moment. With the right myth a man can mould entire peoples to his will. Not that this power of the imagination is a new phenomenon. Every anthropologist knows that among primitive peoples the mythical beliefs are immensely potent. By their means men can be roused to effort, worked into a frenzy, nerved to endure. Fired by their myths they may ravage a whole countryside. Deprived of their myths a people may lose all interest in life and die out. 'Manners makyth man', but it is the myth that moves him.

Nor is it only among undeveloped peoples that a parallel to the ideologies is found. The religions of the world are such living myths. This does not mean that they are 'mythical' in the ordinary sense. The living myth may also be the living truth. But religions have this strange emotive power, working upon individuals and communities, changing their whole way of life.

In the course of the last three hundred years a great new force has come into operation, profoundly affecting the living myth. This force is science. Its influence upon religions and upon ideologies has been fundamental, and fundamentally different. Upon religious beliefs the effect has been caustic. It has undermined, cast ridicule upon, 'debunked', most of the dogma of most of the religions: with the consequence that mankind to a great and increasing extent is now cut off from that means of approach to the living myth. Upon the totalitarian ideologies the effect has been wholly different. Science has immensely increased the possibilities of power—productive power, destructive power, administrative power, power of propaganda, power over others generally. On this the ideologies have flourished. Use the living myth to grasp power, use power to spread the living myth, is the short formula for world dictatorship. And in the ideologies the caustic power of science, so deadly to religion, is quickly dealt with. Dictators write their own science.

As a consequence, at the present time we have a world in which the living myth comes to men very little by way of religion, very much by way of ideologies. From this it results that the peoples whose culture and civilization were originally based upon religion find themselves, in a fashion, cut off from their roots, uncertain, undecided, unsure of themselves and of life. Against them are arrayed fanatical faiths, which to them seem madness or worse, but in which the living myth unquestionably moves. Hesitating between these two ways of life are the great illiterate masses of the world, now moving into the maelstrom of a technological age. To which side their allegiance is likely to go still remains an open question. But this much is certain. Men need the living myth as surely as they need bread. Bread sustains life, but the myth gives life point. Totalitarianism offers both.

Such is the human situation in this mid-twentieth century. In some strange way science, the free search for truth, seems to have betrayed both us and itself. To all appearance, it is helping those who would suppress it. There is, however, another possibility. Perhaps it is not science that has betrayed us but we who have betrayed science. And this, on the whole, seems the likelier hypothesis. So far we have pursued the easy side of science, the side that can be readily 'proved', the side that yields quick results in profit and power, the side giving that comfortable feeling of certainty. The difficult side, the side that does not lend itself to conclusive demonstration, the side that punctures our vanities and does not directly advance our fortunes, the science of man as a spiritual being, this we have not pursued with anything approaching the same ardour. Only now is it beginning to be developed. Particularly is this true of all enquiry into the depths of the human psyche. There we are still in the stage of partisan beliefs. And because of this lack of balance, because we know a great deal about atomic fission but next to nothing about human integration, we are paying the penalty of one-sided development: disruption.

The psychology of the unconscious

Nevertheless, we have not remained completely stationary on the human side. Depth psychology, the psychology of the unconscious, in the course of the last half century has opened up new frontiers of the mind. The first major discovery was made in 1898 when Freud and Breuer demonstrated a novel method of psychological therapy. By getting a mentally sick woman to say freely everything that came into her head, and going thoroughly into the underlying material thus brought to the surface, a neurosis was cured. Since then, this method of free association, the 'talking cure' as the patient herself called it, has come to be recognized as one of the gateways to the unconscious. Another gateway, developed by Freud almost at the same time, was dream analysis: the art and science of penetrating beneath the surface of dreams and detecting the psychological forces at work in the unconscious depths.

Subsequent exploration of this twofold approach has led to certain broad conclusions on which most depth psychologists would probably agree. There seems good reason to believe that everyone in the course of his personal life accumulates a kind of psychological rubbish heap—experiences that were too much for him, issues he dared not face, events, fantasies he felt incompatible with his idea of himself, things contrary to the *mores* of the society in which he had been formed. All these and more fall into the chasm the other side of consciousness; not to be lost there but in secret ways to act back on the man, sometimes with catastrophic force.

Behind this 'personal unconscious', which each of us accumulates in the course of his lifetime, there is what might be called a 'deep unconscious' substantially similar in all people, from which come— among other things—the fundamental drives we share with the animals: self-preservation, the sex urge, the will-to-power, the herd feeling and others. In the human being these instinctual drives encounter no less powerful moral and spiritual forces. The nature and origin of these moral and spiritual forces is a subject of dispute. But on the essential outcome there is substantial agreement. Man is a creature torn between opposites, everlastingly caught in some insoluble problem, propelled to and fro, forward and back, by currents lying far below the surface of consciousness.

Of the three pioneers in the exploration of this new world— Sigmund Freud, Alfred Adler, C. G. Jung—two came to hold specific theories as to the nature of the drives originating in the deep unconscious. Freud saw sex as primal, and based his analyses and interpretations largely upon this belief. Adler gave primacy to the will-to-power, the desire everyone experiences to feel himself somebody, to make good, to be a success, and, openly or surreptitiously, to dominate others. But however different their theories of causation, the basic method of therapy adopted by this new school of depth psychology was substantially the same. It consisted essentially in discovering what was worrying the patient—to this end using the free association method, dream analysis, or any other means in-genuity suggested—and tracing this worry back to its roots: more immediately, to some incident or situation in the past which had set up a complex in the personal unconscious; more fundamentally, to the conflict between the sex drive (or the will-to-power) and the moral and spiritual influences operating in man. By thus bringing the complex in the personal unconscious into the clear light of day and (largely through the authority and influence acquired by the analyst) reducing the conflict between the different drives, cures were successfully effected.[1]

C. G. Jung's essential contribution to the psychology of the unconscious came from the fact that he studied not only the successes of this new therapy, its 'cures', but still more its failures. For a time, as a young man, he applied the free association method, together with dream and fantasy analyses, keeping an open mind as to whether the sex drive, the will-to-power, or some other factor or factors should be held basically responsible. He found that some patients fitted admirably into the Freudian framework, with unresolved sex problems at the root of their troubles. Others no less obviously had the will-to-power underlying their difficulties. In many, the sex drive and the will-to-power were so closely intertwined as to be inextricable. In either case, the complexes once found were subjected to the same type of treatment. By bringing them into the open, talk-ing them over and analysing them down, showing how they had formed in childhood or as a result of some experience which at the time could not be borne, tracing them to their instinctive origins, working them off in many cases upon the analyst himself (the so-called 'transference'), the complexes were gradually dissolved and the neurosis apparently cured.

Certain of these 'cures', though, at times proved little better than the disease. The patient came out of the analytical process with the neurosis gone, but lacking all energy to take up life anew. The

[1] The fact that the Freudian, Adlerian and other systems of depth psychology are not further referred to in the ensuing pages in no way implies that they are looked upon as unimportant. On the contrary, in their respective spheres, they are of the utmost importance. But in the withdrawal-and-return, which is the essential theme of the experiment in depth, it is the Jungian approach that is especially relevant; and for that reason especially considered here. It should be emphasized, however, that no attempt has been made to give a complete account of the Jungian system. For this, Jung's own works should be consulted.

'reductive technique', as Jung calls it, reducing everything to infantile sexuality, thwarted will-to-power, or whatever else appeared
to be responsible, had often this fatal flaw in it: the vitality, the
something that makes life worth living, leaked away in the process.
The operation was successful but psychologically the patient died.

Jung found that this loss of energy appeared to take place whenever especially impressive symbols figuring in the dreams or fantasies
of patients were analysed away by means of the reductive technique.
A man, for instance, might have a key repeatedly appearing in his
dream. This clearly would admit of a sexual interpretation. It could
equally well have a will-to-power significance. But to the patient,
any such explaining away of the symbol as infantile sexuality or
concealed will-to-power, though it might be accepted on the
authority of the analyst, was felt as a great loss. To him it was The
Key; and although he could not give any rational explanation to
himself or anyone else of what The Key meant, he felt that it meant
something vital to him. So long as he could hold on to The Key
which had come to him, life seemed possible; but without that
symbol, that myth, to support him in his struggles, nothing seemed
worth while.

Jung accordingly, when he came across such a symbol in his treatment, instead of analysing it away, encouraged the patient to amplify
it, to seek what The Key meant to him; to establish, as it were, its
mental context, its symbolical background. In other words, instead
of assuming that everything which came from the unconscious was
necessarily bad, Jung treated the matter empirically, and where
unconscious material appeared to be helpful gave it a chance to prove
itself.

The constructive technique

There followed a series of wholly unexpected discoveries. In the
first place, the unconscious progressively responded to this new
approach, elaborating and adding to the symbolical material produced. Dreams and fantasies became richer and more positive. Insofar as consciousness took a co-operative attitude towards the
unconscious, the unconscious itself grew increasingly co-operative.

In the second place, this material had an evident effect upon the
energy and general psychological condition of the patient. The treatment took a new turn, interest going over to the positive symbolical

material streaming in from the unconscious. Accordingly, in place of, or alongside, the reductive technique previously followed, Jung developed a 'constructive technique' in which the neurosis, instead of being (as it were) operated upon and excised by a process of psychological surgery, gradually became outlived, the patient developing new interests, new energy and new aims with the help of the symbolical material coming out of the unknown.

The third major discovery was that the life-bringing symbols being produced by the unconscious were age-old. On examination they proved to be similar to, often identical with, the themes and images found in the mystery cults of antiquity, in classical myth and legend, in folk lore and fairy tales, in Indian and Chinese Yoga, in the rites and practices of medieval secret societies, in the visions of the mystics, in the great world religions. Jung found intricate symbols produced in the course of analysis which neither he nor the patient knew anything about, but which were afterwards discovered in obscure treatises, buried in the depths of time, coming from widely different parts of the world. In short, the unconscious was producing today, in the psychologist's consulting room, symbols which, far away and long ago, had brought new energy and new insights: and the modern Europeans and Americans through whom this activity was operating were likewise experiencing a dynamic renewal of life.

The fourth and fundamental discovery was that this constructive activity of the unconscious was not restricted to neurotic patients. Normal men and women, provided they were prepared to take the trouble and run the risks, also experienced this flow of life-bringing symbols; and underwent a profound change in values and attitude as a consequence. In other words, this source of new energy and new interest was not a kind of psychological antibody, produced by the psyche to combat neurosis. It was an integral part of normal life, at present virtually ignored.

Jung thereupon proceeded to develop this constructive technique, no longer solely as a means of dealing with mental sickness, but rather as a practical enquiry into the nature of life. This enquiry led him into many and various fields of investigation. He found that different types of people encountered reality—both outer reality and inner reality—in widely different ways; these differences in the nature of experience accounting in large measure for the widely different accounts given by psychologists of what goes on the other side of consciousness. He developed new techniques for increasing the flow of material coming from the unconscious and for becoming aware of this material. He studied the whole process of myth and symbol formation as revealed by these techniques, both in neurotic patients and in men and women in good psychological health. He likewise studied parallel processes of symbol formation in the great religions, in primitive tribes, in esoteric societies such as the Alchemists and Gnostics, in practices such as the Tantric Yoga and the Exercises of Ignatius Loyola, in legends such as the quest for the Holy Grail, in works of art and literature such as Nietzsche's *Also sprach Zarathustra*, and in mythology generally, from the Great Mother and death-and-rebirth cults of remote antiquity to the fairy story and folk tales of all peoples. Above all, he studied those factors and forces at work the other side of consciousness making for the integration of the individual personality, the building of the whole man. And there he found himself dealing with essentially the same psychic realities as lie behind the great world religions.

'The intolerable wrestle with words and meanings'

At the same time as Jung was gradually piecing together the constructive technique, T. S. Eliot, in his poetry, was working upon a similar problem from a different angle. Using what he called the 'mythical method', he set forth the essential emptiness of contemporary life against the background of the living myths of an earlier age. Later he found himself constrained to embrace a living myth (in the special sense in which 'myth' is used here), namely the Christian faith. These two events led him along much the same inward journey as that charted by Jung. But whereas Jung's task was essentially one of exploration and the working out of a technique, Eliot as a poet was seeking to express what he experienced. And there, in common with Jung, he found himself caught up in what he calls 'the intolerable wrestle with words and meanings'.

The intolerable wrestle has two main aspects. One is essentially of a scientific nature. Depth psychology uses a number of key terms which either do not admit of strict definition, or, where they can be given a fairly definite meaning, are used in common speech (or by other schools of psychology) to mean something quite different.

Psychology itself is a word possessing a wide variety of meanings. There is not one science of the mind, or soul, but some dozens of different psychologies, many of them having hardly anything in common with one another. The word 'psyche' is an equally good example of the undefinable. It is presumably the central theme of psychology; and we do not know what it is. Jung refers to it as the 'totality of the psychic processes, conscious as well as unconscious'. But this, as he would be the first to insist, is no definition: we have still to know what 'psychic processes' mean.

The term 'unconscious' is an outstanding case of a key word currently employed for widely different purposes. In the ensuing pages it is used (not always with complete consistency) to designate that part of the psyche, lying outside the range of consciousness, from which certain otherwise inexplicable effects experienced by consciousness are assumed to come. But in current usage it can mean almost anything. For some people it is the 'sub-conscious', containing all that is bestial in human nature. Some regard it as a kind of psychological vermiform appendix, which occasionally, like its physical counterpart, gives trouble and requires specialist attention. For others the unconscious is a whole universe which has to be investigated: regardless of the consideration that what is unconscious would presumably not be accessible to investigation by consciousness. Or again, unconscious can be used as adjective or adverb, and it is possible to get such verbal tangles as 'so-and-so used to be unconscious of the unconscious but now he is becoming conscious of it'. While remarks such as 'primitive peoples are virtually unconscious', 'she was unconscious of the effect she produced', 'the unconscious wish', 'it knocked him unconscious', bring in yet other shades of meaning.

This particular aspect of the 'intolerable wrestle with words and meanings' can be a great nuisance. On the other hand, it is not fundamentally important. It provides the raw material of much empty controversy. But in time the dust of controversy settles; particularly as people of good will come to recognize that, since we are all in this verbal mess together, one charitable interpretation is worth any number of split hairs. But the second aspect of the 'intolerable wrestle' is quite another matter.

Language has been devised to give expression to the evidence of our senses, to cope with our experience this side of consciousness. How can it be used to communicate experience encountered the other side of consciousness? Above all, how can it be used when such

few words as do exist for expressing this kind of experience have had
their meaning twisted and dulled until they are virtually useless?
This is the problem to which Eliot addressed himself. And in spite
of the fact that he has a gift of words unmatched in this generation,
he feels he has mainly failed.

> *So here I am, in the middle way, having had twenty years—*
> *Twenty years largely wasted, the years of l'entre deux guerres—*
> *Trying to learn to use words, and every attempt*
> *Is a wholly new start, and a different kind of failure . . .*

> *Words strain,*
> *Crack and sometimes break, under the burden,*
> *Under the tension, slip, slide, perish,*
> *Decay with imprecision, will not stay in place,*
> *Will not stay still.*

But more than any other words spoken in this age, his 'hints and
guesses' convey some impression of a timeless present, an everlasting
now, a living reality interpenetrating this 'twittering world' of
meaningless movement:

> *Men and bits of paper, whirled by the cold wind.*

Eliot, like Jung, seeks above all the creative activity operating the
other side of consciousness, the life-bringing symbol floating up
from the unknown.

> *I said to my soul, be still, and wait without hope*
> *For hope would be hope for the wrong thing; wait without love*
> *For love would be love of the wrong thing; there is yet faith*
> *But the faith and the love and the hope are all in the waiting.*
> *Wait without thought, for you are not ready for thought:*
> *So the darkness shall be the light, and the stillness the dancing.*

But whereas Jung has attempted to develop specific methods for such
'release and realization of experience', Eliot seeks to communicate
the experience itself, the 'timeless moment' when the 'stillness' becomes manifest.

> *Whisper of running streams, and winter lightning.*
> *The wild thyme unseen and the wild strawberry,*

The laughter in the garden, echoed ecstasy
Not lost, but requiring, pointing to the agony
Of death and birth.

And this 'intersection of the timeless with time' is not an individual experience only, but the essential fact, the saving reality, of whole ages and of whole peoples.

The moment of the rose and the moment of the yew-tree
Are of equal duration. A people without history
Is not redeemed from time, for history is a pattern
Of timeless moments.

Challenge and response

At the same time as Jung and Eliot were dealing in their different ways with the creative activity at work in the microcosm of the human psyche, Arnold J. Toynbee in *A Study of History* was dealing with the effect of that activity upon the macrocosm, as expressed in the recorded experience of mankind. Scrutinizing the factors behind the rise, growth, decline, death of civilizations, Toynbee likewise found himself involved with the mythical method. The key to the life history of peoples he discovered in a process of challenge and response. Civilizations regularly encounter challenges of a physical kind: stony soil, swamp, desert, overpopulation, exhaustion of materials, climatic change, savage neighbours, disruption from within. It is trials such as these that bring out the true character of a people and of an age. But as the drama of universal history develops under Toynbee's hand, the factor of major interest becomes not so much the physical challenge as the living myth which enables peoples to stand up to this challenge and emerge triumphant.

Particularly is this true of a challenge that comes when a civilization is already well advanced. During its vigorous period, when the primal vision which gave it birth is still powerful, difficulties are taken in its stride. But when this vision weakens, when the first assurance is gone, sooner or later there comes a 'time of troubles', and the fate of the civilization hangs in the balance.

At such a juncture, according to Toynbee's reading of world events, men and women here and there turn from the macrocosm of the outer world to the microcosm of the human psyche. There, in some manner, they find the answer to the challenge racking their

13

society to death; and, turning again to the outer world, form the nucleus of a 'creative minority' which, if it is successful in transmitting its vision to the great mass of the people, leads the civilization through the time of troubles to new creative achievement.

This process of withdrawal-and-return clearly ties in with Jung's discovery of the constructive activity of the unconscious, no less than with Eliot's 'history is a pattern of timeless moments'. From the clinical experience of the psychologist, from the 'intolerable wrestle' of the poet, from the evidence of a case-study of civilizations, the same possibility emerges: that in the unknown realm the other side of consciousness, creative forces are at work which may at times be channelled into human affairs with life-giving effect.

At a period when the world is in a time of troubles such as never before, these hypotheses have something more than academic interest. It is notoriously difficult to analyse objectively the historical epoch in which one is living, but certain major features of the present age are inescapable. It is patent that the condition into which we have now come is not simply an accident, a run of bad luck which a little forethought here, a little cleverness there, might have avoided. Our problem is that we are caught up in a civilization having immense drive but no direction, marvellous capacity to get there but no idea where it is going.

One segment of the world has reacted against this by a flight into fanatical certainty. As Stalin once put it:

> 'The power of the Marxist-Leninist theory lies in the fact that it enables the Party to find the final orientation in any situation, to understand the inner connexion of events, to foresee their course, and to perceive not only how and in what direction they are developing in the present but also how and in what direction they are bound to develop in future.'

The other segment of the world still has freedom as its lodestar, and looks with doubt upon the doctrinaire. But to the question 'Freedom for what?' we have no answer. When freedom is threatened we spring to its defence. But when freedom is secured we are at a loss what to do with it. As a consequence, we win the wars but lose the peace. If we are ever to win the peace we have to know what freedom is for.

Jung, Eliot and Toynbee are men who, in this time of troubles, have sought new vision in the depths. They are, as it were, the spearpoints of a possible creative minority, dedicated to a new birth of freedom. At present, though, they are spearpoints only. The question examined here is whether and how, on the basis of their discoveries, the peoples of the world can find the means of creative renewal.

In fairness to the reader, it should be emphasized that this is not an armchair pursuit. What is proposed is an experiment, an experiment involving risk, making heavy demands upon those who undertake it, with no guarantee of results. *Mythos* meant originally the words spoken in a ritual, the means of approach to the God. Jung's constructive technique, Eliot's mythical method, Toynbee's withdrawal-and-return are so many modern means of approach to the creative process working in and through man. And, as always, the creative is dangerous.

Superimposed upon this is the fact that, at present, we know very little about this range of activity. For something over a century there has been a tendency to restrict the field of scientific enquiry to those areas where assured results can be obtained. Science has been sacrificed to the pursuit of certainty. As is now becoming realized, science is not primarily concerned with certainty. Its primary concern is that, in the free search for truth, the methods used shall be the most appropriate that can be devised. But because of this undue restriction upon scientific enquiry, large areas of human experience have remained virtually uninvestigated: especially that immense realm of energic phenomena with which religions and ideologies deal. As a consequence, in the ensuing pages there is scarcely a statement of any importance that can be looked upon as scientifically based. We swim in a sea of hypotheses; hypotheses founded upon experience, it is true, but the kind of experience in which the possibility of self-deception is practically limitless.

In such conditions, honest writing, *un livre de bonne foy*, has its difficulties. Montaigne's question, '*Que scay-je?*' is more than ever apposite, but harder than ever to answer. In the first half of the book I have, to the best of my ability, attempted to convey the methods and interpretations (as I understand them) worked out by Jung, Eliot and Toynbee. In the second half, while still holding to the line they lay down, I have more frequently ventured on interpretations of my own.

In sum, this does not pretend to be in any sense a scientific work. It is an attempt to draw attention to certain vital phenomena to which, it is hoped, the scientific method can eventually be applied. But we have first to become aware of these phenomena and their possible relevance to life. The purpose here is, so far as may be, to communicate that awareness.

II

PSYCHOLOGICAL TYPES

I N embarking upon the experiment in depth one somewhat bewildering characteristic of human nature needs particularly to
be taken into account. Anyone who has observed his fellow-
beings at all closely will have noticed how people of ability,
while showing marked strength in some directions, often reveal an
almost incredible weakness in others. Thus, a man of proved scientific
acumen is liable, perhaps, to behave like an adolescent in matters of
the heart. A person of great practical sense may prove completely
devoid of imagination. A genius in philosophy may be capable of
missing his way a few yards from his own front door. An orator,
able to move great audiences with his eloquence, becomes confused,
it may be, when confronted with a few figures. As the French put it,
everyone has *les défauts de ses qualités*; and, it would often seem, the
greater the *qualités* the more abysmal the *défauts*.

When it comes to dealing with the other side of consciousness
there is much the same disparity. A man of great gifts in the outside
world may be childishly credulous in matters of the psyche. The
Newton of the *Principia* and the Newton of the prophecies of Daniel
are as two different beings. In like manner, a man of deep spiritual
understanding may prove hopelessly at sea in the ordinary trans-
actions of everyday life. Furthermore, even where a certain balance
is held between the two worlds, the quality of inner perception
varies. In observing the effects coming from the deep unconscious,
whether in himself or others, a man may show unusual discernment
at some points, coupled with the most absolute blindness elsewhere;
and be at least as dogmatic where he is blind as where he sees.

This phenomenon of uneven development, of high ability in some
directions, little or no ability in others, has two very important
consequences in the present context. For one thing, it means that the
pioneering attempts so far made to chart man's experience the other

side of consciousness are, at best, only partial in their insight. Depth psychologists are as liable to this one-sidedness as anyone else; which goes far towards explaining why they so seldom agree. For another, it means that those undertaking the experiment in depth have great need to discover and be aware of their own blind sides; the more so since the guides themselves are anything but infallible.

Jung's work on psychological types [1] bears directly on this matter of self-knowledge. Most typologies aim principally at providing a means of classifying other people. The great value of Jung's work in this field is that it enables a man to get a better understanding of himself.

Extravert and introvert

It is one of the ironies of fate and fame that what is commonly considered as Jung's chief title to greatness is that he invented the terms extravert and introvert. Actually, the broad distinction had been recognized many centuries before Jung wrote. The difference between an Aristotle and a Plato was too obvious to escape notice. Aristotle takes the world as his laboratory. If he writes on government he makes excerpts from the constitutions of as many actual states and cities as he can lay hands on. Plato goes the opposite way to work. When he writes on government he produces a Republic, spun out of the richness of an informed imagination. His laboratory is the human spirit. In this, as in much else, Aristotle is an extravert, Plato an introvert.

The extravert, as the word suggests, goes out to the visible world with complete assurance, drawn as by an irresistible attraction. To be separated from what is going on around him is punishment and exile. He cannot have too many contacts, too many possibilities, too many facts. On the other hand, when it comes to dealing with the inner life, the picture changes. Introspection, he feels, is unhealthy. That way, morbidity, madness, lie. The soul is a sacredness—or a fiction—which it would be impious—or foolish—to investigate. He circumvents the problem as best he may, usually by some ready-made construct he has found in the outer world—a church, a philosophy, a scientific system; or simply turns his back upon it and, as far as possible, ignores it altogether.

The introvert, on the contrary, remains within himself, putting

[1] C. G. Jung: *Psychological Types*. Kegan Paul, 1920.

together a system of his own with which to cope with the outside world. He has none of the confident approach to things and to people characteristic of the extravert but is inclined rather to entrench himself in his own inner fastness and regard the outside world with a degree of diffidence amounting often to mistrust. With the things of the psyche, on the contrary, he is at home. There he has his ivory castle in which he is king. He may or may not have a formulated religion or philosophy. He may indeed remain speculative in this sphere throughout his life. But he knows that the inner world exists and is not afraid of dealing with it in his own fashion.

Milton's *L'Allegro* and *Il Penseroso* show in lively fashion certain of the typical differences. *L'Allegro* is eager for new experience, new scenes, new ideas. Everything external draws him on. A castle in the landscape is no ordinary castle, but one

> *Where perhaps some Beauty lies,*
> *The Cynosure of neighb'ring eyes.*

Pleasure is to be found in company, amidst jollity.

> *When the merry bells ring round,*
> *And the jocund rebecks sound.*

All is outward and only the outward is real.

Il Penseroso, on the contrary, tends towards solitariness and inner communing, preoccupied with the mystery of life:

> *Or let my lamp at midnight hour*
> *Be seen in some high lonely tower,*
> *Where I may oft out-watch the Bear,*
> *With thrice-great Hermes, or unsphere*
> *The spirit of Plato, to unfold*
> *What worlds, or what vast regions hold*
> *The immortal mind, that hath forsook*
> *Her mansion in this fleshly nook.*

Inevitably the extravert and the introvert take diametrically opposed views as to the nature of reality. The typical extraverted prejudice is that the solid factual world alone is real, the rest 'unhealthy imagination'. The typical introverted prejudice is that the outer world—the mere evidence of the senses—is relatively unimportant; that the things of the inner world—what one believes, what one values, what one is loyal to, what one will die for—are the only true substance. Inevitably also, extravert and introvert take jaundiced views of one another. The extravert looks upon the introvert as morbid, neurotic even. The introvert regards the extravert as superficial, a mere function of his environment. Their pleasures are different, so also their suffering. The extravert likes all the company he can get; left to himself he becomes morose. The introvert, thrown into society, is miserable; his one desire to slink into a corner and pass unperceived.

Nobody is wholly extraverted or wholly introverted. A man in his conscious activities may be as completely outward turning as it is possible for anyone to be. But his introverted side—which has fallen entirely into the unconscious—will nevertheless intrude; in fantasies, as fear of some insidious disease; in melancholy, which afflicts him when left to his own resources; in superstition, or some freak religion; in that total loss of interest and complete sterile introversion which overcomes many extraverts when they can no longer be fully active in the world. For the extravert, introversion all too often actually is what he believes it to be—a neurosis.

The highly introverted person is similarly caught from the side of the unconscious. He may be found indulging in day-dreams of immense extraversion: deeds that will change all history, remake the world, restore the golden age, overthrow tyrants and uphold the just; when actually he is accomplishing nothing. But also, at times, some hurricane of fantasy may carry him into extraverted action— action of the kind which expects to achieve everything at a single stroke—and he becomes miserably defeated when his efforts are misunderstood, despised, laughed at, and nothing achieved.

Quite apart from this compensation—or over-compensation— from the side of the unconscious, relatively few people turn only inwards or only outwards. Most of us have among our acquaintances one or two of whom we could say: 'Yes, he is definitely an extravert': 'Yes, she is introverted in everything she does.' More often, though, it is a matter of being extraverted in some things, introverted in others: eager and outgoing for new ideas, perhaps, but much preferring a pipe and a book to the hilarious party. The reason for this appears on further enquiry into the different psychological functions by which people take account of and react to life.

The four functions

As a matter of empirical observation, we experience phenomena in four main ways. The manner in which this comes about may best be shown, perhaps, by considering a concrete example. We are walking along the street and suddenly hear the loud shrieking of brakes. We look up and see, the other side of the road, a girl knocked off her bicycle by an automobile. People are picking her up. A policeman is hurrying to the scene. These, the brute facts of the situation, we take in by means of the senses. At the same time our thinking gets to work. Evidently the girl was cycling across the side turning, from which the automobile came out. The van parked at the corner probably prevented their seeing one another. Judging by the noise of the brakes the car was travelling fast. Simultaneously we begin making value judgements. Automobiles are a menace. Something should be done to prevent this licensed murder on the streets. The man seems to be taking it pretty callously; he has not even got out yet. Happily she does not seem to be badly hurt. The mind again switches, this time to a troubling possibility. X sometimes cycles home from the laboratory. True, it is on the other side of the city. But if this can happen here . . . We hurry to a telephone and feel an immense relief when the familiar voice answers. Within the space of a few seconds only we have (1) perceived the facts; (2) thought about them, pieced the data together logically; (3) felt about them, made value judgements, taken views—perhaps a little hastily; and (4) looked beyond the facts to certain possibilities, in this case, as it happens, not true.

Plato, in his *Republic*, long ago observed this fourfold character of our means of apprehension. His various translators experienced considerable difficulty in selecting equivalents for the terms he used. The Spens translation refers to 'four faculties in the soul . . . intelligence . . . demonstration . . . opinion . . . and imagination'. Davies and Vaughan speak of 'four mental states . . . pure reason . . . understanding . . . belief . . . and conjecture'. Jowett has yet another version: 'reason . . . understanding . . . faith for conviction . . . and perception of shadows.'

Jung, coming independently upon the same fourfold division some twenty-three centuries later, gave them specific names. The capacity for seeing how things fit together logically ('intelligence', 'reason', 'pure reason' according to Plato's translators) Jung called the *thinking* function. The direct perception of phenomena by means of the senses ('demonstration' and 'understanding' in the Platonic categories) he called the *sensation* function. The ability to make accurate and coherent value judgements, he termed the *feeling* function: a not altogether happy choice, but preferable to the 'opinion', 'belief', 'faith for conviction' which was the best that could be drawn from Plato. The capacity for seeing beyond the facts, sensing the intangibles in a situation ('imagination', 'conjecture', and Jowett's inspired 'perception of shadows') he called the *intuitive* function.[1]

The Four Functions

These four functions may be usefully shown in diagrammatic form since, as becomes evident on some reflection, thinking is both the opposite and the complement to feeling, intuition both the opposite and the complement to sensation.

How this happens may be seen by considering these two pairs of functions rather more specifically. Thinking consists essentially in the making of logical judgements. It sorts, classifies, analyses, synthesizes, argues from premise to conclusion, traces the reason for this, the cause of that. Feeling is likewise a making of judgements, but in a totally different realm—values. Its criterion is not logic but worth. This I like. That I do not like. This is good. That is bad. This is morally right. That is morally wrong.

Obviously, for a rounded judgement—logically right and right in value—both thinking and feeling are required. On the other hand, they can easily interfere with one another. If I want to do some clear thinking on how best to carry out a certain job, but am dogged by the consideration that one way will involve working with a person I detest while another will enable me to work with a person I like, my thinking is liable to be prejudiced. Similarly, if I have to decide whether or not a certain course is morally right, but am all the time

[1] As Jung recognizes, and deplores, none of these terms is ideal. Thinking and feeling, in particular, are words currently used in the loosest fashion to mean almost anything; while intuition probably conveys a different meaning to each different mind. But the alternative device of using out-of-the-way words—cerebration and evaluation, for instance, in place of thinking and feeling—or Latin equivalents (Spinoza's *scientia intuitiva*) is liable to be found cumbrous and, perhaps, pedantic.

obsessed by the consideration that one line of action everyone will recognize as logically consistent, while another will appear contrary to decisions I have taken in the past, I am again liable to be biased.

Much the same is true of sensation and intuition. Both are functions of perception, but of different kinds of perception. Sensation is the *fonction du réel*; it perceives the facts and nothing but the facts, sees what is and what is not, and stops at that. Intuition is at the opposite pole. It is not so much interested in the facts as in the something beyond the facts, the imponderables, the invisible concomitants, the impalpable possibilities, the events still below the horizon, the shape of things to come. Here, also, both sensation and intuition are necessary to a complete grasp of the situation. But the man concentrating on the facts usually has little left over for the possibilities. While the intuitive man is so occupied with the intangibles that the facts for him sometimes almost cease to exist.

From empirical observation Jung found that most people have one of the four functions—thinking, say—particularly well developed; an adjacent function—in this case either sensation or intuition—moderately well developed; while the other two are more or less rudimentary, the one opposite the highly developed function being especially inferior.

This has immense implications for our understanding and conduct of life. The *thinking* type, the man or woman with thinking as the superior function, will tend to use thinking on all occasions. So long as what is needed is the logical handling of a situation, he will do wonderfully well. But thought has only a limited orbit. Let this same man or woman be in a situation where the essential consideration is the perception of the facts. Then, unless he has sensation as an auxiliary function, he will find that he selects the facts which fit in with his thinking and is oblivious to those which do not. And his whole wonderful thought structure will be skewed as a consequence. Or again, suppose the need is not so much for analysis and synthesis as imaginative development. If his auxiliary function is intuition he will readily adapt, thinking in terms of possibilities with accuracy and ease. If, on the contrary, his intuitive side is deficient, then he will be stuck in his thought, bogged down in his theory, static.

But the purgatory of the thinking type comes when the situation requires good feeling. Such a one, with the best intention in the world, will give the matter careful thought. To his pained surprise he will find people against him in whatever he does. His impeccably worked out schemes go wrong. His love-life is all too likely to be chaotic or infantile. In feeling situations he will be continually caught between the opposites of puerile sentimentality and hard-boiled realism, flickering from one to the other, uncertain of what he likes and what he does not like, what he wants and what he does not want. As Jules says in *Pippa Passes*:

> One may do whate'er one likes
> In Art: the only thing is, to make sure
> That one does like it—which takes pains to know.

For the thinking type this is the central problem, in art and in life.

The *feeling* type, the man or woman with feeling as the superior function, is not so handicapped—provided it is feeling that the situation requires. He will know what is of value to himself, and what is of value to others, with the same objective accuracy and coherence as the thinking type achieves in his logical analyses. He will be at home in personal contacts, because an understanding of values is fundamental to that side of life. It does not necessarily follow that he will seek such contacts. Nor does it follow that he will use his capacity for valuing in a kindly fashion. A feeling type knows very well what he wants and what other people want: and often uses this knowledge to see to it that what he wants he gets, whether or not it is agreeable to others. Sometimes, indeed, there seems a certain cold-blooded quality about feeling types. They can handle their emotions so steadily, so naturally, that to people otherwise oriented it appears almost indecent. This does not mean that the feeling type is not subject to passion, cannot be swept away by the forces of the unconscious. But where the thinking type is weak—in the personal, 'real life' situations, where what matters is the heart rather than the head—the feeling type is strong. Pascal's '*Le cœur a ses raisons que la raison ne connaît point*' epitomizes the feeling type's experience of life.

Where feeling has sensation as auxiliary, then this combination of sound value judgement and adequate appreciation of concrete reality results in a man or woman thoroughly at home in all practical matters involving things and people. He will be intelligent, for instance, in political situations, personal relationships, considerations of what is right and what is wrong, what is fair and what is not fair,

He sees life as a human situation to be lived, not a problem to be solved. If the function linked to the superior feeling is intuition, then the combination of value judgement and an appreciation of the intangible is likely to produce the naturally religious person. This does not necessarily mean that he or she will subscribe to any particular faith; but for the feeling-intuitive type the world invisible, the things that cannot be proved, but which he quite naturally knows to be real, are real.

But when it comes to thinking, the feeling type shies away like a frightened horse. To him the resolute thinker is a ghoulish person who 'murders to dissect'; or, at best, one who bespatters the world with unnecessary difficulties that he takes delight in thinking up. Faced with a thinking situation the feeling type will dodge it or, if no other possibility presents, try to get someone else to work it out for him. This is not through any inherent laziness or perversity but from sheer helplessness. One of the most characteristic features of the inferior function, whatever it may be, is that it cannot be summoned at will. It comes, it goes, in its own time, on its own terms. The superior function can be directed, held down to the task. The inferior function cannot. Where thinking is inferior, however much one may wish to think when thinking is required, all too often one can only feel—and flounder.

The *sensation* type is of quite another kind. Thinking and feeling are both rational means of arriving at judgements, the one on grounds of logic, the other on grounds of value. Sensation and intuition, on the other hand, are essentially non-rational. In themselves they decide nothing. They simply take account of what is.

The person having sensation as his strong side is, above all else, an accurate observer. He sees what he sees and automatically records it without even noticing that he does so. In a strange town, when the time comes to find the way back to the station, he will say with complete assurance (and accuracy) no, we went down that road, not this. When revisiting a friend after a long interval she will say, on entering the room: 'Why, you've changed the furniture round; the piano used to be there.' Along with this, the sensation type has an absolute conviction (so absolute that he never questions it) of the essential reality of data coming to consciousness by way of the five senses. Things are real. The proof of the pudding is in the eating. What he sees he believes. Dr. Johnson who demonstrated the reality of matter by delivering a mighty kick at a large rock talks the language a sensation type understands.

Where sensation has thinking as auxiliary the practical man results; the man who understands the way things work, the man who knows how. Where feeling is the auxiliary, another kind of practical man is produced: one who can handle people. He may misuse this gift, of course, but that is what he knows how to do.

It is in dealing with the intangibles that the sensation type is lost. In religion he is likely to profess agnosticism or some creed bequeathed to him from birth. He will be for plain solid sense in all situations, looking with suspicion on anything 'mystical'. That the soul might survive the body after death is a possibility he finds difficult to envisage. For him, matter is so unequivocally real that any other view of reality borders upon the absurd. At the same time, openly if he is naïve, surreptitiously if he is sophisticated, he may be found taking a side-glance (or more) at fortune-telling, spinning a 'lucky' coin to decide which of his two favourite horses he will back, scared in the dead of night that he has appendicitis or worse, turning his money when he sees the new moon.

The *intuitive* type is, in every sense, his opposite number. In the world invisible he is at home. He sees in that world with uncanny prescience—or not so much sees as 'intuits', gathers out of the air, the shape of things unseen. This does not imply that he understands them or knows what to do about them. Intuition is not a means of judging, of arriving at reasoned conclusions, as is thinking or valuing; but an essentially non-rational perceiving, of the same general character as sensation, with this difference, that, instead of being a perception of things, it is a 'perception of shadows' as Plato put it. These 'shadows' may be of all kinds: ideas, possibilities, things impending, the atmosphere of a place, the temper of a meeting, the underlying nature of a new acquaintance; or the intuitive function may explore the depths of the human psyche, as naturally aware of the effects coming from the deep unconscious as the sensation type is aware of the traffic in the street.

Joined with thinking, developed intuition produces the man with new concepts, the innovator, the inventor. He seeks and sees the potentialities in a situation and his thinking enables him to give them form.[1] Where intuition is joined with feeling, this combination of

[1] Referring back to Plato's original discovery of the four functions (pp. 21–2),

possibilities and values is likely to produce the seer, the mystic, the other-worldly *religieux*.

What intuition does not produce is the nice, normal, practical man or woman. The inferior sensation of the intuitive type is a plague to himself and others. He will lose himself in his home town, leave things behind, be buried in a book when the dishes need washing, be chasing the latest prophet and forgetting to pay the bills. The intuitive type lives on and for the impalpables: and at times they yield a poor living. Even if he lights upon a valuable discovery, he can never stay to work it out but is off round the next corner, where a new possibility has just appeared.

Personality orientation

As a matter of empirical observation, the superior function—whether thinking, feeling, sensation or intuition—is either extraverted or introverted. There are, consequently, eight main personality types: extraverted thinking, introverted thinking; extraverted feeling, introverted feeling; extraverted sensation, introverted sensation; extraverted intuition, introverted intuition. Thumb-nail sketches of each of these types is all that can be attempted here; but these may suffice to give a general impression of the strength and weakness of each.

The *extraverted* thinking type collects all facts, data, thoughts, ideas, theories of every kind that come to his hand, lists them, sorts them into categories perhaps, but rarely if ever works them into a coherent whole or arrives at their underlying meaning, causes or laws. Darwin, collecting facts for twenty years, and only seeing the meaning behind the facts when he read Malthus' *Essay on Population*, is a good example of extraverted thinking. The *introverted* thinking type has the opposite urge. Above all he needs to weld his thoughts into a pattern. New data he regards suspiciously until he can see how they fit in. Synthesis is his aim. Where the brute facts are recalcitrant, he is liable at times to take the view, not that his synthesis is perhaps invalid, but 'so much the worse for the facts'. Descartes, with his *Cogito ergo sum* and his *a priori* system-making, is clearly of this general orientation.

it is instructive to note how adequately he describes intuition and thinking, how inadequately he describes sensation and feeling. There can be little question which was Plato's strong side.

The *extraverted* feeling type goes after new experiences, new acquaintances, new relationships—wherever new values are to be found—with the utmost avidity. He is the world's best mixer. He knows everyone by his first name and sometimes not much else. What is widely regarded as the 'typical American' conforms fairly closely to this pattern. The *introverted* feeling type, on the contrary, is shy and reserved; but beneath the surface there is an intense feeling life. The values he holds are held with his life's blood. Too often he finds himself totally unable to give them expression, let alone bring them into reality; and sometimes feels it necessary to shelter behind some acceptable façade.

The *extraverted* sensation type is the forthright goer-out to things in general; the indefatigable explorer, the seeker of new places, new sights, new people, new situations. His decriers would say that he sees everything and understands nothing. The *introverted* sensation type, on the other hand, is the perceptive connoisseur, the appreciator of quality—in food, in wine, in horses, in pictures, or whatever else may take his appraising eye. All too easily he becomes the sterile aesthete.

The *extraverted* intuitive type seeks new possibilities in the outside world. So long as the situation contains such possibilities he is held to it as by the thongs of fate. But once the possibilities have begun to materialize, long before they can be harvested and the hard work on them done, he is away over the next possibility-haunted horizon. The *introverted* intuitive type is the most removed of all men. He is concerned with—often hopelessly lost in—the possibilities hidden in the depths of the psyche; and the outward world for him has little reality in comparison.

This, however, is not all. The auxiliary function—the man's second string—is likewise extraverted or introverted. Accordingly, the neat simplicity of the eight personality types becomes considerably complicated when the auxiliary function is also taken into account.

On the other hand, while theoretically there are now thirty-two possible combinations, the practical problem of distinguishing the superior and auxiliary functions, and which way each of them turns, is not appreciably greater. This does not mean that the task is an easy one, particularly in regard to people one does not know very well— which may always include oneself. But the problem is not four times as difficult, as might at first be thought.

In attempting to arrive at what type a person is, the first thing is to note what he does easily and well, the function into which his energy naturally flows. In many cases this can be checked up by seeing on which side he is inferior. There are here one or two useful rules of thumb which, while far from infallible, may be of help.

Thinking and feeling are alternative methods of weighing up a situation. It is necessary, therefore, to distinguish what form this weighing-up process takes. A thinking type will normally rise to a problem—provided it is within his range of knowledge—and deal with it incisively. Seeing a situation in terms of problems is for him the natural line of approach. A feeling type will not readily take to problems as such, but anything to do with people will at once claim his attention. The human angle is the one he understands.

Sensation and intuition, being alternative methods of perception, may be distinguished by observing how a man perceives. The sensation type, when sizing up an object, narrows his gaze, focuses his eyes upon it, really looks at it. The intuitive, on the contrary, seems to envelop it with his gaze, look round it and through it rather than at it.

Whether the function is extraverted or introverted is more difficult to determine. It is true that the extraverted attitude can be readily distinguished from the introverted attitude by noting whether, in action or conversation, a person is going out freely to the object or audience, or whether he is staying within himself. What cannot so easily be decided is whether the superior function is being used or one of the others. The inferior function, compulsively running the man, may give a completely false impression. Generally speaking, the mark of the inferior function is that it escapes conscious control; comes and goes in its own fashion, at its own time; cannot be summoned at will; brings emotion in its train. The superior function a man will not even know he is using, it works for him so naturally.

These, be it repeated, are no more than rules of thumb. In attempting to distinguish which are the strong and which are the weak sides of a personality, there is a whole series of traps for the unwary, some of which may usefully be examined.

Caveats

As is evident, Jung's work on psychological types is no neat sorting of people into pigeon holes. It is an attempt to distinguish more clearly certain regularly observed variables in the infinite complexity of human beings. Its principal value is to the man who wishes to have a truer picture of himself—Cromwell fashion, warts included —and to gain a better understanding of those with whom he lives and works. And for this purpose it is necessary to distinguish the limitations of the types theory, what it does not do as well as what it does.

In the first place, as Jung is careful to point out, the system does not pretend to be more than it is. It covers introversion and extraversion and the four functions. It does not deal with other exceedingly important human characteristics, such, for instance, as capacity or incapacity for action. At first sight, the extravert seems to be more 'action-minded' than the introvert; but that is no more than the current prejudice that 'action' is something done in the outside world. In fact, the types theory has nothing to contribute on this score: except perhaps this reminder that inward action may sometimes be no less important than outward. Similarly, such matters as goodness of heart, artistic ability, intellectual integrity, sense of responsibility, sense of humour, fall outside these categories.

In the second place, there is the point already referred to at an earlier stage, namely, that the opposite to the conscious orientation is normally piling up the other side of consciousness. Thus, the wholehearted extravert may suddenly be overwhelmed by an avalanche of introversion and not be able to step outside his front door. Similarly, the undeveloped function, the weak side, may spring to active life and for a time run the man. Only on considerable acquaintance, and not always then, can a reliable diagnosis be made. A man is by no means always himself.

In this connection there is a trap which it is particularly necessary to avoid. It should not be assumed that the function which makes the most noise is necessarily the superior function. The truth may be just the opposite. A man, for instance, may have learnt from his environment to put up the semblance of thinking, and will be for ever saying that this is logical and that is not: but be quite incapable of directed thought. On the other hand, in consistent awareness of what he likes and what he does not like, what he values and what he does not value, he may have so little difficulty that the matter never so much as arises. At first sight the uninitiated might put him down as a thinking type. But it is feeling that is really under control. Again, a woman may immerse herself in esoteric literature, talk nothing but mysticism, yoga and the latest development in psychical research, surround herself with spiritual cranks and charlatans, and in every other way proclaim to high Heaven how intuitive she is. But on closer view it will be seen that it is not she using the intuitive function but the intuitive function using her; while underneath all the flummery she may be not at all unintelligent in the practical things of life—clothes, cooking, investing her money and so forth. The sign of the developed function is that the person can use it at will, and use it accurately—accurately within the limits of his personal calibre, of course; but he using it, not it him.

Finally, but by no means exhaustively, there is a general mistake into which one easily falls unless warned. On looking round one's ring of friends and acquaintances with the four psychological functions in mind, the first tendency is to place most of the men on the thinking side of the account, most of the women on the feeling side. This comes from certain normal characteristics of the two sexes, which need to be distinguished from thinking and feeling.

Characteristically, the male human being has a capacity for discrimination, for seeing the differences between things. Jung calls this the *logos* principle. The female human being, on the other hand, has a capacity for relationship, for seeing how things and, still more, people, can be brought together. Jung calls this the *eros* principle. At first sight this male capacity for discrimination looks like thinking, the female capacity for relationship looks like feeling. In fact, the resemblance is superficial only.

To draw a hard and fast line between the thinking function and the *logos* principle, between feeling and *eros*, is difficult, perhaps impossible. But a broad distinction can nevertheless be made. The essence of thinking is well expressed in the word cogitate, with its roots in *co*—'together', and *agitare*—'to agitate'. When we think, we agitate things together. *Logos* concentrates upon the fact of difference, of exclusion, of seeing that fact A is relevant and fact B is not. Occam's razor: *Entia non sunt multiplicanda praeter necessitatem* [4] is a characteristic *logos* statement. No woman would ever have made it. Only a man is capable of mistaking it for an invariable rule.

[4] Things not known to exist should not, unless it is absolutely necessary, be postulated as existing. Or, more currently: hypotheses are not to be multiplied beyond necessity.

There is a similar difference—*mutatis mutandis*—between feeling and *eros*. Feeling is essentially value judgement. *Eros*, as such, has nothing to do with values. Relationship is what it cares about, how things, people, can be brought and kept together, irrespective of value.

The *logos-eros* pair of opposites will need to be considered in its own right at a later stage. In the present context its importance is principally this. Where a man is a thinking type, the concentration of *logos* and thinking is likely to make him formidably and one-sidedly intellectual. Where a woman is a feeling type, *eros* coupled with feeling is liable to make relationship the be-all and end-all of her existence. When, on the contrary, a man has feeling as his superior function, with *logos* to do duty for thinking, he has much more of an all-round capacity—or at least the appearance of it. Similarly, when a woman has thinking as the superior function, and *eros* to make up for the feeling function, there is once more the impression of all-roundness. Or, to put it another way (since everything has its two sides) such rounded personalities are not likely to have the heights and the depths of those less evenly balanced.

Practical application

Anyone undertaking the experiment in depth, indeed anyone wishing to live life consciously, can benefit considerably from a knowledge of the psychological orientation of himself and of others.

In the first place, it is invaluable to know where one is vulnerable. It is on the side of the undeveloped attitudes and functions that the problems of life accumulate. In the first half of life all may go well. A man armed with extraverted sensation and extraverted thinking, for instance, is well equipped to confront the world. But as he grows older, possibly before then, his attempt to deal with feeling situations by thinking them out, his inability to form anything but superficial relationships, his failure to perceive (let alone realize) the possibilities of inner development, will cramp him down to only half a life. Alternatively, the undeveloped side may take matters into its own hands, and he will find himself whirled into situations he has never sought, forced into a life which is not his, a marionette rather than a man. Unless and until he manages to get control of the functions and attitudes gripped by the unconscious, he is at their mercy.

There is no short cut to such 'rounding out' of the functions. Only

in the fundamental coming to terms with the forces of the unconscious, which is the theme of the ensuing pages, can the undifferentiated functions and attitudes be salvaged. On the other hand,
awareness of one's weak side can help in a number of ways, not without their importance. To take a specific example: a man who knows
that his feeling side is inferior does well to keep himself as far as
possible on a short rein whenever a feeling situation arises. His
tendency will be to rush headlong into it, or to bolt from it with
equal precipitancy. As far as possible what he needs to do is neither
to rush in nor to rush out, but to face the situation and experience it
with all the control and awareness he can muster. At the same time,
if he is wise, he will observe those of his friends who have feeling as
a developed function, watch how they do it and pick up what hints
he can. It is true that learning the 'drill' of the feeling type does not
produce developed feeling, but to become even fractionally more
aware of that side is something on the way. Actually it is by making
hideous mistakes, with their accompanying hurt and shame, that
development normally comes. Yet here, also, it is only by being
conscious of what is happening, as far as possible realizing the situation in its entirety, that progress is made.

The second great value of psychological orientation is in working
with others, particularly with others engaged in the experiment in
depth. Once it is realized that the other man is the polar opposite of
oneself, he can be interesting instead of a bugbear. He may eventually come to be one's closest friend. Or again, where two people have
a function in common (the one having thinking and intuition, the
other thinking and sensation, for instance) it is on the function they
both use readily—in this case, thinking—that they can meet: and
each may learn from the other of the function he lacks. In a small
group working together, knowledge of the psychological compass
bearings can go far towards making the difference between finding
the group unbearable and finding it an invaluable means of development. Also, a group embodying the different attitudes and different
functions, if it really works together, can do far more to see a question from all angles than any one person working alone.

Finally, in making what Toynbee calls the withdrawal-and-
return, much depends upon psychological orientation as to which of
the two phases is easy and which difficult. For some the withdrawal
phase, the going inward, is simplicity itself; for others, well-nigh

impossible. Similarly, the return to the outer world is completely natural for some; and for others the hardest thing they ever attempted. Thus, a woman, introverted, with intuition and feeling as her developed functions, will have little difficulty in making the withdrawal. Everything in her is attuned to the call of the inner world. A man, extraverted, with sensation and thinking as his developed functions, is likely to find the withdrawal utterly incompatible with everything he is and does. As a man, his *logos* will be all on the side of keeping clear of the unconscious, of holding on, first, last and all the time, to that great deed of discrimination, the emergence of human consciousness. As an extravert, with the whole

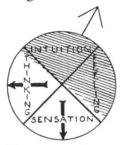

The extraverted man

interesting world before him, what has he to do with 'morbid introspection'? As a sensation type, with the *fonction du réel* at his command, why should he concern himself with these unrealities? As a thinker he will pronounce it unscientific and the matter will be closed; unless, also as a thinker, he finds it impossible to ignore the chaos of the age. Possibly he may satisfy himself with some strictures on the earth being the cosmic lunatic asylum and rest content with that; but he may also conclude that, since he is in it too, something must be done. Even then, unless the unconscious hits him in his own life so hard that he cannot put it entirely behind him (such a one, perhaps, was Saul on the road to Damascus) a man with this psychological orientation will find it very hard to begin.

On the other hand, should he succeed in making the inward journey, when it comes to the return phase his way is plain. As an extraverted sensation and thinking type he asks nothing better than to set forth what he has found. It is the woman, introverted, with developed intuition and feeling, who now has the hard way. She is at home in the unconscious. There she is free. She is the one who, in Plato's famous image of the cave, has come into the daylight. Why should she go back? Here in the world of the spirit everything is real with a reality the world

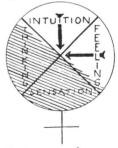

The introverted woman

ignores. Down in the cave of everyday existence everything is murky, cramped, uncertain, obscure. Plato, who wanted to make his Republic work, said that such people must be made to go back. Only in this way could the full light of consciousness come to mankind and the reality of the spirit triumph over the shadow world of mere appearance. But why should she heed Plato? And yet, in the end, *eros*, a feeling of oneness with others, may possibly bring her back. But the return will be as agonizingly difficult for her as was the withdrawal for her opposite number.

These two cases are the two extremes. Broadly speaking, *logos*, extraversion, sensation and thinking make the withdrawal hard, the return easy; *eros*, introversion, intuition and feeling make the withdrawal easy, the return hard. In between are all the other possible combinations, each with its particular difficulties and particular aptitudes.

The above brief description of psychological types is, needless to say, no more than impressionistic, and, as such, wholly inadequate. Happily, for those who wish to pursue it further, there is available Jung's own detailed work on this question. The types theory richly repays study. At first sight this sorting out of one's strong and weak sides, the strong and weak sides of one's acquaintances and friends, seems rather like a parlour game. Actually, it is wisdom vital to the understanding and living of life. It enables a man to see himself in the round, it may be for the first time. It makes possible a new relationship between people, a relationship based upon better mutual understanding. It gives a preliminary insight into the fundamental requirement of life: the linking of the inner and the outer worlds. For all these reasons it is the necessary initial step in the experiment in depth. Also it indicates one of the principal reasons for making the experiment: the development of the inferior functions and attitudes, by winning from the unconscious those parts of the personality at present submerged.

III

THE CONSTRUCTIVE TECHNIQUE

THE theory of psychological types, by bringing into awareness the weak side of the personality, the side in the grip of the unconscious, leads directly to the central purpose in the experiment in depth: how consciousness and the unconscious can be enabled to work together. Jung's constructive technique is designed to this end. It consists essentially in developing certain latent faculties—the inward eye, the inward ear, the inward understanding—enabling a man to become increasingly aware of what is happening the other side of consciousness.

In a sense, as Jung has pointed out, technique is a somewhat misleading term to apply to the various psycho-perceptive methods used. It suggests a more or less automatic functioning. Actually the constructive technique is in the main a matter of attitude. This is not to suggest that the methods employed are in any sense unimportant. On the contrary, for most people they are indispensable. But unless the basic attitude behind them is right, they will not work.

What then is the right attitude? This, in a sense, is for each person to discover for himself. There is no universally valid prescription. Expressed in general terms, though, I should say that it is an attitude compounded of serious attention, involvement and objectivity: together with a basic steadfastness of spirit. At first sight, involvement and objectivity may appear difficult to reconcile. What I mean by this is that a man must be wholly committed to the experiment, not regard it merely as an intellectual excursion; but at the same time repeatedly stand back from it, bring to bear upon it the maximum of conscious awareness. For unless he is wholly committed he will get nowhere. And if he fails to bring to bear upon it the maximum of conscious awareness, the experiment is liable to run away with him.

Of the other two components—an attitude of serious attention and a basic steadfastness of spirit—each has its special importance. So

36

far as can be judged, it is the attitude of serious attention that stimulates the constructive activity of the unconscious. For instance, to attempt to recall one's dreams is a first step towards serious attention. To write them down is a step further. To record them systematically in a special book kept for that purpose is a step further still. To do one's best to analyse them and get at their meaning carries the process a long stage beyond the mere recording. To realize, from experience, that the dream images represent in their own fashion the vital forces at work the other side of consciousness carries the process full circle.[1]

Serious attention requires as its counterpart a natural steadfastness of spirit. Without this, the experiment in depth can be unduly dangerous. When we deal with the deep unconscious, we are dealing with the depths from which, only yesterday as it were, consciousness emerged. In doing so, inevitably, we place consciousness in peril. To take it upon oneself to apply the constructive technique in one's own life, a man needs not only resolution but psychological stamina. Without it, the risk is too great. If you do not have it—and we are all made as we are made—keep away. To recognize that there are some things one is not fitted to do, is not cowardice but wisdom.

Finally, in this attempt to characterize the general attitude fundamental to the constructive technique, the word attitude itself may usefully be annotated. Not only in practising the constructive technique but in everything appertaining to the experiment in depth, attitude is what matters most. A sure counsel at all times, whenever things go wrong, is 'examine your attitude'. By this, needless to say, is not meant the attitude one is assuming, one's mental pose, so to speak. What is meant rather is the poise, balance, disposition of the total psyche. Jung defines attitude as 'a readiness of the psyche to act or to react in a certain direction'. In the experiment in depth this readiness needs to be a steadfast readiness, a determination and an ability to hold on to the last gasp, the attitude of Jacob at the ford:

'And Jacob was left alone; and there wrestled a man with him until the breaking of the day.

[1] It should not be inferred from this that for anyone at any time serious attention given to dreams is necessarily the right course. For a particular person, at a particular time, it may be. But dreams are only one aspect of the activity the other side of consciousness. For a particular person at a particular time, other aspects may be of greater importance.

And when he saw that he prevailed not against him, he touched the hollow of his thigh; and the hollow of Jacob's thigh was out of joint, as he wrestled with him.

And he said, Let me go, for the day breaketh. And he said, I will not let thee go, except thou bless me.

And he said unto him, What is thy name? And he said, Jacob.

And he said, Thy name shall be called no more Jacob, but Israel: for as a prince hast thou power with God and with men, and hast prevailed.

And Jacob asked him, and said, Tell me, I pray thee, thy name. And he said, Wherefore is it that thou dost ask after my name? And he blessed him there.

And Jacob called the name of the place Peniel: for I have seen God face to face, and my life is preserved.'

Dream analysis

Dream analysis is the keystone of the constructive technique. Most depth psychologists would probably agree that dreams show, in their own manner, the situation in the unconscious. This manner is a figurative one, a picture writing, a language of images. The problem is to know what these images mean.

There are three principal methods of interpreting the dream images. There is the old wives' method: 'If you dream of a cat, it means that someone is coming to tea who will tell you interesting news.' There is no warrant for considering it scientific although, like all such lore, it may occasionally have interesting, inexplicable insights.

There is the *a priori* method, which starts with an established theory as to the nature of dreams, and deduces from that what the images represent This is excellent, provided the theory happens to be right. But if it is not right, then it involves a circular deception of the type of the conjurer triumphantly producing from the hat the rabbit he has previously put into it. To take an imaginary example. Let our theory of dreams be that they are wholly concerned with nutrition, eating and drinking. Then practically all long and rigid objects can be interpreted as knife, fork or spoon; every concave object as glass, cup, goblet or mug; every circular object, a plate; every rectangular object, a tray; while the combination of knife, plate, tray and mug will constitute the central symbol of the Square

Meal. Within this framework, the various kinds of food and drink, their absorption, digestion and elimination, will be symbolized in endless profusion. Our theory will also give us the clue to the great art and literature of the world—which will be seen as cunningly disguised descriptions of Gargantuan appetites—to say nothing of such classics as Little Jack Horner, Hey-diddle-diddle, Simple Simon, and others. Accordingly, to such extent as we adopt an *a priori* method of dream analysis we need to be very certain that our basic theory is accurate. Otherwise, the possibilities of self-deception become almost infinite.

There remains the empirical method, which starts with the data, argues from the facts. It says, in effect, if there is any reason in dreams at all, there is presumably some reason why in this particular dream the man climbs through a window instead of going through the door. Well and good, let us see what we can find out—from the person having the dream—what climbing through the window means to him. Has he ever done it? If so why, where, when? Has he heard of people doing it—Romeo, cat burglars, returning roysterers or what not? Is there perhaps some window he would like to climb through? Does climbing through a window perhaps symbolize something to him? In brief, what is the mental context *for him* in which this image is contained?

In using this empirical method it is necessary, therefore, to seek first of all the personal amplifications of the different images appearing in the dream and then to piece the meaning together with the help of the background material thus obtained. As need hardly be said, it is the dreamer's personal amplifications that are sought, not somebody else's personal amplifications. It was to him that the dream came. It was from his mental equipment, as it were, that the images were taken. It is his development of the context of these images that stands a chance of being relevant.

At this point it needs to be emphasized that it is amplification, not free association, that is sought. This is highly important because otherwise a most convincing 'interpretation' may be arrived at which owes nothing to the dream.

For instance, a man dreams that he is staying in a farmhouse. His amplification for this may strike off in all sorts of directions: maybe, he stayed for a while in a farmhouse when he was a child; maybe, farmhouse has an idyllic ring for him, all the townsman's longing for a cottage in the country; maybe, farmhouse raises in him bitter memories of years lost in fruitless labour, striving to reclaim derelict land; or again, it was at a farmhouse that such and such a girl was staying . . . and he is off and away in some sentimental episode of the past. These are all genuine amplifications, probings into the mental tissue, as it were, in which the image is embedded. Now suppose the request for amplification to be wrongly put. The dreamer is asked, 'What does farmhouse remind you of?' 'Cows,' he replies. 'And cows, what do they make you think of?' 'Cows? Cows? Women—just what they are, lot of cows.' And in all probability he has found a rapid associative route to some complex just beneath the surface, with which, it may well be, the dream has nothing to do. If, instead of farmhouse, the Eiffel Tower or the Atlantic Ocean had been given to him as a starting point, he would have got to the same place. Such 'interpretation' of dreams, while rather convincing to anyone who does not know better (after all, has it not led to the complex?) is widely removed from genuine dream analysis. The dream, figuratively speaking, may have come from the very depths of the unconscious, thousands of feet down. By using it to set up an associative chain all that is discovered is the current complex a few inches deep, which could just as easily have been dug out by any other associative technique.

The amplificatory method starts, therefore, with such background material as the dreamer himself can supply to each of the dream images. A second source of amplification is to be found in previous dreams. Wherever possible, it is much more satisfactory to work upon a dream series rather than upon a single dream. A method can then be employed analogous to that used to decipher unknown languages. Where the same sign is found in a number of different passages, the philologist has the task of imagining what it is that could fit into each of these contexts and so arrives at some approximation to its meaning. In like manner, if 'farmhouse' turns up in dream 7, dream 16, dreams 53, 54, 55 and again in dream 59, as well as last night, there is a much better chance of getting at its significance.

There is yet a third source of amplifications: the dreams, as it were, of mankind. Particularly when the dream introduces images totally strange to the dreamer's everyday life—human sacrifices, temples, the bottom of the sea, prehistoric reptiles—the amplifications coming from myths, religions, folklore, fairy-tales, may prove relevant. If, for instance, a townsman who never actually sees snakes continually dreams of them, possibly some of the serpent-lore to be found all over the world may help in the interpretation.

Where none of these forms of amplification is able to throw light on a dream image, Jung's counsel is to see that image as literally, as primitively and naïvely, as possible. As he says, naïveté is a fault in the conduct of life but it is a virtue in the elucidation of the dream image. On the other side of consciousness it is as if we were still at the primitive level, and the more we can see the images with complete absence of sophistication the nearer we get to their meaning. Thus, a weapon is something we may use to protect ourselves, to enforce our will, to dominate others. A tool is a means of making something, of working more effectively. A motor-car is something which carries us about (important to know who is driving) with a motor, a drive, other than our own. A bus or a tram or a train, likewise; but this is something everyone goes by, a collective way; and trams and trains run on rails, have to follow a set course. A bicycle is an individual way of going about, where one has to supply one's own drive and keep one's balance. The kitchen is a place where the cooking is done, where raw food is made assimilable, able to be digested. If in the dream I look in the mirror and see I have acquired a great shock of red hair, red hair is what is coming out of my head (and such sayings as: 'Keep your hair on', 'It got in his hair', 'She took her hair down', give some impression of how hair appears to the popular mind which we all share). If I am out in the street without shoes, then my feet are liable to suffer; shoes protect one against the asperities of the way. If I find myself in public insufficiently clad, that is the comment the dream is making—that I am not dressed to go out, yet am doing so. Long experience with dream analysis makes many of these figurative uses familiar. But this naïve, child-like, interpretation of the dream image, immensely important as it is, should only be used if more direct amplification is lacking. To be in a train, for instance, may have relevant personal meaning: for one man, a means of escape; for another, the fulfilment of his heart's desire; for yet a third, a symbol of disaster.

Dream analysis is still in its infancy. Half a dozen different psychologists are quite capable of giving half a dozen different interpretations to the same dream. Many dreams yield no more than the

merest hints of what may be behind them. The four methods used in
the constructive technique—the dreamer's own amplifications, the
philologist's device of deducing the meaning of an image from its
appearance in different dreams, the mythical background of an
image and the naïve interpretation—have this immense advantage.
They do not rely on any dogma as to the nature of dreams. There
is no forcing of the meaning. The dream images are enabled to speak
for themselves. This is a standpoint to be preserved at all costs.
Otherwise, inevitably, one falls into some form of the *a priori* self-
deception—the conjurer-rabbit-and-hat fallacy of dream analysis.

Dealt with by these means, what do the dreams show? This
depends in great measure upon the depth of the dream, a rather
elusive quality, but in practice not so elusive as at first it sounds.
Many dreams appear to be relatively superficial, a straight reaction
of the unconscious to the standpoint of consciousness. For instance,
we take on a new job and feel we are doing rather well. The dream
shows us bogged down in a marsh, lost in a city we do not know,
trying to catch a train and unable to collect our luggage, going back
to school and being scolded for lateness, caught again in some
situation of the past we hate to remember. Or, conversely, our
attitude in actual life is pessimistic, despairful. The dream shows us
running like an Olympic champion, throwing opponents about
with the ease of a practised all-in wrestler, moving into a new house
wonderfully designed. Or again, we meet someone during the day
and form a low opinion of him. In the night we dream of him and
he is having the freedom of the city conferred upon him, while we
are in the crowd looking on. This reaction type of dream is one of
the commonest. It shows consciousness and the unconscious at vari-
ance. It is not to be assumed that the statement of the unconscious is
necessarily right. But it is wise in such circumstances to re-examine
the conscious attitude; and in any case the divergence itself is something we need to know about and bear in mind.

At the opposite pole to this reaction type of dream is what the
primitives call the 'great dream'. The reaction dream characteristically uses for its imagery things and incidents drawn from our
ordinary daily life, now or in the past. It may perhaps be somewhat
bizarre in its action, but the general *mise en scène* is of a familiar type.
The 'great dream', on the contrary, has a vividness and reality all its
own. Often there is a special kind of light about it. Or it may be in

bright colour, when the ordinary dreams are in neutral shades. The characters themselves may perhaps be unknown to us, but men and women of personality, not mere dummies. Strange beings may come in, gods and goddesses, mythological creatures, wild animals, or there may be metamorphoses from man to animal or vice versa. The whole action has a special impressiveness, even though, as sometimes happens, the events and surroundings themselves are ordinary. Or the setting may be completely strange: back in the Middle Ages, in Greek or Roman times, in some country and among some people unknown, beneath the ocean, in the bowels of the earth. Such great dreams characteristically bring with them symbols, living myths, opening up new possibilities, new means of action, which, as it were, the unconscious proffers to consciousness, for consciousness to make of them what it can.

Between the reaction dream and the 'great dream', with no distinctive dividing mark, are the dreams of which it can best be said that they show an aspect of the unconscious as it is at that time. To some extent such dreams may be tinged by a negative reaction against the conscious attitude. To some extent they may be positive intimations from the possibility-bringing depths. For this reason it is difficult at times to distinguish whether the dream statement has, so to speak, a minus or a plus sign in front of it; whether it is counterbalancing the conscious attitude or prompting it to new endeavour.[1] In this matter there can be no rule-of-thumb interpretation, no general formula to be automatically applied; only the careful and tentative setting of the dream in the total life situation of the man or woman to whom the dream came.

A like difficulty frequently arises as to whether some person appearing in a dream—one's mother perhaps, or a long-ago school-days friend, or some casual acquaintance—is actually the person indicated, or an activity operating in the psyche most appropriately represented by such a figure. As a broad generalization, where such a person is in fact part of one's normal life and appears in a normal fashion, then the dream image is best taken as actually standing for that person. If, on the other hand, the figure is no part of one's

[1] One of the central hypotheses of analytical psychology, as developed by Jung, is the 'compensatory' character of the activity of the unconscious. A question which may usefully be applied to any dream is: what does this compensate in the outer attitude?

normal life, or, though part of normal life, appears in an unusual fashion—an image like one's mother, for instance, but ten feet high and arrayed in Greek robes—then it is best taken as representative of a power constellated in this form.

A good deal of patience is needed in dream analysis, especially at the outset. Many dreams say practically nothing to us, appear meaningless, and yet these same dreams, looked at afterwards, as part of a series, make astonishingly good sense. To use a somewhat fanciful analogy, it is as if the unconscious were showing several films at once, films taken at different levels. Each dream is a brief 'shot'. A particular 'shot' at a particular time may be meaningful: or it may leave us completely nonplussed. It is only when we piece together the 'shots', and have a wider knowledge of the living background, that we get some idea of what the total performance represents.

These, needless to say, are no more than the roughest indications of how the meaning of dreams can be to some extent understood. Later, it may be, our knowledge will have advanced to the point where a definite technique can be worked out. At present there is nothing of the kind. By and large, however, there are these four things that may be said about dreams and dream analysis with some confidence. In the first place, since we do not know much about the dream process, a highly empirical, non-dogmatic approach would seem appropriate. In the second place, provided we give them serious attention, dreams appear to perform their function to a considerable extent, even if we signally fail to 'understand' them in an intellectual sense. It has been well said: 'The dream is its own interpretation.' Even though we can make nothing of a particular dream, if we turn it over in our minds the images seem to have their effect upon our attitude and actions. In the third place, by some strange dispensation it is very difficult to deal satisfactorily with one's own dreams, at least during the next few hours or days. Later, when they have 'gone cold', it is more possible to make an analysis. But, as a general rule, the dream at the moment it comes seems to fall on a blind spot; which means, if we are to do good work on it, we are dependent upon the help of others. Finally, the man or woman who gives serious attention to these 'magic casements', but does not permit himself or herself to be spirited into the 'perilous seas, in faery lands forlorn' on which these casements open, is likely to find a subtle change occurring in personality and attitude. Consciousness and the unconscious are, to some extent, working together in partnership; and something akin to a change in the psychological centre of gravity, an approach to wholeness, tends to take place.

'Be not afeard, the Isle is full of noises'

The only satisfactory way of demonstrating dream analysis is to analyse actual dreams. Unfortunately, it is virtually impossible to analyse actual dreams satisfactorily as a demonstration. There are several reasons for this, each of them crippling. For one thing, any particular dream selected has the appearance of having been especially chosen, of being more or less a unique specimen. This is not so. There are literally hundreds of other dreams that might have been used in its stead. But the reader—who perhaps himself hardly dreams at all—has little means of knowing this. Another grave handicap is that, to demonstrate a dream adequately, it is necessary to give a large part of the life-history of the dreamer as background; and this, for a variety of reasons, is hardly feasible. Most handicapping of all is the fact that, in analysing a dream, one cannot say positively, this means that, so-and-so is obviously such-and-such. There is no certainty, only surmise; with now and then a convincing 'click' as pieces fit into place. But that 'click' cannot be reproduced in writing. With two people working over a dream in which both are deeply interested, the one because it has come to him and apparently means something, the other because he feels such ingenuity and insight as he may possess directly challenged, there is a certain dialectical interchange, a living process, which no descriptive account can convey. Consequently, the ensuing analysis is presented not as a specimen designed to convince, but simply as a none too satisfactory means of illustrating how to set about the operation and the kind of interpretation that may emerge.

The following is the dream of a man of British nationality, living in Switzerland, high above average in education and experience, in good psychological health, with no more than the intelligent layman's knowledge of depth psychology. The title to the dream I myself have added, as it seemed appropriate. Otherwise the dream is as recorded at the time.

'The Villains in the Villa

Episode I. I read a newspaper article which charms me by its deliciously light fantasy and humour, but of which I can remember but one passage, and that absurd: that America can be properly explored only on a bicycle.

Episode II. I am sitting in the kitchen of my villa alone. I realize that there are two villains upstairs. There are, for the moment, two staircases, at the top of each of which is a villain, and somehow there is a clock at the top of each staircase, too. These villains threaten my life—I am in deadly danger and frightened as in a nightmare. Somehow I have got a glimpse of one of the villains; he is visible through the open door in a room at the top of the (real) staircase. (At the bottom of this staircase I examine a "clock" with a peculiar dial, hand-written in ink.) He is a dark, but not unpleasant-looking Oriental, in Oriental garb. He squats, gazing out of the window tranquilly.

Back in the kitchen I realize that the awful moment of attack has arrived. I am not so much concerned about the other villain, who is at the top of the (imaginary) staircase: I feel that the friendly author of the humorous article will be able to cope with him. But the dark villain is now coming down the (real) staircase.

I leave the kitchen and walk towards the foot of the stairs, sweating with fear. I let drop the motor paper I have been reading (I have been reading such papers for the last 30 years, and they represent something infantile), and feel for a weapon. From my right hand pocket I produce a pipe which, for a moment, I think will look like a revolver (this is a well-known trick, which my grandfather once used with success against a burglar), but change my mind and produce from my left hand pocket a tiny leather case (such as contains my tyre-pressure gauge), and from the case draw a tiny automatic about the size of a cigarette lighter. There is an agonizing instant as I fumble with the safety-catch—the villain is almost on me, when I succeed in cocking the weapon, and then I woke up.'

One or two amplifications have been incidentally included in the description of the dream. For the rest, only the vaguest indications were forthcoming. A bicycle, for some reason which he cannot explain, the dreamer associates with 'life'. He has not been to North America. His villa means a great deal to him—it is home. The oriental man suggests nothing; likewise the clocks—apart from the fact that there actually is a clock at the foot of the stairs and that he is interested in clocks. He is a good shot with a revolver; it is a weapon he knows how to handle. Beyond that, the dreamer himself had nothing to suggest, except that the dream seemed to mean something and made a great impression upon him at the time.

In dealing with a dream of this sort it is advisable to divide it into scenes and to take each scene separately. Not until the successive phases have been worked through in detail should an attempt be made to see the dream as a whole.

'*Episode I.* I read a newspaper article which charms me by its deliciously light fantasy and humour, but of which I can remember but one passage, and that absurd: that America can be properly explored only on a bicycle.'

The writer of this article is again referred to at a later stage in the dream as the one who can tackle the second villain. The dreamer himself has, in fact, a detached, fantastic, humorous side and it is reasonable to assume that it is this side making the remark that America should be seen from a bicycle. For 'America' a possible meaning might be the new and strange world of the unconscious—the land of unlimited possibilities. This, in fact, is an image frequently occurring in dreams. The bicycle for the dreamer means 'life'—a simple way of travelling, one in which the traveller has to keep his balance and supply his own drive. The dreamer deprecates the idea of exploring the New World in this fashion, calling it absurd. He is set against it; when in fact, though a slightly unusual idea perhaps, there seems no reason to dismiss it out of hand. Actually, in consciousness, he is the kind of man who might do such a thing.

This possible course having been rejected, there comes the alternative:

'I am sitting in the kitchen of my villa alone. I realize that there are two villains upstairs. There are, for the moment, two staircases, at the top of each of which is a villain, and somehow there is a clock at the top of each staircase, too. These villains threaten my life—I am in deadly danger and frightened as in a nightmare.'

The dreamer is sitting in the kitchen, not a thing he would normally be doing. The kitchen repeatedly appears in dreams. It is the place where materials are prepared, transformed, rendered assimilable, the place of change. The dreamer feels the villains to be a fearful menace. They threaten his life. He is, in fact, making the discovery that his house—the place where he lives, his personality—has strange presences in it; that he is not the sole inhabitant. 'You know,' he commented, 'those fellows had their own furniture up there too.' They are not merely intruders. They are part of his household, but a part of which he has hitherto been unaware.

The staircases and the clocks are especially interesting features. The staircase often appears in dreams as representing a way to the upper part of the house, something above the conscious standpoint. In this case, at the top of the staircases are the clocks. The dreamer himself, considering the dream afterwards, had no idea what they might represent, although they were an important feature of the drama. For the moment it will be best to leave the symbolism of the clocks aside, since it would involve too long and detailed a discursion at this point.

The fact that everything is doubled—two villains, two staircases, each with a clock—may indicate that similar events are occurring on two planes, as it were. That other aspect of the dreamer, the one with the sense of humour and of fantasy, who is interested in the New World, is later assumed to be able to deal effectively with the second villain. There is a *sous-entendu* here, perhaps, that the dreamer's instinctive feeling of terror and of opposition is not necessarily the appropriate way of coping with the situation. The detached, humorous, enquiring spirit of the writer of the article is another possible attitude towards the 'villains'.

'Somehow I have got a glimpse of one of the villains; he is visible through the open door in a room at the top of the (real) staircase. (At the bottom of this staircase I examine a "clock" with a peculiar dial, hand-written in ink.) He is a dark, but not unpleasant-looking Oriental, in Oriental garb. He squats, gazing out of the window tranquilly.'

The 'villain' then is not so villainous after all. He is Oriental, tranquil, meditative. He may, perhaps, be taken as a personification of the unconscious, the 'mysterious East'. There would seem no great reason for fear, but the dreamer sees him as the intruder in the house that he thought was wholly his; and he is not in the least reassured. There are then two views of the situation. The writer of the article sees the unconscious as the New World, the land of infinite possibilities, to be explored by means of the bicycle, the humble unassuming method of approach. The dreamer himself sees the unconscious as an invasion by the dubious, dark and Eastern aspect. And again there is the 'clock' motif, this time evidently not so much an actual clock as something like a clock, with the dial 'hand-written in ink' the peculiar feature.

'Back in the kitchen I realize that the awful moment of attack has arrived. I am not so much concerned about the other villain, who is at the top of the (imaginary) staircase; I feel that the friendly author of the humorous article will be able to cope with him. But the dark villain is now coming down the (real) staircase.'

Things are about to happen on both planes. In the inner world the situation can be held. The detached, humorous author can deal with the second villain. He has the means of coping with the situation. But down the real staircase, actually coming into life, is the dark Easterner. And the dreamer can see him only as a horrible menace.

'I leave the kitchen and walk towards the foot of the stairs, sweating with fear. I let drop the motor paper I have been reading (I have been reading such papers for the last 30 years, and they represent something infantile), and feel for a weapon. From my right hand pocket I produce a pipe which, for a moment, I think will look like a revolver (this is a well-known trick, which my grandfather once used with success against a burglar), but change my mind and produce from my left hand pocket a tiny leather case (such as contains my tyre-pressure gauge), and from the case draw a tiny automatic about the size of a cigarette lighter. There is an agonizing instant as I fumble with the safety-catch—the villain is almost on me, when I succeed in cocking the weapon, and then I woke up.'

The dreamer is shaken to the depths, but nevertheless advances to meet the situation. The motor paper, a mere distraction, an escape from life, is dropped. The pipe—a comfort-loving, meditative attitude towards life—might conceivably serve; it is a traditional method; but this is a situation where bluff will not work. Instead, from the left pocket comes an altogether unexpected weapon. In all esoteric lore the left hand means 'from the unconscious'. In this particular case, though, the meaning is doubtful, since the dreamer happens to be left-handed. But whether from the conscious or the unconscious side, a miniature pistol emerges. Quite unexpectedly he has come upon a weapon he can wield. He was the best shot with the revolver in his battalion. It is something by which his will can be enforced, with which he is effective—if only in a small way. There is an agonizing moment when it is doubtful whether he can have the weapon ready in time for the attack. But he manages that too: and, in the way of dreams, the drama ends.

In a single dream, such as this, there can be no certainty as to the interpretation of particular details, but the general drift is reasonably clear. The time has come when the dreamer has to deal with the unconscious, the villains are in the villa. The detached part of him suggests looking upon the unconscious as the new world, the land of possibilities, and of dealing with it in a simple, everyday fashion. But the attitude of the dreamer is quite otherwise. He can think only of resistance. His glimpse behind the scenes shows that the unconscious, although strange, is not terrible; and there are the clocks, the meaning of which is still to be explored. But he is horribly afraid. He searches for means of defence against this menace to his life. The old devices—the hobby, the comfortable meditative attitude—are not sufficient. To resist the unconscious he brings into action a weapon, an effectiveness, he did not know he possessed. Actually, over the ensuing years, that is substantially what happened. The dreamer declined the adventure of the unconscious. He did not become neurotic—the friendly author held the imaginary staircase all right. He gave up the easy-going comfort-loving life. He became effective —in his own *cuisine*—to a far greater extent than before.

A dream of this kind, with a minimum of amplifying material, is to a great extent its own interpretation. The theme itself—the burglar, the invader—is a regular one. It is the unconscious, saying, so to speak, here I am: a thing very likely to happen around middle age, when a man passes over the meridian and starts the second half of the journey. The presentation of alternatives, first the major alternative—New World on bicycle or Eastern villain in the villa—later the possible choices of the motor paper, or the pipe, before the pistol is discovered, is likewise typical. Most characteristic of all is the dreamer's attitude in the dream. In consciousness he is of a curious, enquiring turn of mind, interested in metaphysics, just as likely to stand a burglar a drink as to shoot him—especially such a meditative villain as this Easterner. But in the unconscious there is a very different attitude constellated; and it was that attitude which prevailed.

There remain the clocks. Here, as a matter of record, it has to be said that some months after this dream, two burglars did actually break into the villa while the occupants were away on holiday. The trail of candle-grease left by the burglars led as far as the foot of the famous staircase, where in fact a rather special clock did stand. There it ceased. Examination of the house showed that nothing had been taken. Apprehended some time later the two men confessed to the burglary. They had been told that the people were away, and had broken in. They had reached the foot of the staircase, when suddenly the clock struck. And they had fled, supposing the occupants returned.

If this had happened before the dream occurred, then the source of the dream images, especially the clocks, would have been obvious. But it happened several months afterwards. Coincidence? In a case like this it is impossible to say. But there is considerable evidence (J. W. Dunne's *An Experiment with Time* a notable example) to indicate that the dream occasionally goes forward instead of back to find its material.

This, then, is one, highly inconclusive, pointer towards the significance of the clocks. The clock defeats the burglars. The other possible meaning of the clocks goes back to one of the great primordial images of mankind. As will be explored later at some length, the principal religions, as also the 'secret doctrine', of the world make free use of a geometrical pattern the

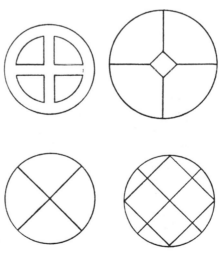

Typical *mandalas*

essential features of which are the square, the circle, four radii (or some multiple of four) quartering the figure, and a centre—the centre being of especial importance. Jung calls this figure the *mandala*, the Sanskrit name for this type of design. Judging from an impressive mass of empirical evidence, its broad significance is that of integration, of wholeness, all the disparate parts of the human personality—conscious and unconscious—held together around the centre and protected from the outside by the circle and/or square. The clock, with its square face, its round dial, its twelve divisions, its centre (moving the clock hands, yet itself unmoved and timeless), is a characteristic *mandala* figure. At the foot of the staircase the dreamer looked at this symbol of integration, 'a peculiar dial, handwritten in ink', but made nothing of it. And there were the clocks among the villains' furniture; as if to say that with them came wholeness as well as disintegration.

As a foil to the Villains in the Villa, a dream dealing with much the same psychological situation, but from a different standpoint, may be of interest. The dreamer is substantially similar in material circumstances to the one just considered, but with diametrically the opposite attitude towards the unconscious. The dream was self-analysed long after it had 'gone cold'.

'THE LEFT FORK TO LAUSANNE

I dreamt that we were in a car going from Geneva to Lausanne. There were four of us, my father, mother, younger brother and myself. My father was driving, my brother and myself in the back seat. The car was of a rather ramshackle old-fashioned type. As we came near to Lausanne there was a fork where one used to be able to go straight on. But now the road had been made one-way and we had to take the left fork.

This led up to the top of a strange mound. The car stopped and we got out. There were two guardians of the mound, mighty-limbed men clothed only in skins, the flesh an unhealthy greenish-white. They said nothing. The whole mound was in some uncanny fashion alive, or as if life of a kind moved in it. I had the impression that it was made up of corpses and there were rats among the corpses. The guardians, I thought, probably fed upon the decaying flesh. Below the mound, where the one-way road ran which we had not been allowed to take, I saw a motor bicyclist and some other traffic, driving along quite normally.

The mound overlooked a broad level plain reminiscent of Holland—there was a windmill far away in the middle of it. I looked to see how we could continue and realized that my father had stopped because, if we were to get off the mound, it would be necessary to drive down a flight of rustic steps, built of earth and logs. I realized that to do it I should have to drive and that going down that flight of steps would be a perilous business, since even with the brakes full on the car would slide down them with locked wheels.

Still turning this over in my mind I suddenly had the impression that something extraordinary was about to happen. Over to the left a large flock of birds rose up and flew away; among them a porpoise-like creature that propelled itself through the sky by doubling up and straightening out. I recollected that there used to be things like this about, but I had forgotten them. Suddenly, from the left, there came a great rush of water, fathoms deep, flooding the whole land over which we looked. The water, which had been rushing from left to right, suddenly reversed and rushed from right to left. I reflected that it was as well we had not gone on.'

'This dream made a considerable impression upon me at the time and I tried hard to puzzle out the amplifications. These were difficult to get, but over a period of months I managed to piece together most of them. The first part is fairly clear:

> *We were in a car going from Geneva to Lausanne. There were four of us, my father, mother, younger brother and myself. My father was driving, my brother and myself in the back seat. The car was of a rather ramshackle old-fashioned type. As we came near to Lausanne there was a fork where one used to be able to go straight on. But now the road had been made one-way and we had to take the left fork.*

I have several times made the run from Geneva to Lausanne, going beyond to Berne and Zürich. Jung lives near Zürich and on one of the occasions, at least, it was to visit him there. It is the psychological road perhaps.

I always disliked going through Lausanne—never sure I should find my way. But this time it is my father, not I, doing the driving. Actually my father (who had died some years earlier) never drove and we never had a car in his time. Presumably, then, this is the family situation, and I am travelling in it still.

We come to the left fork—left, I knew, meant the unconscious. We can no longer travel along the ordinary high road, normality and all that. So off we go, to the left.

> *This led up to the top of a strange mound. The car stopped and we got out. There were two guardians of the mound, mighty-limbed men clothed only in skins, their flesh an unhealthy greenish-white. They said nothing. The whole mound was in some uncanny fashion alive, or as if life of a kind moved in it. I had the impression that it was made up of corpses and there were rats among the corpses. The guardians, I thought, probably fed upon the decaying flesh. Below the mound, where the one-way road ran which we had not been allowed to take, I saw a motor bicyclist and some other traffic driving along quite normally.*

For me the mound telescopes two war-time situations. One in France, in the First World War, at a place where the trenches were dug in ground thick with corpses and where there were the most disgusting rats. The other, a large tumulus I camped on for some while, during the same war, in Greece. General background, therefore, death and putrefaction, life feeding on death, prehistory —heroic prehistory, perhaps—and war.

The guardians of the mound likewise telescoped two amplifications. On the one hand, Michelangelo's statuary. I always look upon Michelangelo as a man having a special insight into the unconscious. On the other, some dimly recollected book on anthroposophy, read many years before, which referred to "Guardians of the Threshold". I thought the book foolish at the time, but the phrase had stuck.

Turning the dream over with these amplifications in mind, I found that, rightly or wrongly, I was becoming convinced that the mound stood for what Jung calls the collective unconscious, the outcome of countless generations of man and his forbears, in which life still moves; and that the "guardians" stood for the primordial forces of the unconscious, who derived their sustenance from this still-living deposit.

The fact that, just a short distance away, life was going on quite normally struck me very much at the time. All was as before except—I had taken the left fork.

The mound overlooked a broad level plain reminiscent of Holland —there was a windmill far away in the middle of it. I looked to see how we could continue and realized that my father had stopped because, if we were to get off the mound, it would be necessary to drive down a flight of rustic steps, built of earth and logs. I realized that to do it I should have to drive and that going down that flight of steps would be a perilous business, since even with the brakes full on the car would slide down them with locked wheels.

Holland for me is a rather magic land, with sentimental associations. The light there is beautiful. When I was going there for the first time, an old Belgian in the train asked whether I had been there before and, finding I hadn't, said: "Hm. You'll be surprised. *Ils sont tous fous.*" After that I always called it the "fou" country. With the windmill in the centre, particularly, it stood well for the other side of the looking glass, the other side of consciousness.

The flight of rustic steps eluded me for a long time. Then I remembered where I had seen them. It was at the mountain hotel where we stop when we go skiing to the *Col Infranchissable*. I remembered, too, that my friend's car jibbed just at the foot of those steps, and in getting it started we came near to having it over the edge. The meaning of those steps then would seem to be, the pass you cannot cross, the place of danger.

Still turning this over in my mind I suddenly had the impression that something extraordinary was about to happen. Over to the left a large flock of birds rose up and flew away; among them a porpoise-like creature that propelled itself through the sky by doubling up and straightening out. I recollected that there used to be things like this about, but I had forgotten them. Suddenly from the left, there came a great rush of water, fathoms deep, flooding the whole land over which we looked. The water, which had been rushing from left to right, suddenly reversed and rushed from right to left. I reflected that it was as well we had not gone on.

The flock of birds I took to represent ideas, intuitions, winged creatures pursuing their own independent life. They were flying away. The porpoise-like creature was much more extraordinary: but I found almost at once what "porpoise" meant to me. It was the "porpoise" of *Alice in Wonderland*; and it struck me that for many years, until relatively recently, I too had travelled with a purpose: but that, like the birds, it had now flown away leaving me in a sterile patch.

The great rush of water I took at once to be the spirit (water, in its meaning of spirit, being an almost stock symbol with me) but the spirit in its destructive aspect. Its flowing first one way and then the other put me in mind of the strife of the opposites.

The chief points I had out of the dream, rightly or wrongly, were: I can no longer drive in the family car; in future I have to do the driving. I have to take the left fork. It is a queer uncanny place, like being back in the war, but the normal world goes on just the same close by. Don't try driving over the Col Infranchissable—the boundary of consciousness—or you will find it is *infranchissable*. The "porpoise" is gone for good. The *"fou"* land beyond the mound is very interesting, but no place for tourists. Look out!'

Upon this self-analysis of a dream two comments may usefully be made. It is sound practice to 'get inside' the dream, as has been done here. The dream comes alive; and not only is the analysis itself facilitated, but the effect upon the dreamer is enhanced. He is able to 'eat the dream' in a way otherwise impossible.

At the same time, what the dream says should always be subjected to the criticism of consciousness. The dream is not an oracle. It is (at least, this the hypothesis) the point of view of the unconscious. For consciousness to accept this point of view uncritically is to be caught in a particularly insidious form of superstition. On the other hand, to learn of the attitude of the unconscious is valuable knowledge. It is the first step towards inner co-operation, the forming of the whole man.

The active approach

Dreams and dream analysis are fundamental to the constructive technique. But the dream is an essentially passive means of approach. It comes to us, or does not come, in its own time and own way. Sometimes the way it comes, moreover, is so involved, so recondite, that we can make nothing of it. For those committed to the 'left fork' there are more active methods, each of which has its special advantages and drawbacks. These are dealt with in more detail in later chapters, so that only a cursory description need be given here.

The method most closely allied to dream analysis Jung calls 'active imagination'—the voluntary seeing of visions. The technique of active imagination consists essentially in withdrawing the energy normally flowing through the conscious functions, directing it into the situation the other side of consciousness, and observing the results. When this is successfully accomplished one sees, as with an inward eye, a play of images (in something of the same way as in a dream) while at the same time remaining fully awake and aware.

Such visions are essentially different from the more or less pathological phantasies to which some people are subject, where the unconscious breaks in unasked. With active imagination, the act of seeing with the inward eye is deliberately willed. On the other hand, what is seen is completely unwilled, being just as autonomous in its operation as a dream. Because of this, it is sometimes called the *rêve éveillé*. But there is one very important difference between the dream and the product of active imagination. Whereas the dream expresses the standpoint of the unconscious only, active imagination apparently presents something more in the nature of a synthesis of the conscious and the unconscious standpoints. Because of this, although such visions are expressed in the same picture-language as the dream, they are, nevertheless, nearer to consciousness, and as such more readily interpreted. Furthermore, active imagination, in which consciousness and the unconscious have collaborated, does not call for the same degree of criticism as does the dream, but primarily for understanding; and in this respect is a considerable advance on dream analysis as a means of arriving at a working partnership between consciousness and the unconscious.

To some people, this technique of active imagination is likely to savour unpleasantly of the occult. They feel that it is handing over the citadel of consciousness to the enemy, the unconscious; and are profoundly antipathetic to anything of the kind. Such a feeling is understandable. Man during his chequered history has had a hard fight to draw his small fragment of consciousness out of the great unconscious. To risk losing it, as it would seem, is akin to madness. But there is another and perhaps more accurate point of view; namely, that active imagination is a faculty we have lost and are now recovering. T. S. Eliot, in his essay on Dante, has some interesting and relevant comments on this.

'Dante's is a *visual* imagination. It is a visual imagination in a different sense from that of a modern painter of still life: it is visual in the sense that he lived in an age in which men still saw visions. It was a psychological habit, the trick of which we have forgotten, but as good as any of our own. We have nothing but dreams, and we have forgotten that seeing visions—a practice now relegated to the aberrant and uneducated—was once a more significant, interesting, and disciplined kind of dreaming.'

It may be apposite, also, to recall what a tremendous part visions have played in the drama of history, not least of our own civilization. The vision that came to Saul on the road to Damascus, Peter's vision of the knotted sheet justifying the preaching of the gospel to the Gentiles, Constantine's vision of the *Labarum*, before the battle of the Milvian Bridge, leading to the official adoption of the Christian religion, together changed the whole course of human life, from then to the present day.

For many people the most practical method of starting active imagination is to permit a dream to continue. The following is an instance, as recorded at the time. The dreamer was a woman of middle age, interested in depth psychology, but with no specialist knowledge.

'I dreamed that I was on a holiday in France with a number of friends, one of whom suggested that we should go to the theatre. We saw a play by Molière, which I know we enjoyed, though I remember nothing about it. Then, where the stage should be, there was a harbour with a curving jetty on the left; it was rather like the harbour at B—— (a town in France), where I had recently been, though there the jetty is on the right. I noticed a black and gold altar with candles near the end of the jetty, and said, "I suppose that's there for Lent, it's not always there." Suddenly there are gold and silver wheatsheaves—or are they fireworks shaped like sheaves?—alternate, one gold and one silver, held or sent up by choir boys or acolytes standing on the altar—a striking and beautiful sight, of which I subsequently made a painting. (The picture showed three silver and three golden sheaves with four white-robed figures.)

Then it is a theatre again; we are in one of the galleries. Great crowds of people swarm in behind us; some of them wear carnival masks, covering the whole person, which make them look like primitive idols. Groups of three are announced in German by an unseen master of ceremonies: *die drei Grossen; die drei Trotzigen* (I don't think that was the actual word, but there was some suggestion of a defiant or aggressive character. These announcements seem to be some sort of allusion to the Second Part of Faust). The "three big ones" were in ordinary clothes and did not seem to me to be as big as some of the others.

Then a general move was made; there were to be festivities somewhere else. We wanted to go, but we had to go round by a back entrance because we were not Catholics. We were negotiating for admission when I awoke.'

The general purport of this dream is fairly clear. It is presenting three ways of life. There is the rational French outlook, symbolized by Molière—enjoyable but nothing retained. There is the diametrical opposite to this, the religious outlook but in a bizarre setting—the 'jetty on the left', and the acolytes with sheaves of corn, or possibly fireworks. There is the German, Faust Part II, *Weltanschauung*, the artistic philosophical insight into the unconscious, but somehow falling rather flat. The dreamer's account then continues:

'I was sleepy and did not want to write down the dream at once, but I twice dreamed I was writing it, so as it was spoiling my sleep I got up in the early morning and wrote it.

It was suggested to me later that as this dream was an interesting one I should use it as the starting point of a phantasy. The phantasy which resulted was as follows:

I went with the friends who had been with me in the dream to the side entrance, and explained that we were not Catholics, but wanted to be admitted, and on that understanding we were allowed in. It was a kind of park with grass and large trees. There was a broad alley, and all the people who had come in by the main entrance were walking along it; you could hear the sound of their feet and they were talking in low tones. It was rather dark, though not deep night. They came to a place where there was a large oval amphitheatre of turf set at a lower level, with grassy banks sloping down to it. They seated themselves all round in groups of three, two men and a woman, or two women and a man. The men were dressed in red and the women in blue; rich dark colours. I did not specially distinguish the shapes of their clothes; they might have been cloaks.

There was some sort of structure at one end of the oval. Three heralds came out; they had golden trumpets on which they blew a blast. Then several other groups of three emerged. They went to the middle of the oval, and there they dug a deep hole. Then they poured water into the hole from ewers. As they poured, there emerged from the hole a dull gold shape, like an enormous crocus bud; it rose up—it was like a poplar tree—it opened out and exfoliated, and it was a great golden tree with upturned branches.'

The phantasy takes up directly the central problem of the dreamer —the need, of which she was well aware, for some kind of religious understanding. She has to explain that they are not Catholics, they have not the direct link with the pre-Christian faiths which Roman Catholicism, by its syncretistic tradition, affords. But they want to be admitted to the mystery: and, through their insistence (the carrying on of the dream by active imagination) they are.

In the phantasy everything is designed to evoke that fourth possibility which the dream did not afford. The groups are in threes, sometimes a man, sometimes a woman missing. The something that is to come is, as it were, both male and female. The men are in red cloaks, characteristically the colour of the instincts, of passion; the women are in blue, characteristically the colour of the spirit. Something is to be elicited which is neither instinct nor spirit, yet both. The deep hole is dug, the place of birth. It is fertilized from the ewers. And what comes is the golden tree. To the dreamer the tree has a profound personal meaning. A dream when she was a young girl, which made a lasting impression upon her, was that of a marvellous tree. At the deep level of the unconscious the tree is a persistently recurring symbol for the impersonal life, the something totally different that may grow in a man from the union of earth and sky, the conscious and the unconscious. And here it is neither red nor blue, neither instinct nor spirit, but gold—the highest value. The dreamer's persistence, refusing to stop short where the dream ended, has enabled her to visualize a new way of life—the one in fact that she eventually took.

Active imagination may assume many other forms. The action may take place not as here over a period of minutes, but of months or of years even. In such cases a long symbolical process may be worked out in a series of incidents, each incident continuing more or less where the preceding one left off. (An example of this is given in a later chapter.) Or it may take the form of a split-second vision, when we ask ourselves whether we really saw it or not.

Some people acquire active imagination with the utmost ease. For others it is a complete mystery. To attempt to give instructions is thus liable to be either unnecessary or useless. But there are some general working rules which may be of use to those coming somewhere between these two extremes.

It is useful, as in the case cited above, to start with some dream image or inner situation which, so to speak, has a certain life of its own. This image or situation should be visualized and held relaxedly yet firmly—relaxed in body but firm in mind—just as one might the recollection of last night's sunset or some far away memory of childhood. The next step is to give energy over to it, so that it is free to move and develop in its own way. To do this it is necessary to collect the energy normally going into the outer life, and to let that energy flow into the image. This does not mean forcing the action in any way, pushing the figure around. One must be actively passive—active in giving over the energy, passive in observing. The outstanding characteristic of the true vision is its complete autonomy. The images go their own gait, not yours. It may well be that you do not like what comes. The instance recorded above was, for the seer, a joyous experience. It might easily have been otherwise. One is not given the choice. You start with the image, which must be conscientiously held in the mind's eye with the utmost of awareness; you give over the energy; and you see what happens.

There is a further development of active imagination in some ways more valuable still and for many people much easier to do. This consists in concretely depicting—drawing, painting or modelling—the inner image. Here also a beginning may be made by taking some striking episode in a dream and proceeding to paint it. In the course of the painting, details—sometimes more than details —proceed to fill themselves in, thereby developing the dream images in a fashion achievable in no other way. A still more useful method of using the painting technique is to seize a time when the unconscious feels heavy with unexpressed contents, and to paint what is there, letting the contents depict themselves upon the paper. For instance, when a black mood descends, or when something is gnawing at one beneath the surface, it is possible to paint the mood and so to bring the 'something' into the outside world. This can give an immense relief, in that it exteriorizes the inner image. By separating oneself from it, by objectifying it in this way, one is in a better position to cope with it. The picture itself, moreover, acts back upon the unconscious. It enables the unconscious to see itself, as it were, in the light of consciousness; with great integrative effect.

The type of drawing or painting so made varies from geometrical patterns to fantastic figures and scenes, from the most childish or primitive representation to compositions having obvious affinities to modern non-representational art. The value, however, lies not so much in its artistic quality as in its essential truthfulness. The painter, however skilled or unskilled, must put everything he has and is into the work. When this is done, it provides one of the most effective and by far the safest of all methods of making contact with the unconscious, for here consciousness and the unconscious are purposefully working together. It has indeed only one major drawback. Methods are a means to an end. The end in this case is an effective working partnership between consciousness and the unconscious. But the fascination of the images coming from the unconscious can be such as to turn this technique into an indulgence, a playing with the unconscious, with no real work done, because the integration embodied in the picture is not carried over into life.

As with active imagination, some people readily acquire this technique of painting or drawing from the unconscious, while for others it is almost inconceivable. To these latter Leonardo da Vinci gives some advice, which as he says,

'might seem trivial and almost laughable, yet is of great value in quickening the spirit of invention. It is this, that you should look at certain walls stained with damp or at stones of uneven colour. If you have to invent some setting you will be able to see in these the likeness of divine landscapes, adorned with mountains, ruins, rocks, woods, great plains, hills, and valleys in great variety; and then again you will see there battles and strange figures in violent action, expressions of faces and clothes and an infinity of things which you will be able to reduce to their complete and proper forms. In such walls the same thing happens as in the sound of bells, in whose strokes you may find every named word which you can imagine.'

The 'divine landscapes' and 'strange figures in violent action' Leonardo himself saw—as, for instance, in the background to the *Gioconda* or the sketch of St. George in his fight with the dragon—breathe the spirit of the deep unconscious.

Voices

There remains still another method, in some ways the most impressive of all, but also involving the most risk. It is possible not only to paint, but also to write from the unconscious; or, still more directly, to speak with the figures constellated there. If, for instance, a personality of a definite kind appears in a dream, it may later be interrogated and will answer. The following is a more than usually dramatic example of this kind of communication. The dreamer is a woman of middle age, deeply interested in the psychology of the unconscious, but having no special knowledge of it at the time.

'THE BLACK MADONNA

Dreamed I had some contact with a curious dark woman, in a kitchen of a house. I seemed to be staying with her; or she with me. We had had an ordinary meal round a table in the kitchen. The woman was tall, with dark straight hair parted in the middle and drawn into a low knot behind and some kind of white cap, long oval face, large dark opaque eyes, white lace round the neck, plain black dress. After the meal, a dreadful sense of impending danger. She took a candle and went out of the kitchen and up the stairs. I knew that she wanted to kill me, would do so if she got me alone. A. (the dreamer's husband) was there, I resolved not to leave him. We put the kitchen straight. He stood by the door into the hall and I called to him to wait for me while I went into a scullery and put the light out. While I was doing so, the woman came down again and did something in the kitchen. I had to cross the kitchen which seemed all in shadows, and the woman stood among the shadows looking at me. Even then I felt she might spring and strangle me. Those few steps were ghastly terror until I reached and touched, clung to A.'s shoulder and we went out together. Only his presence saved me and even that could not take away the awful fear.'

Here follow the dreamer's written comments:

'I can't get any association to the woman in real life, but the words that come into my mind as I think of her are "The Black Madonna". She was impersonal, deadly and sinister. A. seemed unconscious of the danger. He seemed to stand for something absolutely safe and "ordinary". Something concretely normal that would protect me.

It was as if I were split in two parts at the time. One part of me was a young girl, taking a meal, talking to an older woman, clearing up. The other part was an onlooker who watched the woman take the candle and leave the kitchen and go upstairs, and it was the onlooking part who realized fully the danger as I watched her mount the stairs and look back with a terrible look. It was the onlooking part who realized the safety in A.'s presence. It was the onlooking part watching the young girl put out the light in the scullery. Then the two parts joined in the terror of crossing the shadowy kitchen with the shadowy woman looking out, with the feeling "she will strangle me", and the rush to reach A. at the door and clutch his shoulder.

Why do I realize the woman's danger and power when she took a candle and started to go upstairs?'

There follows the record of a written conversation with the Black Madonna.

'Why do you inspire me with terror?

'Why do I feel sure you will strangle me and that you mean evil?

'Who are you with that Victorian dress?

'Why do you carry a candle, and give me that malevolent glance when you go upstairs?

'Why are your eyes so opaque? If it were not for that you could be beautiful with your oval face and dark eyes.

'But there is something fixed and rigid about your form and face.

'That black, close-fitting dress seems tight and uncompromisingly severe. The white at your throat and head does not soften, it only relieves and shows the black up more clearly.

'Why do I call you Madonna? You have the Madonna form of face, and if instead of being opaque your eyes were large and soft and full of feeling that would change your whole character.

'But why do I feel evil and terror in connection with you?'

Madonna: 'You are young and irresponsible. You are frightened of me because I touch dark instinctive things. I belong to the very deeps of life, and you are young and superficial. How could I do otherwise than seem terrible to you because you are not capable of touching my world. I am a woman who has lived and suffered, who has been wronged, put on one side—denied the expression of that which is within. You are an undeveloped creature, your youth is superficial, you flee for protection to the normality of the daylight—of course you feel I should strangle you because of the depth of life and knowledge I have in me, both of you and of the world. But too much would suffocate you.

'My eyes are opaque because you have not lived enough to reach me and change that expression. I hate you because of your youth and frivolity and superficiality. Because you are choosing the safe and easy path and you daren't turn and face me.

'My black dress and white cap and Victorian respectability are symptoms of servitude. They are what creatures like you have made of me. Yet without me, you frivolous ones are nothing, you can do nothing, be nothing. I am in your house because I am the mainstay of it; but because of you I am not free. I, the older, experienced being, am clothed in garments of the last century, tied down to a conventionality which is not my true nature.

'It is because you like to have me uniformed and taped, that I am dressed like this; but it is not my true nature. You feel evil and cruelty in me, and you are frightened. That is due to your own repression of me because I am dependent on you. I am irrevocably tied up with you and so long as you take refuge with the normal you will relegate me to the shadows. A little candle-light shows up what I am to you; "The spirit of man is the Candle of the Lord". That is the flame that lights up my face, and shows the hatred that is in me because of the part I am forced to play in your life.

'I am the Mary Magdalene. If, instead of wearing this stiff black dress and respectable white cap, my hair was flowing loosely and wildly, my dress was a loose robe and you saw me thus in the daylight, I would seem a vagabond, a woman of sorrows and acquainted with grief, and belonging to a wild life which you wish to deny. Because I am part of you you cannot live with me in this form, and so you have tried to relegate me to the shadows in conventional dress.

'All criminals shut away from life, all those in whom ordinary life is dead, develop an opaque look in the eyes. It is part of the mask of conventionality and repression.

'There is the criminal in me—that is why you felt evil: but there is also sorrow and experience and instinctive life. If you do not give these things their place some day they will suffocate you: you suffocate your normal life in the dark kitchen of the unconscious. I must come upstairs and meet you, and live with you in daylight, and you must hold intercourse with me because I *am* part of you: and without me, the normal "you"—the young bride in her honeymoon grey dress who flies to reality for safety—that young girl will be suffocated by her own instinctive life.'

Colloquy with the unconscious, such as the above, need not be related to a dream, or to a specific figure constellated, as here. Whenever the typical 'insoluble problem' starts to weigh life down, the unconscious has a view on it. At such a time, by questioning the unconscious and giving over to it the necessary energy, this view will be expressed.

The actual procedure of writing from the unconscious varies from one person to another. With some people it approximates to the automatic writing of the medium. More generally, it is something between word-by-word dictation and the spontaneous rising of thoughts and phrases in the mind which set themselves down with remarkable ease and speed. Characteristically, the writing from the unconscious is in a different literary style from that of the conscious individual. Almost always the statements made appear to have been carefully worked out in advance and often have remarkable intellectual or dramatic qualities.

In all such direct dealing with the unconscious, criticism by consciousness is absolutely essential. The contents of the unconscious are putting up their point of view. This point of view is important for two main reasons: because in some things the unconscious has insights going far beyond those of consciousness; and because the point of view put forward by the unconscious indicates the kind of action it is likely to initiate or support. But to accept such communication as if it were oracular is the crassest and most elementary of errors. The temptation to do so is nevertheless exceedingly strong. Consciousness becomes so weary of responsibility that when it finds something which can reel off decisions with complete assurance it is all too ready to sit back with a sigh of relief and refer everything to the inner mentor. Also, the unconscious speaks with such authority, and at times with such extraordinary wisdom, that it is hard for consciousness to assert its own feeble and vacillating standpoint. But for consciousness to give over control in this fashion is disastrous. The *dicta* of the unconscious lose their insight and turn to foolishness: and the man who accepts them uncritically will find himself paying the price of his irresponsibility.

None of these four methods of perception—dream analysis, active imagination, painting or drawing the inner image, direct communication with the unconscious—is anything new in the world. In one form or another they have always been the means by which prophets, seers, artists, mystics have made contact with the unseen. What is different is that, in the experiment in depth, these methods are used to a specific end. The essential aim of the constructive technique is to make possible a fundamental re-adjustment of the personality, an organic linking up of consciousness and the unconscious. This purpose is achieved by action from the two sides. From the conscious side, the man has to use his understanding, his capacity for objectivity, his steadfastness of spirit, to the utmost. He needs to recognize and realize, to the fullest extent possible, activities emanating from the other side of consciousness which had previously passed him by. At the same time he has to hold his own against the tremendous pull and disintegrating tendencies of the forces of the unconscious. This is the task of the conscious being and it is a hard one. But the real work, the organic linking of consciousness and the unconscious, is done from the other side. The man is worked upon and inwardly transformed.

Part Two

THE DEEP UNCONSCIOUS

IV

AUTONOMOUS COMPLEXES

NYONE who uses the constructive technique sooner or later makes the same discovery as did the dreamer of the Villains in the Villa: one is not alone in the house. There is the ego, the complex of consciousness, the entity one refers to as 'I'; and around it there are a number of other complexes, enjoying a considerable measure of autonomy.

The term 'complex' is one that has suffered considerably in the 'intolerable wrestle with words and meanings'. It has come to be looked upon as more or less synonymous with 'kink', a bee in the bonnet. As Jung originally used it, the meaning was exactly that of the roots from which the word derives: something *com-plex*, twisted together. One of the characteristics of psychic contents is that they do get twisted together in strange fashion. The ego, so far as can be seen, is a particularly complicated twisting together, having the unique capacity for consciousness. The personal unconscious, the living rubbish heap of the repressions, is full of such twistings together: sore points, explosive topics, earlier attitudes we have failed to assimilate. And there are other 'twistings together' of a more permanent kind, essential parts of the human psyche, which behave like so many independent personalities. The Villains in the Villa are indeed 'such stuff as dreams are made on'; but in their own way they are just as real as the ego.

These disembodied beings the other side of consciousness may appear as one or they may appear as legion. They are like figures of the mist, continually forming and re-forming; at one moment taking definite shape, the next disappearing again into the undifferentiated energic mass that is the deep unconscious. In the course of the ages, however, it is as if mankind had gradually succeeded in con-cretizing to some extent certain of these figures. They have taken form and can be encountered, as it were, on a 'being-to-being' basis. The autonomous complexes, thus constellated, provide one

71

of our principal means of making contact with the unconscious depths.

In the normal course of everyday living an autonomous complex is encountered in any or all of four main ways. It may be projected upon somebody in the outside world. When this happens we are compulsively bound to that somebody. The ties may be of love, or they may be of hate, or they may be of both; but bound we are. An essential part of the psyche has gone out from us and settled upon some other person; and we are held to that person as by the bonds of destiny.

The autonomous complex, instead of being projected (or besides being projected) may invade and more or less take over the conscious personality. To some extent the man may be aware of this invasion and struggle against it. More often he will identify with the invader and believe that it is he himself producing these tremendous impulses, doing these unusual deeds. When this happens the man is thoroughly possessed, rapt, carried away—possibly to greatness, possibly to madness, more often to empty foolishness. But whatever his fate may be, this thing is certain: so long as the invasion lasts, he is not himself.

The third type of interaction with an autononous complex is, to put it paradoxically, where there is no contact made. The complex simply disappears, all touch with it is lost. At first sight, for people who do not appreciate villains in their villa, this seems a most desirable condition. Actually it is not. A man so abandoned is left derelict. The life has gone out of him. The ego is alone in an empty house, a burden to himself and a bore to others.

The remaining form of relationship consists in a fundamental coming to terms with the autonomous complexes, thereby bringing about at least an approximation to wholeness of the total personality, conscious and unconscious. How this coming to terms may be effected is an essential part of the experiment in depth.

There remains one other general characteristic of the autonomous complexes which needs to be mentioned at the outset. The nature of these beings is one of manifold ambivalence. They are infantile, undeveloped, semi-animal, semi-reptile even, and at the same time, semi-divine. They are completely indispensable and an insufferable nuisance. They have immense energy, extraordinary insight; and (so long as no adequate relationship is made with them) they will endeavour to use this energy and insight to run the man their own way—which will not be his way. They are immensely wise and can give the worst possible advice. They can be the truest guides and the most arrant deceivers. They are the light and the darkness, inspiration and madness, the new life and a perpetual distraction. Only as and when they take their proper place in relationship to consciousness do they carry out their true function as part of the whole man.

The shadow

The shadow, or shadow-ego, is the autonomous complex first calling for description; but in many ways is the hardest of all to describe.

It normally appears in dreams as a personality of the same sex as oneself, in some manner like oneself, but inferior: a younger brother or sister, a junior colleague, a schooldays' friend, *protégé* or *bête-noire*, a foreigner, a servant, a gypsy, a prostitute, a 'little' man, a 'little' woman, the person next door. It may be a weak, colourless figure. Or it may have the whole force of the deep unconscious behind it; in which case it will bear strong resemblance to the Devil —an adversary in the path, a dogger of one's footsteps, a burglar, a sinister figure lurking in the dark. The 'Black Madonna' of the preceding chapter is a particularly highly-charged and impressive example of the shadow.

Broadly speaking, the shadow is made up of the negatives of the ego's positives. It is the something which comes between a man and his fulfilment: his laziness, his fecklessness, his tendency to let things slide or to over-do things, his cowardice, his rashness, his self-indulgence, his carping and envious nature, his murkiness and smut. In a sense the shadow is a personification of the personal unconscious, the negative expression of all those things in our life which belong to us, but which we have not been able, have not dared, to live. But it is also much more than that: the dark background from which we have emerged, the primitive, the animal, the non-human.

The following account of the appearance of the shadow in dreams, while necessarily peculiar to the man concerned, gives some impression of how this figure may be encountered and also how it may develop.

'I have, over the last fourteen years, experienced five different "shadow" figures in dreams. The first and most regular is my younger brother—sometimes more or less as he was some years ago, sometimes as he was as a child. It is never quite my brother, though, but someone like him. In the dream he is sometimes helping, sometimes opposing, but for the most part passive. This, as I take it, is the shadow in its acceptable form: an autonomous complex, own brother to the ego, but almost devoid of energy. For years, although this figure appeared in scores of dreams, he never spoke a word.

The second figure is the shadow in its unacceptable aspect: a dark, disreputable tramp-like fellow, sometimes shabbily, sometimes flashily dressed. He is untrustworthy, thoroughly dislikable; but virile enough in an unpleasant way. In the dream where I first came upon him he had been chasing little girls and, in concert with a number of neighbours, I helped round him up. When we captured him, he and I stood by a deep still pool and I had to decide whether or not I would throw him in and drown him (i.e. thrust him back into the unconscious). Fortunately, in the dream I had the sense not to—or I should have had trouble. Instead, I recognized that there might be that about me which was like him.

This had an interesting sequel. In a later dream the younger brother and the tramp-like man coalesced to their mutual advantage. I dreamt that I found myself sharing a bed with some man I did not know. I got up at once, he also. I looked at him and saw the most extraordinary combination of the better aspects of the "younger brother" shadow and of the "tramp" shadow: tall, decently dressed, a little *louche*, but a man-like sort of person. I was on the point of congratulating him on his transformation, when, to my intense astonishment, he anticipated me, speaking for the first time. He said: "You are twice the man you were." Which was precisely what I was going to say to him.

The third figure is a soldier, the transmogrified tramp in uniform, perhaps. Again, anything but a trustworthy character, a man who considers his own interests, first, last and all the time; a rash and dangerous man, who could be very vicious if cornered. His presence I recognize easily enough, every time I put on any sort of uniform. For the time being I am subtly different from myself—rougher, coarser, taking a special pleasure in using bad language; and it is not hard to recognize who it is speaking. On the other hand, unpleasant though he is in many ways, he has a certain toughness of fibre which I appreciate.

The fourth figure is of a dark, stocky peasant; quiet, steady, versed in the things of the earth, instinctively wise. This aspect of the shadow goes beyond the purely personal, down to the primitive origins. The fifth and most recent figure goes deeper still. In the night, in something between a dream and a vision, I saw a great stone pillar, inclined at a steep angle, part of an ancient ruin. Up this pillar a shadowy figure was climbing, someone whom I knew to be myself and yet not myself. He climbed expertly. The last part, over the great capital of the pillar, was especially difficult and I admired the way he got first a hand, then an elbow, then the chest, above the top. At that moment he gave a spring and was standing erect upon it. He had goats' feet. It was Pan—or a satyr?'

Ideally, the shadow-ego should be an integral part of the personality—the dark side, it is true, but part of one's wholeness; that something not altogether admirable in a man which nevertheless gives him solidity, shade as well as light. More often, though, the shadow side of ourselves is the last thing we wish to accept, the 'ugliest man' as Nietzsche called it. Instead of being integrated, it is projected upon the outside world.

When we project the shadow upon an actual person, we detest in him just what is most detestable in ourselves; and because it is part of ourselves that we are projecting it is no ordinary detestation. There is a kind of feverish, high-temperature feeling about it, so that the very thought of the person irritates us beyond bearing. We fume about him inwardly, can hardly be civil when we meet, get irritable whenever his name is mentioned. He becomes an itch in the mind that we cannot let alone. We must always be thinking or talking about him, seeing malignancy and evil in his every action. It may well be that the person on whom the projection is cast has something about him to justify our dislike. There is almost always a hook on which the projection hangs—he is arrogant, sniffs continually, cheats at golf, does not wash his ears, or something like that. But it is the projection, not the hook, that we hate.

75

Mass projections of the shadow can be particularly ugly. The religious bigot projects his own religious doubt upon the heretic and burns him. The Nazi projects his own inferiority upon the Jew and does his utmost to wipe out this 'impurity' in the race. The white man projects his dark side upon the negro, treats him as sub-human, and himself becomes sub-human when he feels it necessary to keep the 'nigger' in his place. The political doctrinaire, perfect in his infallible creed, projects his shadow so completely upon the 'class-enemy' that nothing short of total liquidation will suffice.

The commonest of all mass projections of the shadow is that upon the foreigner. It is one of the major tasks of war propaganda to mobilize this projection and transfer it to whatever quarter is required. Especially where one's own cause is not too good, by far the best line is to get the people to identify whole-heartedly with some exalted ideal. This produces a complete separation from the shadow. The next step is to supply an appropriate hook for the projection of the shadow. And thereafter keep the name of the hook always the same; so that what started by being the sub-human Jews can be successfully extended to include the sub-human Judaic-pacifists, the still more sub-human Judaic-pacifist-democracies and eventually any other race, nation, party or creed against which hate needs to be mobilized. Adolf Hitler, in *Mein Kampf*, specifically prescribed this technique of propaganda, and practised it with sinister (but ambivalent) success.

Projection, individual or collective, is normally the initial form in which the shadow is encountered. But this complex can also enter into and possess a man. Such possession by the shadow, the virtual replacement of the ego by the shadow-ego, may be violent. If a man is completely out of touch with the unconscious, then the whole pent-up energy of the deep unconscious in its negative aspect overtakes him from behind. In such case he becomes capable of the most inhuman cruelty. The youth in Hitler's Germany, who had been taught to identify with a Siegfried ideal, to look upon himself as a budding superman (and so to lose all contact with his own reality), who had learnt to project everything that was vile in himself upon the 'race enemy': when that 'race enemy' fell within his power, was all too liable to become wholly possessed by a demonic shadow—with what results the concentration camps revealed. And what was true of German youth, given the necessary means of conditioning (both ability to condition and readiness to be conditioned) can be true of any other people, not excluding ourselves.

Normally, though, when a man is not altogether out of touch with his psychological roots, the shadow has relatively little energy. Its typical 'activity' is the negative one of neglect, failure to rise to the occasion. It is the sins of omission rather than of commission that it takes as its own.

> Between the idea
> And the reality
> Between the motion
> And the act
> Falls the Shadow.
>
> Between the conception
> And the creation
> Between the emotion
> And the response
> Falls the Shadow.
>
> Between the desire
> And the spasm
> Between the potency
> And the existence
> Between the essence
> And the descent
> Falls the Shadow.

How to deal with one's shadow is a psychological problem to which there is no short answer—except to say that it is a life's work. Something can be done by perceiving the projection, recognizing that what one so fervently detests in the adversary is one's own shadow side. This does not mean that the projection will thereby be lifted, but at least one begins to take some responsibility for it. Still more can be done by recognizing the nature of the shadow, not merely in general terms but specifically, by coming to know it and understand its point of view. For this, dream analysis and the other psycho-perceptive techniques are invaluable. What is necessary, so far as it is possible, is to give the shadow a chance to live instead of seeking to suppress it completely. It is with the shadow that a man's unused capacities lie, his hidden life, the side that is kept in the dark. Admittedly, enabling the shadow to live is rather like taking a gorilla out walking on a string. A man has to judge for himself what he can and what he cannot do in this way. But to know of and recognize the activity of the shadow; to say as Prospero did of Caliban 'this thing of darkness I acknowledge mine'; above all to give it scope, within reason, instead of driving it underground: these are things which are due and necessary both to oneself and to one's neighbour—who otherwise bears the brunt. Moreover, when the shadow is faced, it changes in character, progressively becoming more assimilable.

Only by dealing with the shadow can the depths be reached. George Fox, the founder of the Society of Friends, has a remarkable passage in his Journal bearing on this:

'The Lord showed me that the natures of those things which were hurtful without, were within, in the hearts and minds of wicked men. The natures of dogs, swine, vipers, of Sodom and Egypt, Pharaoh, Cain, Ishmael, Esau, etc., the natures of these I saw within, though people had been looking without. I cried to the Lord saying, "Why should I be thus, seeing I was never addicted to commit those evils?" and the Lord answered, "That it was needful I should have a sense of all conditions, how else should I speak to all conditions?" and in this I saw the infinite love of God. I saw also that there was an ocean of darkness and death; but an infinite ocean of light and love which flowed over the ocean of darkness. In that also I saw the infinite love of God, and I had great openings.'

It is in facing and dealing with the shadow, the dark gateway to the deep unconscious, that a man realizes himself for the first time; and with that realization may find a sense of community with others and come upon the 'great openings' of the spirit. But facing the shadow is not a happy experience. To some it brings a feeling of insufferable guilt; to others, hopelessness; to all a heaviness of spirit, hard to bear. Some people find it well-nigh impossible even to look upon this 'ugliest man', let alone accept him. Yet, as Fénelon well says: 'It is mere self-love to be inconsolable at seeing one's own imperfections.' And, in the last analysis, the shadow is also one's substance.

Belladonna, the Lady of the Rocks, the lady of situations

The shadow-ego normally appears in dreams and phantasies as of the same sex as oneself. There is, also, a no less typical autonomous complex of the opposite sex. With a man this figure normally takes the form of a mysterious, elusive woman: sometimes the same in appearance over a period of years, sometimes differing from one dream to the next. This 'woman in the unconscious' Jung has called the anima.

The anima appears frequently in literature and in the arts—a quasi-magical creature with the mysterious light of the unconscious playing around her; fascinating, intriguing, enigmatical, unreal. A highly attractive anima figure is Rima in W. H. Hudson's romantic novel *Green Mansions*. He comes upon her, appropriately, in the depths of the primeval forest:

'It was a human being—a girl form, reclining on the moss among the ferns and herbage, near the roots of a small tree. One arm was doubled behind her neck for her head to rest upon, while the other arm was held extended before her, the hand raised towards a small brown bird perched on a pendulous twig just beyond its reach. She appeared to be playing with the bird, possibly amusing herself by trying to entice it on to her hand; and the hand appeared to tempt it greatly, for it persistently hopped up and down, turning rapidly about this way and that, flirting its wings and tail, and always appearing just on the point of dropping on to her finger. From my position it was impossible to see her distinctly, yet I dared not move. I could make out that she was small, not above four feet six or seven inches in height, in figure slim, with delicately shaped little hands and feet. Her feet were bare and her only garment was a slight chemise-shaped dress reaching below her knees, of a whitish-grey colour, with a faint lustre as of a silky material. Her hair was very wonderful; it was loose and abundant, and seemed wavy or curly, falling in a cloud on her shoulders and arms. Dark it appeared, but the precise tint was indeterminable, as was that of her skin, which looked neither brown nor white. Once for a moment she raised herself to reach her finger nearer to the bird, and then a gleam of unsubdued sunlight fell on her hair and arm, and the arm at that moment appeared of a pearly whiteness, and the hair, just where the light

79

touched it, had a strange lustre and play of iridescent colour. So vivid was the image left on my brain that she still seemed to be actually before my eyes; and she was not there, nor had been, for it was a dream, an illusion, and no such being existed, or could exist, in this gross world: and at the same time I knew that she had been there—that imagination was powerless to conjure up a form so exquisite.'

Epstein, when he came to reproduce Rima in stone, instead of copying Hudson's description, reached down to his own corresponding image in the unconscious and produced an anima figure as totally unlike that portrayed in *Green Mansions* as could be imagined —a powerful, primitive, Semitic woman, with exaggeratedly large hands—but in her way as completely authentic as Hudson's fairy-like creature. The two Rimas between them give a fairly accurate impression of the more favourable aspect of this 'woman in the unconscious': infinitely attractive, yet primitive; of the air, yet of the earth.

In poetry there are innumerable examples of the anima. She is Helen of Troy:

> *the face that launch'd a thousand ships,*
> *And burnt the topless towers of Ilium.*

She is Cleopatra, the 'serpent of old Nile':

> *Age cannot wither her, nor custom stale*
> *Her infinite variety.*

Keats' *Endymion*, telling the love of the Moon Goddess for a Greek shepherd, is a complete anima phantasy. So also is *La Belle Dame Sans Merci*:

> *I met a lady in the meads,*
> *Full beautiful, a faery's child;*
> *Her hair was long, her foot was light,*
> *And her eyes were wild.*

Anima portrayal in novels is likewise frequent. Jung cites Rider Haggard's *She* and Bénoit's *Atlantide* as interesting examples. Taken as literature, these books are not remarkable. But their theme, centring around the semi-immortal figure of the mysterious woman, comes unmistakeably from the unconscious. The fact that both authors place the scene of their novels in Africa—the Dark Continent as it was then known—is completely in keeping. Significantly, Rider Haggard records that he wrote *She* at 'white heat' in a little over six weeks. Another favourite anima figure in novels is that of the gypsy girl: Esmeralda in Victor Hugo's *Notre Dame de Paris*, Mirabell in Walpole's *Rogue Herries*—strange, elusive, half-unreal figures to whom men are bound as if by a spell.

Of the many anima pictures, Leonardo's *Gioconda*, much of Michelangelo's work (particularly the *Delphic Sybil* of the Sistine Chapel and the figure of Eve accompanying the Creator in the famous *Birth of Adam*), Van Eyck's *St. Barbara* and innumerable Madonnas are among those showing this figure in some of her more pleasing aspects. But the anima can also be otherwise. The terrible human-inhuman figure in Pieter Bruegel's *Dulle Griet* is authentic anima. She may be crabbed, witch-like, half-animal or half-fish, a human-headed serpent, a vampire, a harpy. She is the siren that can turn men into swine; the mermaid that drowns the sailors; the Lorelei; the false lady who feigns distress to lead true knights astray, Duessa of Spenser's *Faerie Queene* no less than Britomart; 'Belladonna, the Lady of the Rocks, the lady of situations.' Yet at the same time she is a source of inspiration, the poet's muse, the semi-divine Lady of the Troubadours,

> *Who walked between the violet and the violet*
> *Who walked between*
> *The various ranks of varied green*
> *Going in white and blue, in Mary's colour. . . .*
> *In blue of larkspur, blue of Mary's colour,*
> *Sovegna vos.*

In actual life a man normally encounters the anima first in the form of a projection. There is a sudden overwhelming 'falling in love' and for a while nothing else in the world matters. The woman on whom the projection is cast becomes for him no creature of flesh and blood, but a divinity, an enchantment. From her he expects everything. She knows the Great Secret, she holds the key to life. The thought of separation is impossible; existence would be meaningless without her. They have met in some previous life. They have known and been fated for one another throughout the ages. A special light pervades the whole landscape, illumining especially the woman on whom this projection from the unconscious has fallen. Clods who have never attempted any such thing before take to writing verse. So long as the projection lasts, the man is held by a completely irrational attachment. His thoughts and his footsteps lead persistently in her direction—and inevitably so, for she has upon her an essential part of his inmost being.

A few weeks or months or years later the projection goes, gradually perhaps, or vanishing in a flash. What was almost a goddess, in any case no mere mortal, becomes a rather ordinary member of the female sex. Looking back, the man can see that the object of his attachment was totally different from what he imagined at the time, had different physical features even.

Such projections of the anima may come about in a great variety of circumstances. In adolescence they are a normal, in fact a necessary, first step towards eventual relationship with the anima. But some men pass practically the whole of their lives in one long succession of compulsive projections. Others, more fortunate, are likely to find the projection operating only in rather special circumstances. One of the most frequent is where a man and a woman pass through some exciting or dangerous experience together—a fire, a shipwreck, an accident in the mountains—in which event, almost certainly, at least a partial projection will result. Again, when a man takes on some great task he may find himself automatically projecting the anima upon a woman, as if he needed her support in order to bear the additional burden. There are also the split-second projections. Most men have probably had the experience of momentary dissociation when unexpectedly introduced to some strikingly beautiful woman—a 'dizzy blonde' to use the expressive term. Projections of this sudden kind are of no special importance; but it is at such moments that the woman in the unconscious can be almost visibly distinguished—vanishing Cinderella-like down the corridors of the psyche—as the man pulls himself together and makes the polite response.

The anima may also invade the man. Here the picture changes. So long as she is projected, the anima is all that is most wonderful. But when the anima seizes upon the inferior, unconscious side of the man's personality, the other aspect appears. Such invasion usually takes the form of a peevish mood, a mood in which the man will sulk, make remarks (or more accurately, find remarks making themselves) which are petulant, weak, nagging, 'womanish' in the worst sense of the term. If the man is sufficiently aware to notice his condition, he will feel himself a kind of wraith, paper-thin, without depth or substance, going about things in a febrile and futile fashion. He is, at one and the same time, angry and miserable, resentful and self-pitying. Especially when a man is a little over-worked or off-colour, and feels he is not being sufficiently sympathized with and looked after, the anima can make him exceedingly sorry for himself. And although he may be fully aware of his condition, if it is a thorough-going case of anima invasion he will not be able to get out of it by will-power alone, however hard he may try.

The man's part in the familiar 'lovers' quarrel' often shows both the projection of and invasion by the anima in an almost bewildering succession. He sets out to meet the lady of his heart, treading on air, feeling that never was life so good or man more fortunate. The lady keeps him kicking his heels for half an hour in the rain. At last she comes with a rather feeble excuse and her complexion somewhat ravaged by the weather. Instead of being the semi-divine creature he supposed her to be, she is suddenly revealed as a stupid and incon-sequent encumbrance who has probably caused him to catch his death of cold. He brushes aside all her reasons, declares that every-thing is over and is resolved never to see her again. As the next train he can catch is not for another hour, he agrees grudgingly that they might as well get something to eat together. And under the influence of food and warmth, with his feet dry again and her com-plexion restored, she is once more the altogether magical being he set out three hours ago to meet.

The anima is not always the goddess. She can also be projected in her negative form: the witch, the whore, the harpy, the predatory female, the devouring mother; that in a man which enables him to see woman as a direct emissary of the Devil. But, positive or nega-tive, the anima in projection has certain characteristic features. There is always something magical about her and, at the same time, in some indefinable fashion, she is 'dubious'. When interrogated by written question and answer, the anima shows substantially the same ambi-valent traits. She can say exceedingly pertinent things, infused with a kind of wild wisdom for which she finds haunting words. She can also talk the most arrant nonsense, a hysterical woman at her worst.

Some men learn from the anima only by the way of the fool— a succession of anima projections, one after another, each more empty than the last. There are few more fruitless ways of wasting life. Those, on the contrary, who are able to get on to terms with the anima, find her a complement to consciousness of inestimable value. In establishing such a relationship a man has to steer a difficult and dangerous course. If he attempts to assimilate the anima, integrate this figure of power into the ego-personality, he will find that it is not he who assimilates the anima but the anima—in all her ambivalence—who assimilates him. What he needs to do is, on the one hand, to learn from her, so that the *eros* side of his personality may find its right development; and, on the other, to enter into something in the nature of a working arrangement with the anima herself. How this may come about is the subject of later chapters. But the first, essential step is to become aware that the anima is real: and not merely as an intellectual concept but as an autonomous complex existing in her own right—a 'twisting together' of psychic contents every whit as authentic as the ego.

'The obstinate, unconscious, sub-human strength that some women have'

In a woman's psychology, the autonomous complex corresponding to the anima is what Jung calls the animus. The animus-image is quite definitely male in its characteristics, but subject to manifold and frequent changes in form. Almost anything embodying the male principle, from a prancing stallion to an army on the march, may stand for the animus. With some women, however, a specific personality (or series of personalities) is constellated—a man, complete with name, profession, and all the appurtenances of life—which may be intensely active for a number of years, possibly a whole lifetime.

In dreams and phantasies, the animus typically plays one or other of two rôles. In the unfavourable rôle he is the villain, the seducer, the sinister figure holding the woman in prison, leading her into peril, handing her over to the torturers. In the favourable rôle he is the guide, the deliverer, the protector, the man who shows how the work can be done. Mr. Greatheart, who accompanies Christian's wife and children on their long pilgrimage from the City of Destruction to the Heavenly City, is the prototype of the positive animus. He is the one who, coming to the Valley of the Shadow of Death, can give comfort and strength:

'This is like doing business in great waters, or like going down into the deep; this is like being in the heart of the sea, and like going down to the bottoms of the mountains; now it seems as if the earth, with its bars, were about us for ever. But let them that walk in darkness and have no light, trust in the name of the Lord, and stay upon their God. For my part, as I have told you already, I have gone often through this valley, and have been much harder put to it than now I am, and yet you see I am alive. I would not boast, for that I am not mine own saviour; but I trust we shall have a good deliverance. Come, let us pray for light to him that can lighten our darkness, and that can rebuke not only these, but all the Satans in hell.'

The quasi-demonic figure of Heathcliff in Emily Brontë's master-piece is a remarkable phantasy of the animus in its sinister and for-bidding aspect. Charlotte Brontë, in her Preface to the 1850 edition of *Wuthering Heights*, speaks of him with insight:

'Whether it is right or advisable to create beings like Heath-cliff, I do not know: I scarcely think it is. But this I know; the writer who possesses the creative gift owns something of which he is not always master—something that at times strangely wills and works for itself. He may lay down rules and devise principles, and to rules and principles it will perhaps for years lie in subjection; and then, haply without any warning of revolt, there comes a time when it will no longer consent to "harrow the vallies, or be bound with a band in the furrow"—when it "laughs at the multi-tude of the city, and regards not the crying of the driver"—when, refusing absolutely to make ropes out of sea-sand any longer, it sets to work on statue-hewing, and you have a Pluto or a Jove, a Tisiphone or a Psyche, a Mermaid or a Madonna, as Fate or Inspiration direct. Be the work grim or glorious, dread or divine, you have little choice left but quiescent adoption. As for you—the nominal artist—your share in it has been to work passively under dictates you neither delivered nor could question —that would not be uttered at your prayer, nor suppressed nor changed at your caprice. If the result be attractive, the World will praise you, who little deserve praise; if it be repulsive, the same World will blame you, who almost as little deserve blame.'

Charlotte Brontë's own melodramatic Mr. Rochester, like

Dorothy Sayers' Lord Peter Wimsey, presents a much more attractive picture of the animus. Here is the essentially male person: in the one case authoritative, determined, ruthless even, but completely vulnerable on the side of feeling and *eros*; in the other, a model of quiet good taste and impeccable appearance but, behind the façade, an infinitely resourceful mind and infinitely resilient frame. More than any other autonomous complex, the animus has the two characteristic marks: energy and ambivalence. More than with any other it is true that everything depends upon the relationship effected.

The projection of the animus is similar in its essentials to anima projection and does not call for special description. Under the influence of such a projection, a woman endows a man with glamour, heroism, intellect, charm, to which he can make little or no pretence. The hook on which this projection is hung is often of the slenderest —he has wavy hair, good teeth, a pleasant smile, shakes hands nicely, or some such small feature or mannerism. She is henceforward bound to him as by a magical and compulsive bond. Many women have the animus incarnated in some well-known tenor, violinist, pugilist, or, above all, film star; and will 'fall in love' with a man through some resemblance, real or imaginary, to this hero.

The man on whom the animus projection is thus hung feels himself called upon to perform the rôle of hero, prophet, deliverer, worker of miracles, romantic lover or whatever other characteristic is demanded. If he is running a counter-projection of the anima at the time, he will probably attempt to live up to the part thus thrust upon him: and make a considerable fool of himself in the process. If he does not return the attachment, his one idea will be to get out as fast and far as he can. An unwanted animus projection is an intolerable burden to bear. Nothing is openly said, nothing openly done, but there is the woman expecting all heaven and earth from him. And it is a weight like a tomb.

As with the anima, the animus may and does invade the conscious personality. The effect, while equally characteristic, takes a very different form. Invasion by the animus drives a woman to opinionating. In such a condition she—or rather the animus speaking through her—will make the most positive statements on questions of which she has little or no real knowledge, and for which, often, there is no basis in fact. Traced to their origin, such statements usually prove to be a version of something heard once from some impressive male person—her father, an elder brother, a minister, a man with a beard, or some like authority. But in spite of the complete lack of substance, the animus-possessed woman will withstand, correct, criticize and argue down any opposing point of view, particularly if put forward by a man; and often, the less she knows of the question, the more positive she—or rather, it—will be.

Besides their lack of adequate foundation, animus opinions are usually just that amount beside the mark which makes them particularly infuriating to the male mind. Inability to keep to the point is a failing not peculiar to the animus, but the animus turns the failing into a fine art. Moreover, in line with its masculine character, the animus tends always to be aggressive and is continually trying— usually with success—to provoke the anima in the men around. And for this there is no better means than to shift ground continually, bringing in every irrelevancy to confuse the issue. The nagging wife, the woman who always has the last word, the uncanny gift by which a woman manages to fasten upon a man's pet weakness and drag it into the light, the ability to make a man feel that what he has just said is probably the most vapid remark ever made, are all characteristic aspects of the animus.

> You, madam, are the eternal humorist,
> The eternal enemy of the absolute,
> Giving our vagrant moods the slightest twist!
> With your air indifferent and imperious
> At a stroke our mad poetics to confute. . . .

With most women the animus invades only on occasions, but with some it is a quasi-permanent condition. Such animus-possessed women—'animus-hounds' as one of them called herself—make animus attacks upon the men about them, living upon argument and conflict, seeking always to force their opinions upon others by sheer unreason, invariably refusing to get down to fundamentals where these baseless statements would collapse. A 'masculine' woman of this sort is sometimes looked upon as having intellect, a 'mind of her own'. In point of fact, as she herself may in moments of lucidity recognize, it is not she who has the so-called 'mind', but the 'mind' that has her. And that mind is a contentious mind, wounding and lacerating to every-one around.

In much the same way as a man in the grip of the anima will not admit that he is moody, over-sensitive, a woman possessed by the animus is usually unable—at least at the time—to see that she is opinionating without any real knowledge. Afterwards she may, perhaps, have the impression that she was rather sweeping in her statements. If she is particularly aware, she may realize, on looking back, that something not herself was speaking. On the other hand, she may be so completely identified with the animus that she regards his voice as herself; as with the woman who, when asked to give an opinion on a matter new to her, rejoined: 'But how do I know what I think till I hear what I say?'

Such animus-possessed women are liable at times to 'animus panics'. There is a sudden breakdown of the masculine attitude, a fearfulness over nothing, a bursting into tears, in vivid contrast to the previous hectoring. These panics, though, are usually of short duration; in due course the animus reappears and the opinionating recommences. And with the return of the animus, the suppressed human being, momentarily visible, again disappears. Where a woman is completely identified with the animus—or a man with the anima—one has the feeling that anything one says to them is somehow ineffective. Nobody is there with whom a contact can be made.

Often, in later life, the animus characteristics of the woman, the anima characteristics of the man, plainly get the upper hand. The woman 'wears the trousers', becomes peremptory and domineering; while the man degenerates into 'just an old woman', peevish and complaining, all his fire and energy gone. It is one of the great possibilities of the experiment in depth that this lamentable metamorphosis is rendered not inevitable.

So much for the negative aspects of the animus. They are stressed here with intent, since they may serve a most valuable purpose. Often, with a man, it is the wound inflicted by the animus that first makes him realize such beings may exist. And when a woman discovers what murder she has done with her opinionating, she too may be ready to recognize that strange forces are at work. But if the animus has its negative, wounding side the positive aspects are no less remarkable. The woman who is in good relationship with the animus conveys the impression of infinite reserves. And it is not impression only. The animus can enable women to stand up to adversity and privation before which a physically more powerful man goes under. Edward Chamberlayne in *The Cocktail Party*, speaks of 'The obstinate, unconscious, sub-human strength that some women have'. 'Obstinate', 'unconscious', 'sub-human' are all completely apt designations of the animus: but the fundamental characteristic is 'strength'.

Second only to strength is insight.

> *But there's wisdom in women, of more than they have known,*
> *And thoughts go blowing through them, are wiser than their own.*

This capacity for insight may take various forms. Some women orators, for instance, speak directly from the animus having no clear idea in advance of what they intend to say, but nevertheless delivering an eloquent and powerfully argued address. The animus, too, can be a source of inspiration. George Sand, in a letter to Flaubert, writes:

'The wind plays my old harp as it lists. It has its *high notes*, its *low notes*, its heavy notes—and its faltering notes, in the end it is all the same to me provided the emotion comes, but I can find nothing in myself. It is *the other* who sings as he likes, well or ill, and when I try to think about it, I am afraid and tell myself that I am nothing, nothing at all. . . . But a great wisdom saves us; we know how to say to ourselves, "Well, even if we are absolutely nothing but instruments, it is still a charming state and like no other, this feeling oneself vibrate." '

'It is *the other* who sings as he likes.' Not perhaps an ideal relationship with the animus. A little too much like invasion. But since she is conscious of it, recognizing that 'we are nothing but instruments', very far from the dangerous state of identification.

Particularly in dealing with the forces of the unconscious, the animus is a power. Jung maintains that in the exploration of the mysteries of the psyche it is women, through the animus, who are destined to do the great things. However this may be, it is certain that for every one man who masters the constructive technique and makes something of it there are perhaps half-a-dozen women. Speaking very generally, the man is not psycho-perceptive. The woman is, and has the courage of her convictions.

On the other hand, for the animus to serve the woman, a right relationship must be achieved. How is this to be done? There is no single answer to this question any more than there is to the corresponding one, how is a man to get on with the anima. But there are two or three general points of special importance. The ensuing dream illustrates one of them:

'I am with several friends in some kind of a house or chalet where we are to do the work ourselves. There is a man with a short grey beard who has some kind of association with an Elizabethan sea-captain or explorer. He and I have had a quarrel. A great friend of mine, a man, who is the chief personality in the party, says, "Are you two on speaking terms? Because if not, I don't know how you'll do the work." I think the bearded man and I are to do the cooking, and he is good at it and is to tell me how. The bearded man does not reply. I say, "Well, I am, anyway, so I can ask him things and he can nod or shake his head." My attitude is humorous and a little self-righteous; I'll show that I can give way and not be quarrelsome.'

This is a typical animus figure: beard (the dreamer's father wore a beard); atmosphere of enterprise, adventure; above all, the man who 'knows how'. The woman, very wisely, is willing to learn, intent on getting his aid and, above all, doing the 'cooking' herself. This is the right attitude, the attitude of responsibility, to which the animus can hardly fail to respond. The woman knows she needs the animus. At the same time she is taking charge, not leaving things to him.

But the animus is not always thus potentially amenable, nor is it always a peaceful chalet and a pleasant house party in which he appears. A frequently recurring situation is where the animus has joined forces with the shadow. In dreams they appear as married, or bound together in some more questionable union. When this happens the animus may become demonic, and the woman fall completely under his sway. The deep unconscious is then highly ambivalent:

A savage place! as holy and enchanted
As e'er beneath a waning moon was haunted
By woman wailing for her demon-lover!

A woman thus compulsively bound to the demonic animus is evilly possessed. To free herself is a hard task. Here, as with most other things in dealing with the unconscious, the question of attitude, of steadfastness, is fundamental. If in consciousness she determines to break this liaison between the shadow and the animus, and takes every practical means of doing it in the course of everyday life, the situation in the unconscious gradually, changes. To do this, two things are necessary. The shadow in all its blackness needs to be seen, acknowledged, and, as far as may be, assimilated. When this is done, the positive aspects of the shadow appear. At the same time, the animus as far as possible must be depotentiated, the woman insisting on her own individuality, refusing to follow his lead blindly. In particular, when the animus makes the barbed negative criticisms characteristic of animus possession, the woman does well to examine these statements to see what it is she has neglected in her outward life. If, for instance, something she should have done herself she has omitted to do, left it to be done by someone else, these neglected things feed the animus and increase his hold upon her. Careful scrutiny of the animus statements will often reveal these neglected things: and that particular hold can then be prised loose by remedying the omission. But it may be many months, or years, before a wrong relationship of this kind can be set straight.

For the woman who has the necessary quickness and courage, there is a valuable counsel in dealing with the animus, applicable on all occasions. Time and again she will hear herself saying something which inwardly she knows is not exactly what she means. Often it will seem too insignificant to matter. But what the animus says in this fashion always does matter. It is not what is said, but who says it. And if the animus is saying it, there will be trouble. At such a time, if she has the presence of mind and greatness of spirit to say 'Stop a minute, that isn't what I mean' and herself re-phrase what the animus has just said, the beneficial effect, not only upon the situation, but upon herself and upon her relationship to the animus, can be out of all proportion to the apparent importance of the incident itself.

In subsequent chapters other means of coping with the animus appear. For the woman it is the great need and the great duty, and not merely from her own personal standpoint. The animus is the most powerful of all the figures the other side of consciousness. In the experiment in depth, to a great extent, it is he who leads the dance.

V

ARCHETYPAL IMAGES AND THEMES

THE shadow-ego varies considerably in force and nature from one person to another. It may be utterly demonic; or it may be no more than those failings and weaknesses in a man which his friends find almost lovable. Much the same is true of the anima and the animus. It is not only that they are experienced in widely different ways by different people. There would seem every reason to suppose that the complexes themselves are widely different, as the ego in one man is widely different from the ego in another. But in each case, with the shadow, with the anima, with the animus, there is an underlying typical pattern of behaviour. To use Jung's term for them, they are archetypes.

Most people who have studied Jung's work—still more, those who have given it only a cursory glance—find considerable difficulty in the concept of archetypes. Jung has been at considerable pains to define this concept in the only way that it can be defined: by reference to man's experience of it. But what it is that lies behind this experience escapes definition. These elemental powers are, indeed, one of the deep mysteries of life. Why and how living creatures should have built into them typical responses to typical situations we simply do not know.

The broad facts, however, are reasonably clear. There are a number of basic, instinctive drives actuating living creatures: notably, self-preservation, the reproductive urge, the will-to-power, the herd instinct. These fundamental drives follow certain characteristic patterns, varying from one species to another. Thus, birds, in common with other creatures, have the reproductive urge. They have also a nest-making archetype. And that archetype varies from one kind of bird to another. Swallows build different nests from robins. The cuckoo does not build a nest at all. Young weaver birds, whose ancestors over several generations have been kept on sand, at once start tying the same complicated knots to make their nests the moment the necessary material is again available. And these are only minor marvels. Such phenomena as the spawning archetypes of salmon and eel, the migration of birds over thousands of miles of trackless ocean, the mass suicide of lemmings, raise in our minds a sense of incredulous wonder; but we can hardly refuse to recognize the facts. When it comes to ants and wasps and bees, the well-nigh unbelievable patterns of response may dumbfound us, but there they are, however inexplicable they may seem.

In man, the archetypes are, as it were, characteristic aspects of the psychic energy flowing through the human being, energy deriving not only from the instincts but also from the spiritual, moral, ethical drives which, in the main, oppose the instincts. Possibly because of this divided origin, they are neither so specific nor so open to observation as in the creatures still wholly activated by instinct. On the other hand, by means of the constructive technique, it is possible with some practice to perceive the archetypal forces operating upon the human personality. One gradually becomes aware of a strange array of archaic figures, themes and objects appearing and disappearing the other side of consciousness, all in their various ways making their characteristic impact upon one's attitude and action. As awareness develops, the archetypal powers can be brought into a certain relationship with consciousness; and thereby gradually enlisted in the service of life.

This said, a series of problems arises as to how this aspect of the experiment in depth can most usefully be presented. The archetypal patterns in man are far more fluid and manifold than in the other creatures. They are consequently so much the more difficult to describe. In the end, choice lies between one or other of two bad courses: to be circumspect and erudite, citing specific examples only, whether from mythology or from actual experience, leaving a very diffuse impression of what it is all about; or to give a fairly definite description, usually much more definite than the facts warrant. I have chosen the second course, while at the same time keeping the sketch as brief and as light as possible. My reason for doing this is twofold. In the experiment in depth what matters is direct experience, and the fullest possible awareness of that experience. Those encountering the archetypal figures and themes need to know that this is what is happening and that it is something demanding their utmost attention. Otherwise they may pass the experience by un-recognized and the necessary relationship will not be made. At the same time, it would be altogether wrong to impose some pre-formed pattern upon the living experience. Consequently, what I have aimed at is to say enough to enable the phenomena to be identified if encountered, but not so much as to do violence to the experience itself.

At this point the second problem arises: ignorance. Our present knowledge of this type of phenomena is rudimentary in the extreme. Only as and when we have brought together and funded a wide and varied body of experience showing how men and women in good psychological health actually encounter the archetypal forces can we hope to give a reasonably reliable and specific account of what these forces are and what they do. In the meantime, such rough notes as are proffered here should be regarded as indicative only. They are unquestionably incomplete, very possibly inaccurate.

The greatest problem of all, however, is to find the right personal introduction, so to speak. A man or woman making the experiment in depth certainly needs to know of the existence of these forces. On the other hand, in the early stages at least, he probably does well to keep clear of them as far as possible. The defensive attitude of the man in the 'Villains in the Villa' dream, the warning given to the man in 'The Left Fork to Lausanne', are both highly pertinent. Normally, it is through the direct encounter with the archetypal forces that a man first realizes he is dealing with realities. But he needs to be well rooted psychologically before he proceeds to this stage. Otherwise, instead of his dealing with them, they may deal with him.

Accordingly, in the ensuing brief descriptions, I have sought to present the archetypal images as quasi-mythological concepts rather than as the living forces they actually are. In this way, when they come to life in a man's own experience, he may know what is happening and take due account. Until then, 'let sleeping arche-types lie' is probably good counsel for most—provided always that this does not mean shutting one's eyes to their presence and pre-tending they do not exist.

The Wise Old Man

In dreams and visions, in mythology and folklore, in religion and esoteric cults, in the history of peoples and civilizations, in the living experience of individual men and occasionally of women, there appears a figure most conveniently subsumed under the title of the Wise Old Man. He takes many shapes: god, prophet, sage, law-giver, king, counsellor, philosopher, priest, professor, judge, head-master, doctor, alchemist, medicine man, magician, sorcerer, wizard, necromancer, warlock, and others of like kind. He is, as it were, the embodiment of the age-old experience, wisdom, *logos* of mankind.

Historically, the image of the Wise Old Man in its projected form has played an immense rôle in the shaping of men's minds. Confucius, Aristotle, Karl Marx are typical recipients of this projection. For their disciples and followers the least of their *dicta* have a more than human sanction. Aristotle's first beginnings of scientific enquiry, instead of being taken as beginnings only, were accepted for hundreds of years as dogma which it would be absurd to question. Marx is seen not as a fallible human being, industriously making notes in the British Museum, but as a latter-day prophet to whom the ultimate verities have been revealed. This, indeed, is one of the great dangers of the Wise Old Man archetype. In its projected form it can induce entire peoples to drape the panoply of absolute truth around some 'human-all-too-human' figure: and to remain caught, perhaps for a whole era, in some plausible but erroneous myth.

As a personal experience, projection of this figure typically results in an aberrant form of master-disciple relationship, stultifying to master and disciple alike. The master feels impelled to live up to an absurd omniscience. The disciple, instead of dealing with life himself, in his own way, ekes out a parasitical existence, made up on the one hand of uncritical acceptance of all the master does and says, on the other of petty quarrels with his fellow-worshippers.

Projection of the Wise Old Man, however, can be a valuable stage in psychological growth—provided it is a stage and not a stagnation. If the would-be disciple is fortunate, the revered teacher for some reason ceases to be a fitting hook for the projection. The man perhaps outgrows him, or the recipient of the projection (if he is a truly wise teacher) enables the man to see that such syco-phancy is a little absurd. The time has then come for the advance. Normally this advance will take the shape of invasion by the Wise Old Man: which brings its own perils. The man will now feel that it is he who has the great secret and will be impelled by a tremendous urge to communicate it to the world. If he is foolish, he will look upon the activity of the archetype as his own wisdom; will come to the conclusion (in all modesty) that he is really rather a remarkable person; will feel the world should recognize him as such, and be bitterly hurt that the world does nothing of the kind. He is likely to find pretentious—or, as he would regard it, prophetic—phrases rising to his lips or flowing from his pen; and (if he is very foolish) he may start acting and dressing the part.

Such a situation is a perilous one. Identification with the Wise Old Man can have tragic consequences. The invasion of Nietzsche by the figure of Zarathustra resulted in one of the world's great masterpieces; but Nietzsche, the man, was destroyed. What it feels like to be so visited may be judged from Nietzsche's autobiography:

'Has any one at the end of the nineteenth century any distinct notion of what poets of a stronger age understood by the word inspiration? If not, I will describe it. If one had the smallest vestige of superstition left in one, it would hardly be possible completely to set aside the idea that one is the mere incarnation, mouthpiece, or medium of an almighty power. The idea of revelation, in the sense that something which profoundly convulses and upsets one becomes suddenly visible and audible with indescribable certainty and accuracy—describes the simple fact. One hears—one does not seek; one takes—one does not ask who gives: a thought suddenly flashes up like lightning, it comes with necessity, without faltering —I have never had any choice in the matter . . . Everything happens quite involuntarily, as if in a tempestuous outburst of freedom, of absoluteness, of power and divinity. The involuntary nature of the figures and similes is the most remarkable thing; one loses all perception of what is imagery and metaphor; everything seems to present itself as the readiest, the truest, and simplest means of expression.'

These are the authentic signs of the archetype. It would have been better for Nietzsche if he could have realized that, in fact, he was no more than a 'mere mouthpiece'. He might then, perhaps, have held his own against the invasion.

The Wise Old Man frequently appears in company with the anima. In folklore, painting and literature the theme of the ancient sage and the young maiden—Joseph and Mary, Prospero and Miranda, the Old King and the Beautiful Princess—is typical. In actual life these two archetypal images repeatedly appear together. Rudyard Kipling's *Wressley of the Foreign Office* sets out in perfect miniature one of the commonest variations on this theme, *viz.* anima projection and simultaneous invasion by the Wise Old Man. Wressley, the confirmed bachelor, is suddenly crazed by a minx of a girl running around Simla. He feels he must do something worthy of her; goes away for a year and writes a remarkable work on the Indian rajahs, a masterpiece such as no one would have imagined coming from his pen. He lays the book at her feet. She, disappointedly, lisps: 'But it's all about your howwid old Wajahs.' The anima projection disappears in a flash. The match is off. Wressley destroys all the copies of the book he can lay hands on. And never does anything out of routine again.

The means of dealing with the Wise Old Man archetype are essentially the same as for the anima and the animus: recognize the figure for what it is; differentiate oneself from it; give what it has to say the most careful attention; accept only those things which belong to oneself. In short, be responsible. As always in dealing with the unconscious, prescription is easy, practice hard. Broadly speaking, though, dealing with the Wise Old Man (once the figure has been recognized) is not so difficult as dealing with the anima and animus. And the wisdom he brings is true wisdom; provided always that the human being, through whom this insight of the deep unconscious is manifesting, does not hand himself over to, identify himself with, this power. That way lies—not necessarily madness—but, more probably, a pitiful kind of folly; that of the crank, the fanatic, the half-baked man with a message.

The ensuing account gives some impression of how, more or less unknowingly, a man may learn:

'Three times the projection of the Wise Old Man has basically affected my life. The first was when I was in the late twenties. It fell upon a revered leader who was, indeed, wise beyond most. But the effect upon me was ludicrous. I at once ran a strong anima projection upon his daughter, this rapidly usurping the place of the projection of the Wise Old Man. It was an absolutely compulsive attachment; and not until she did something totally out of character with the projection (when the attachment vanished as if it had never been) could I do anything about it. The second came some years later, when I had embarked upon a task far above my capacity. This time the projection fell upon a man, in a distant land, whose work in my chosen field was outstanding. Later I was able to work with him and was quite prepared to fall into the master-disciple relationship. Happily for me he was far too wise to permit this. The projection gradually faded as progressively I realized that, in this matter, I must stand upon my own feet. I did the best I could by myself, not wisely, but not altogether foolishly. Later, in the middle forties, the projection came again; and again on a truly wise man. By this time I had acquired the rudiments of psychological knowledge. I found the strange urge come to me to write the epitaph of the man on whom the projection had fallen. I turned this over, saw what it might mean, wrote the epitaph. And again the projection, as it were, "came home"; and I did the best I could on my own resources.'

The figure of the Wise Old Man has its own characteristic theme: the great work, the discovery of the hidden treasure of wisdom, the knowledge that can miraculously transform. Like the anima, he has the secret: but he has it by virtue of *logos*—learning, wisdom, insight; while she has it by virtue of *eros*—charm, fascination, allure. This theme that the Wise Old Man brings with him is, in a sense, the archetype behind all invention, research, scientific and philosophical enquiry. As William James says, once a certain maturity is reached, there is one thought only: 'the work, the work.'

An archetypal theme such as the 'great work' can be projected, or can invade a man, in much the same way as an archetypal figure. Jung's enquiry into the semi-mystical, semi-chemical speculations and experiments of the alchemists, shows this theme in action. For some seventeen centuries, in labour and prayer, laboratory and oratory, men strove to discover the philosopher's stone, that magical substance which would transmute base metals into gold. Certain of the wisest of them (and there were truly wise men among the alchemists) recognized that it was not so much a chemical as a psychological change they were seeking: not ordinary gold, but 'our gold'. But most of them were helplessly caught in the mystery. As Jung points out, they were projecting upon matter and chemical trans-formation the whole gamut of the deep unconscious; and, all too often, the archetype of the 'great work' swallowed them whole.

Over the last two or three hundred years, matter, under the scrutiny of science, has yielded up many of its secrets and is no longer a suitable hook for projection. To a considerable extent politics has taken its place. Belief in the philosopher's stone has gone over to ideological beliefs. Living matter, the collectivity, has re-placed inert matter as the *materia* which can be magically trans-formed. The consequences for the world have been considerable. As Max Weber has pointed out, Karl Marx (on whom a large fraction of mankind now projects the image of the Wise Old Man) and Nietzsche (an outstanding case of possession by the Wise Old Man) have probably done more than any others to shape the present age. Communism on the one hand, Fascism and Nazism on the other, are striking products of the modern alchemy—the 'great work' become demonic.

The Magna Mater

The Wise Old Man is, predominantly, an archetype in a man's psychology. The corresponding figure in a woman's psychology is the Great Mother. This is by far the most difficult of all the arche-typal images to describe adequately, since it is at one and the same time immensely powerful but impalpable and diffuse.

In mythology, folklore and religion the Great Mother has played a mighty and continuous rôle from the earliest times. The female figurines found in cave deposits of the Upper Palaeolithic, with their stylized exaggeration of the sexual features, are almost certainly representations of this image. In the historical era the *Magna Mater* has appeared under many names: Ishtar of Babylon and Assyria; the Anatolean Cybele; the Cretan Rhea; the Phoenician Astarte; the Egyptian Isis; Demeter; the triple Hecate; the Ephesian Diana: to mention only a few around the Eastern end of the Mediterranean. She also has many guises. She is the maiden. She is the earth mother. She is the queen of the underworld. She is the goddess of war, the goddess of nature, the goddess of love, the goddess of marriage, the mountain goddess, the goddess of the chase, the goddess of herds, goddess of agriculture, goddess of fecundity, goddess of the moon.

Sometimes a single figure will combine several of these rôles. Thus, in the Christian tradition, Mary is both the Virgin and the *Mater Dolorosa*; while in the form of the black virgin, to be found in many Roman Catholic shrines, she also fulfils the rôle of the earth mother and the queen of the underworld—*Notre Dame de Sous Terre* as in the great crypt of the Cathedral of Chartres. The special honours accorded to the Virgin in recent years by the Roman Catholic Church attest to the continuing power of this majestic figure.

The *Magna Mater* is not exclusively the woman's archetype. The fact that the Great Mother is also the Virgin, Persephone no less than Demeter, links this figure to the anima in a man's psychology—in much the same way as the animus, in one of its many forms, is the equivalent in a woman's psychology of the Wise Old Man. The following account of a vision, reproduced from the *Journal* of George Fox, is illustrative:

'And I had a vision about the time that I was in this travail and sufferings, that I was walking in the fields and many Friends were with me, and I bid them dig in the earth, and they did and I went down. And there was a mighty vault top-full of people kept under the earth, rocks, and stones. So I bid them break open the earth and let all the people out, and they did, and all the people came forth to liberty; and it was a mighty place. And when they had done I went on and bid them dig again. They did, and there was a mighty vault full of people, and I bid them throw it down and let all the people out, and so they did.

And I went on again, and bid them dig again, and Friends said unto me, "George, thou finds out all things," and so there they digged, and I went down, and went along the vault; and there sat a woman in white looking at time how it passed away. And there followed me a woman down in the vault, in which vault was the treasure; and so she laid her hand on the treasure on my left hand and then time whisked on apace; but I clapped my hand upon her and said, "Touch not the treasure." And then time passed not so swift.

They that can read these things must have the earthy, stony nature off them. And see how the stones and the earth came upon man since the beginning, since he fell from the image of God and righteousness and holiness. And much I could speak of these things, but I leave them to the right eye and reader to see and read.'

This encounter with the feminine principle in a man's psychology—the deep creative purpose of earth and of time—while not unusual, is nevertheless not characteristic. It is upon women, in the main, that this archetypal figure of the *Magna Mater* exercises its influence.

In its projected form the Great Mother is typically seen in the compulsive attachment girls and younger women often have for some older woman, sometimes their own mother, sometimes a school mistress or other person of authority. For such a one no sacrifice is too great, no care too tender. Should the older woman die, the loss is felt as if something in the younger woman had died with her.

Should a woman be invaded by the *Magna Mater*, there is a tendency for her to go over to the negative aspect of this archetype, the devouring mother, often represented in dreams and visions (as well as in fairy tales and traditional lore) as the sorceress, the child-eating witch. Under the influence of this figure a woman is capable of mothering to death anyone unfortunate enough to come into her clutches. Her sole motive, as she believes, is love; but it is a love with talons. The tragedy of a woman thus possessed, holding tenaciously to son or daughter, refusing to let them live lives of their own, is the theme of innumerable plays and novels—Eliot's *The Family Reunion* and Barrie's *A Window in Thrums* notable among them—and still more the theme of innumerable lives.

Where a woman effects a relationship with this figure she is capable of extraordinary activities. The lives of Queen Victoria, Mary Baker Eddy, Annie Besant and certain of the founders of famous *salons* may well have owed much to this archetype. But the tendency to identification is an ever-present danger, especially when the rôle assumed is a religious one. Mrs. Eddy, for instance, normally referred to herself as 'Mother', and hymns written by her—still reverently sung in the Christian Science churches—bring in the mother image unmistakably. The detailed history of the Church she founded, on the basis of universal harmony and the non-existence of evil, is a striking commentary on the power, and ambivalence, of this figure.

As might be expected, a whole cluster of archetypal themes centre around the *Magna Mater*, most of them in one way or another related to the key theme of death and rebirth. Sometimes the myth is that of the marvellous impregnation of the Great Mother and the birth of the hero. Sometimes it is the protection of the child-hero against the dangers which encompass him. Somet mes the Great Mother is found with a god-like consort—Ishtar and Tammuz, Cybele and Attis, Isis and Osiris, Aphrodite and Adonis—who is also the dying and resurrecting hero-saviour. Frequently, various of the themes are combined. But, however figured, death-and-rebirth is as naturally the province of the *Magna Mater* as the great work is the province of the Wise Old Man.

The Miraculous Child

Since Jung has published a detailed account of the archetype of the miraculous child,[1] little need be said about it here. In many ways this figure is more in the nature of a symbol—the symbol of promise—rather than a personality such as the anima-animus, the Wise Old Man and the Great Mother. But whether it comes as figure or symbol, miraculous it is in nature and appearance, the day-spring from on high, the joyous renewal of life, the vision of the new beginning.

> *Piping down the valleys wild,*
> *Piping songs of pleasant glee,*
> *On a cloud I saw a child . . .*

The following dream, from a man in early middle age, gives some impression of the sense of youth and delight this archetype brings. The dream is of particular interest in that it links the miraculous child to other archetypal figures and themes: on the one hand, to an archaic form of the Great Mother; on the other, to the 'City'—in this case, Edinburgh, a royal city with its citadel built on the rock.

'I was in a pleasant country spot, the sun shining, a kind of small sequestered valley in the hills. The first intimation I had that something strange was happening was when Highlanders, in kilts, and on skis, came down the hillside, sliding over the grass and rocks as if on a kind of slow but smooth-running snow. In the valley there was now a ruined church and the Highlanders were arresting a strange half-naked woman with two enormous breasts and a number of small subsidiary breasts.

[1] C. G. Jung and C. Kerenyi : *Introduction to a Science of Mythology.* Routledge & Kegan Paul, London. Bollingen Foundation, New York, 1950.

Without knowing how it came about, I now had in my arms a marvellous child, a boy of perhaps nine months, but perfectly formed and with the delight of all the ages in his smile. There was also, just behind me, a bent, black-coated old "Dominie" with his nose running. It was now night and a whole company of us—I, with the miraculous child in my arms, followed by the "Dominie" and a cloud of friendly presences—were dancing down the road to Edinburgh.

We ran into adventures on the way. At one moment the sea swept in on us and I was waist-high in the waves.

At another we were making our way through a series of rooms and scrambling through the transom over a locked door. But the miraculous child smiled always and the dance to Edinburgh went on.'

The miraculous child is the archetype of the new possibility, the new attempt. It is that which brings the good news to man of the possibility of regeneration, the promise of the Christmas eve:

As I in hoary winter's night stood shivering in the snow,
Surprised I was with sudden heat which made my heart to glow;
And lifting up a fearful eye to view what fire was near,
A pretty Babe all burning bright did in the air appear.

A figure not unlike the miraculous child, but widely different in other aspects, Jung calls the *puer aeternus*, the enterprising youth, the boy who never grows up. With some men (and some women) this is in the nature of a first approximation to the anima-animus, ranging all the way from the radiant figure springing up behind the plough to the difficult and perverse gutter-urchin. Ariel and Robin Good-fellow, Peter Pan and Puck of Pook's Hill are characteristic figures in literature. With some people this is not so much the archetype of the new beginning as a retarded psychological development. But, as always with the archetypal figures, any absolute statement is danger-ous. For one person the *puer aeternus* is something he or she needs to out-grow. For another it may be the means of development. Con-ceivably it may be both. Here, as throughout, there can be no neat fitting into set categories. Each individual experience requires to be taken and considered as a thing in itself, the archetype having its own appositeness in each unique situation.

A strikingly different, yet not dissimilar image, is that of the hermaphrodite, a figure with both the male and the female sexual attributes. Here again, whether it stands for an unsuccessful union of the opposites, or the opposites before they have fallen apart, or some other aspect of the *coniunctio*, depends upon the circumstances. These relatively uncommon archetypal forms are mentioned here with a minimum of description, so that if they are encountered they may be recognized for what they are. At present little is known about them: which makes them, from a scientific standpoint, so much the more interesting. But behind both the *puer aeternus* and the hermaphrodite is the possibility of development, ambivalent though it may be; and in this sense they have a certain kinship with the miraculous child.

The Hero-Saviour

The hero-saviour, the knight-errant, the warrior-saint, the deliverer, is an archetype linked both to the Miraculous Child and to the *Magna Mater*. The birth of the hero is typically of the stupendous kind, with wonders attending—signs in the heavens and prophecies on earth. Even as a child the hero does marvels. Hercules grappling with the serpents in the cradle is in the right heroic tradition. The *Magna Mater* is either the mother of the hero or (in her form as maiden) his consort. To some extent the hero-saviour merges with the Wise Old Man. The figure of the King—as for instance King Arthur, Charlemagne, Barbarossa—partakes of both.

But while thus characteristically blending into the other archetypes of the deep unconscious, the hero-saviour is more clear-cut than most. His characteristic theme is the quest, the adventure, the great deed. It is he who fights the dragon, is swallowed by and destroys the sea monster, encounters and worsts the false knight, rescues the maiden, frees the captives, delivers the waste land, discovers the priceless treasure. He is magically armed and equipped. Arthur has his sword Excalibur, Roland his Durandal; Perseus has the Gorgon's head, Siegfried his cloak of invisibility; there is the bow of Ulysses and the bow of Robin Hood; and a whole stable of magical and demonic horses, from Pegasus to Rosinante, Sleipnir to Black Bess. Jason and the Argonauts seeking the Golden Fleece, Hercules and his labours, Orpheus, Ulysses, Aeneas descending to the land of the shades, the Archangel Michael in his conflict with the powers of darkness, St. George slaying the dragon, the Knights of the Round Table in the quest of the Holy Grail, all are so many facets of the hero and the heroic task.

One single strand in this theme of the hero—his conflict with the bull—may give some idea of the multiplicity of possible meanings grouped into a single image.

In the Dordogne, among the cave paintings of Lascaux (attributed to the Upper Palaeolithic and as such presumably some ten to twenty thousand years old) there is, in a deep hole in one corner of the cave, the most remarkable of all the records of remote antiquity. It consists of four figures. There is a hairy rhinoceros making off into the undergrowth, having apparently gored a giant bison whose entrails are dropping out. This bison, in its death agony, is charging and about to trample to death a roughly sketched figure of a man, whose spear has been cast in vain and whose throwing stick has fallen to the ground. But it is no ordinary man. He has the face of a bird and the four-fingered hands of a bird. Surveying the whole scene is a bird on a stick (an image rather than an actual creature) with the same face as the man. The penis of the bird-man is erect. The rhinoceros is defecating.

Any reconstruction of the meaning of this scene is necessarily hypothetical. From analogies with primitive tribes the bird on the stick may with some assurance be taken as a totem bird, whose flesh is ordinarily forbidden as food but from time to time is ceremonially eaten by the whole tribe as the sacred bond between them. Here such a rite would presumably commemorate the great bird-man ancestor whose legend the painting sets forth. The nature of this legend can only be inferred. Presumably the great bird-man ancestor went out to hunt the bison. But the hairy rhinoceros, the villain of the piece (for Palaeolithic man, with his puny weapons, the hairy rhinoceros might well have stood for the Evil One) had gored the bison; and the bird-man was killed in its mad rush. But only his body was killed. His spirit lives on in the totem, and is imparted to the tribe when they partake of it together. The erect penis (actually, a physical consequence of the spine being broken) symbolizes this great creative act: the hero is at one and the same time dying and giving life. The rhinoceros, defecating, makes the appropriate diabolical comment.

Whether or not this interpretation is approximately valid, there is the undoubted fact that already in the Early Stone Age the conflict between the hero and the bull is depicted. Leaping from the Upper Palaeolithic to the classical epoch, there is Theseus in the Labyrinth fighting the Minotaur, half-man, half-bull, a figure exercising a strange fascination upon modern painters and sculptors. There are the winged bulls with human heads of the palace of Sargon, where apparently the hero and the bull have become one. There is Mithras, the God of the Roman Legions, sacrificing the bull; and the *Tauro-bolium* where the initiant was washed in the blood of the bull. Among men and women of the present age, and of all ages where records of dreams and visions have been kept, there is the persistently recurring image of the bull; sometimes the bull coming as the hero, as Jove came to Europa; sometimes in the fight to the death with the bull, such as the one George Fox records:

'. . . . a fierce bull did chase me sore, and would have devoured me . . . And I had many with me and little children, and I was loath they should be tired or hurt with the bull, and I did set the children upon my horse that they should not tire because of the bull's chasing them, I was so tender towards them. And the bull met me in a place where he thought he had me sure as his prey. I got a great hedge stake and chopped it down his throat to his heart and laid him still.'

To this present day, in many of the Spanish-speaking countries, the bull-fight, with its colour and its cruelty, its squalor and its heroism, remains as a strange survival of the age-old conflict.

The hero and bull theme is taken here, not for its special importance, but primarily to illustrate the unity-in-diversity of the archetypal image. Other typical incidents of the hero-saviour theme include the forging or finding of the magical weapon; the meeting with the women who help the hero and the women who tempt him out of his way; the vigils and pilgrimages, the Chapel Perilous, the Dark Wood, the Valley of the Shadow of Death, the bitter journey, the hard task. There is the hero chained to the rock, as was Prometheus, or hanged upon the tree, as when Odin invented the runes.

> *I know I hung on the wind-swept tree*
> *Nine nights through,*
> *Pierced by a spear, dedicated to Odin,*
> *I myself to myself.*

There is, above all, the self-sacrifice of the hero-saviour: as Toynbee puts it in *A Study of History*,

'A very god who dies for different worlds under diverse names—for a Minoan World as Zagreus, for a Sumeric World as Tammuz, for a Hittite World as Attis, for a Scandinavian World as Balder, for a Syriac World as Adonis ("Our Lord"), for an Egyptiac World as Osiris, for a Shi'i World as Husayn, for a Christian World as Christ.'

The hero, like the Wise Old Man, is primarily an archetype in a man's psychology. With a woman the corresponding rôle is played by the positive animus, who goes ahead and shows how the necessary thing can be done. As an individual experience the hero image is normally first projected upon some figure in the outside world: a games captain, football player, boxer, toreador, general, religious leader, dictator, film star. If it stays there, then little or nothing of value is accomplished—there is one more worshipper, one more letter added to the fan-mail. The next stage—invasion by the hero figure—may drive a man to extraordinary feats of bravery, or to fantastic madness. But if by good chance some relationship to this figure is effected, its value may be gained. The following is perhaps a fairly typical instance of how the projection may be 'brought home' in a modest fashion, according to a man's calibre.

'When the 1914 war broke out I felt myself utterly at a loss. I had not the remotest notion of how one fought wars. I had never so much as fired a rifle. And here was England in the midst of a war, a war to the death.

Then came Kitchener. There he was on every hoarding, with piercing eye and pointing finger, saying—it's you I want. That was all right. Kitchener knew how to fight wars. All one had to do was to join up and do what he said. So I did that and all was well. But only for a while. There came the news one evening that Kitchener was dead—gone down off the north of Scotland. What now? By that time, though, I was in uniform, had hardened up, could handle a rifle. And I knew the answer. Kitchener was no longer there. In my miniature way it was I who had to do it.'

Of all the manifestations of the hero-saviour archetype, however, none is so striking, or so disastrous, as that coming from mass projection. The present age has shown in a fashion well-nigh unbelievable what this image, backed by modern methods of propaganda, can do to whole peoples. Few things are more incredible in the history of humanity than the manner in which the German people cast the mantle of the hero-saviour upon Adolf Hitler. Yet such are the forces evoked that, in the course of twenty years, this sixth member of an obscure political party, meeting in a Munich beer-house, was within an ace of becoming the master of the world.

As with the other archetypal images, the figure of the hero has his characteristic theme: the quest, the deliverance, the discovery, the great deed. Much of what is noblest in the world derives from this theme, and much that is basest: from the self-sacrifice of men that set out on a forlorn hope, to the sacking of whole continents in the search for treasure. Also the hero brings with him the pattern of chivalry, the 'verray parfit gentil knight', the idea of the gentleman as in Sir Ector's memory of the dead Sir Launcelot:

> 'Said Sir Ector . . . Sir Launcelot . . . thou wert never matched of earthly knights' hand; and thou wert the courteoust knight that ever bare shield; and thou wert the truest friend to thy lover that ever bestrad horse; and thou wert the truest lover of a sinful man that ever loved woman; and thou wert the kindest man that ever struck with sword; and thou wert the goodliest person that ever came among press of knights; and thou wert the meekest man and the gentlest that ever ate in hall among ladies; and thou wert the sternest knight to thy mortal foe that ever put spear in the rest.'

The archetypal object

Accompanying the archetypal figures and themes there are numbers of archetypal objects, animate and inanimate. Dreams and visions, folklore and fairy tales, myths and legends, religions and magical practices, regularly bring in such forms as the dragon, the snake, the bull, the horse, the dog, the fish, the bird, the tree, the phallus, the sword, the spear, the stone, the jewel, the treasure, the flower, the wheat, the seed, the cauldron, the philtre, the poison, the secret, the sign, the cup, the blood, the land, the island, the city, the volcano, the well, the spring, the sun, the moon, the star, the sea, the ship, the desert, the mountains, the pass, the ford, the sunken way, the wood, the road, the door, the key, and many others, each with a rich and manifold mythological background.

To give the full archetypal context of any one of these objects would require a chapter to itself. But some broad impression of their meaning can be had without any elaborate description or research. The snake, for instance, appears in the Christian scriptures as the tempter, the Adversary, the Evil One. By many peoples in the past, though, the snake has been worshipped: there are the serpents inscribed on the sarcophagi of the ancient Egyptians; there is the plumed serpent of Mexico; Indian religion is full of serpent lore. Snake-bite is poisonous. At the same time, the snake, from the time of Aesculapius, has been associated with healing; and is to be found in the present-day badges of pharmacists, ambulance units and the like. The snake is cold-blooded, with forked tongue, reputed to fascinate, hypnotize, its prey. Many people have a feeling of horror towards snakes, a repulsion not based on actual experience but apparently innate. Yet, from time immemorial, by reason of its ability to cast its skin, the snake has been looked upon as immortal, as the symbol of rebirth. Snakes played a part in the antique mysteries: the initiant had to kiss the snake, sometimes to simulate eating it. The hero has snake-like eyes. Dead people are sometimes thought to re-appear in serpent form. The snake is a creature utterly unlike man and yet, in our spinal column, we are, as it were, linked to a common ancestor. Because of these manifold, ambivalent and uncanny meanings, the snake often stands for the unconscious in its chthonic aspect—a man's 'other side'.

A more ordinary object, often associated with the snake, is the tree. Here also, the archetypal content within the range of ordinary knowledge is considerable. In the Garden of Eden stood the tree of the knowledge of good and evil and the tree of life. The eating of the fruit of the tree—'The bitter apple and the bite in the apple'— was the cause of man's fall. But the tree also appears in Revelations, in the New Jerusalem, the four-square City of God. There, set in the midst of the city, it is 'for the healing of the nations'. Thus, the tree and its fruit is the symbol of the coming of man to consciousness, the separation from God; and at the same time of the new at-onement between God and man. The cross of Jesus is sometimes called 'the tree'.

In classical myth, there is the tree bearing the golden apples of the Hesperides. In Scandinavian myth, there is Yggdrasil, the world tree, binding together heaven, earth and hell. As Eden has its snake, the Hesperides their dragon, Yggdrasil has its serpent, gnawing at the root. The tree is another form of being. Unlike man and the animals, it draws its subsistence directly from the soil and the air. With its roots clutching earth and its branches outspread to heaven, the tree is a living symbol of the reconciliation of the opposites. It is life, yet a wholly different kind of life from ours; and time and again appears as such in dreams, visions and the products of the unconscious generally, standing for the impersonal life, the life transcending the ego.

These are typical examples, set out with no pretence of pattern or completeness, of the mythological and quasi-mythological lore behind what at first sight appear quite ordinary things. Not all archetypal objects, however, are matters of common knowledge. In the 'Villains in the Villa' dream, full consideration of the 'clocks' motif was deferred to a later stage. This may usefully serve as an illustration of a highly symbolical archetypal object, found in every age and all parts of the world, immensely meaningful, yet by most people virtually unrecognized: the *mandala*.

In its simplest form the *mandala* consists of a sacred enclosure, a *temenos*, having some 'great value' at the centre. Normally, this enclosure is circular or square; or combines the circle and the square, as for instance the square within the circle or *vice versa* (cf. diagrams p. 51). Normally also, the *mandala* has four ways in—or the 'great value' at the centre has four objects around it—characteristically at the four points of the compass: or the ways in may be some multiple of four, but always with the fourfold character emphasized.

The oldest type of *mandala* is the sunwheel, a circle with two diameters set at right angles, as in the Celtic cross. This image goes back into the mists of prehistory and is to be found in a variety of forms, the swastika being one. The symbolism of esoteric societies, the so-called 'secret tradition', abounds in *mandalas* of this kind. But it is in the great religions of the world that this symbol is most notably found.

The Christian Bible begins with a *mandala*: the Garden of Eden, having the four rivers going out from it, north, south, east and west, and with the great value—the tree of life and the tree of the knowledge of good and evil—at the centre. The Bible also ends with a *mandala*, the New Jerusalem coming down from Heaven.

'And he carried me away in the spirit to a great and high mountain, and showed me that great city, the holy Jerusalem, descending out of heaven from God,

Having the glory of God: and her light was like unto a stone most precious, even like a jasper stone, clear as crystal;

And had a wall great and high, and had twelve gates, and at the gates twelve angels . . .

On the east three gates; on the north three gates; on the south three gates; and on the west three gates . . .

And the city lieth foursquare, and the length is as large as the breadth . . .

And the building of the wall of it was of jasper: and the city was pure gold, like unto clear glass . . .

And I saw no temple therein: for the Lord God Almighty and the Lamb are the temple of it.

And the city had no need of the sun, neither of the moon, to shine in it: for the glory of God did lighten it, and the Lamb is the light thereof . . .

And he showed me a pure river of water of life, clear as crystal, proceeding out of the throne of God and of the Lamb.

In the midst of the street of it, and on either side of the river, was there the tree of life . . . and the leaves of the tree were for the healing of the nations.'

The whole of the imagery of this vision—the city, the jasper, the gold, the stream, the tree—is typical *mandala* symbolism.

In the subsequent development of Christianity the *mandala* repeatedly appears. Some of the earliest Christian Churches, notably St. Vitale at Ravenna (sixth century), were built on the *mandala* pattern. The first plan of St. Peter's at Rome was a perfect *mandala*. Many Gothic churches and cathedrals have above the main porch a *mandala* structure: the Christ at the centre, with the four evangelists, one at each corner, in their symbolical form, the Lion, the Eagle, the Ox and the Angel. The great rose windows of the cathedrals are *mandalas*. Behind the heads of saints, or sometimes in their hands (as in the Sainte Chapelle in Paris) are *mandalas*, all similar in form but each with its individual structure. The cloisters, which formed an integral part of the mediaeval religious establishment, are normally *mandalas*. The Cathedral at Chartres has an intricate *mandala* let into the stone floor of the nave, taking the form of a maze along which the devout on their knees worked a hard and winding way to the centre. The primitive Abyssinian churches are regularly built on the *mandala* model, consisting of two concentric circles with a square structure at the centre having four entrances. In Wales it is possible to find, on a chapel wall, the sunwheel *mandala*, of immemorial antiquity, with the trefoil representing the Christian Trinity at the centre.

In other religions and cosmologies the *mandala* pattern is no less evident. Buddhism has perhaps the most remarkable *mandala* in the world, the Barabudur in Central Java, attributed to the ninth century A.D. This is a marvellously sited stone structure, built round a hill, having the characteristic four gates, north, south, east and west; six square walks (the lowest underground) each rising above the other; these leading upwards and inward to three successive circles of 32, 24 and 16 stupas, each containing an image of the Buddha; the whole encircling the great central stupa. An idea of the size and magnificence of this *mandala* may be gathered from the fact that there are over two miles of frescoes along the rectangular walks.

In certain of the more esoteric cults, mythical *mandalas* are to be found of the most diverse kind. In Lamaist cosmology, Mount Meru forms an intricate multi-dimensional *mandala*. The mountain itself is conceived as towering 84,000 miles above the Central Ocean, extending below the surface for a like distance. The eastern face is of silver, the south of jasper, the west of ruby, and the north of gold. Around it are seven circles of oceans and seven intervening circles of golden mountains, each successive ring of mountains decreasing in height. Beyond that are the continents, the four chief ones in the Four Directions. The whole system is girdled externally by a double iron wall. Outside, all is void and in perpetual darkness.

The Muslim creed, with its predilection for geometrical forms, lends itself naturally to the *mandala* pattern. Much of the decoration of mosques takes this form. The famous Dome of the Rock on the Temple Platform at Jerusalem is a *mandala*. The great Muslim tombs in India are regularly constructed on the fourfold principle, with the tomb at the centre.

Other examples, taken at random in space and time, include the great Neolithic-Bronze Age circle at Avebury in Wiltshire; the design on the 'Battersea' bronze shield in the British Museum; the famous Calendar Stone of the Aztecs; the turquoise mosaic plaque of the Mayan civilization found at Chichen Itza in Yucatan; the pre-Colombian Mexican religious designs; the sand paintings of the present-day Navajo Indians in the United States; Tibetan *mandalas*, to be seen at any exhibition of Tibetan art, or in such accounts as Evans-Wentz' *The Tibetan Book of the Dead*; the vision described in the first chapter of the prophet Ezekiel; the Book of Kells; the exquisite tree *mandala* on the 7th Century binding of the St. Cuthbert gospel; Tom Quad at Oxford; the ancient game of the Nine Men's Morris; the 'rosie crosse' of the Rosicrucians; the English Good Friday hot cross bun; the aid to meditation used by Father Joseph in Aldous Huxley's *Grey Eminence*; Leonardo's mural of the Last Supper; the diagram in W. B. Yeats' *A Vision*; T. S. Eliot's *Four Quartets*; and, most interesting of all perhaps, the blotting pads and scribbling blocks on desks and committee tables where present-day civil servants, business executives, professional men and the like unknowingly record their inner preoccupation with this archetypal form.

The *mandala* repeatedly occurs in dreams, phantasies and in painting from the unconscious. In *The Secret of the Golden Flower* by Richard Wilhelm and C. G. Jung, *The Integration of the Personality* by C. G. Jung, and *Studies in Analytical Psychology* by Gerhard Adler, some examples are given of the intricate patterns produced by modern men and women, in the course of psychological analysis. These are not, as might be supposed, rare or unusual products. As soon as effective contact is made with the deep unconscious, the construction of *mandalas* normally begins.

An account as brief and sketchy as the above is obviously open to every criticism. On the one hand, it shows certain of the archetypal images in a fashion far more definite and clear-cut than they are actually experienced. On the other, it conveys little or nothing of their subtlety and power. It would be much simpler, of course, if the archetypes in human beings appeared consistently in the same form, as they do in creatures other than man. It would be much simpler, also, if our mode of apprehension of these forces were more direct, less mythological, in character. As it is, we have to relate to them as best we can. In by-gone ages men endeavoured to do this by representing them as some combination of man and beast, which was also a god: the bird-man of Lascaux; the bird and animal-headed gods of Egypt; animals having human heads, such as the Sphinx and the winged man-bulls of Nineveh; the Minotaur of

Crete; the goat-god Pan. We of the present age need a different approach to the archetypes, in keeping with our time. Simply to ignore them is to lose our roots. For with all their vagueness and impalpability, their ambivalence and many-sidedness, the arche-typal images hold out this great possibility: by their means it is possible for consciousness to effect a certain relationship with the forces of the depths. So long as the deep unconscious is a kind of highly-charged storm cloud enveloping a man, little can be done about it. But when it takes form in these images, something in the nature of a contact can be made. There is danger. Projection of the archetype, invasion by the archetype, identification with the arche-type, are situations beset with peril. But the greatest of all dangers is where archetypal projection and invasion take place uncon-sciously; as time and again has happened in this twentieth century when whole peoples, archetypally possessed, have run amok in the world. One of the essential features of the experiment in depth is that, in place of this unconsciousness, this failure of awareness, we may progressively gain knowledge of these forces and so convert them from the menace they at present are to the strength they can become.

VI

THE TRANSFORMING SYMBOL

THE principal means by which the creative possibilities of the deep unconscious may be reached is the transforming symbol. Anyone wholeheartedly engaging in the experiment in depth will find, as a normal fact of experience, that the unconscious repeatedly produces shapes, objects, phrases, ideas, which have this peculiar quality: if put to their right use they make possible a re-direction of energy and, by so doing, progressively transform the man who uses them.[1]

Rilke, in his sonnet on an archaic torso of Apollo, conveys some impression of the nature and effect of the transforming symbol. One may walk through the Louvre and glance at the headless Apollo—many times perhaps—admire its vigour and its 'wild beast grace', perceive perhaps that it has that essentially Greek quality—the whole body speaks—but never be stirred beyond a certain aesthetic appreciation. Till one day it is different:

> *Although we never knew his lyric head*
> *from which the eyes looked out so piercing clear,*
> *his torso glows still like a chandelier*
> *in which his gaze, only turned down, not dead,*
>
> *persists and burns. If not, how could the surge*
> *of the breast blind you, or in the gentle turning*
> *of the thighs a smile keep passing and returning*
> *towards that centre where the seeds converge?*
>
> *If not, this stone would stand all uncompact*
> *beneath the shoulders' shining cataract,*
> *and would not glisten with that wild beast grace,*

[1] The classical exposition of the function of the transforming symbol is given in Jung's *Psychological Types*, particularly Chapter XI, 'Definitions'.

and would not burst from every rift as rife
as sky with stars: for here there is no place
that does not see you. You must change your life.

In one way or another, sometimes with force brooking no denial, sometimes unobtrusively, perhaps unobserved, the symbol says: 'You must change your life.' Furthermore—the vital point—it musters the energy by which this may be done; and not only in consciousness but the other side of consciousness also.

'By this sign . . .'

Symbols assume an almost infinite variety of forms, ranging from the most ordinary object or phrase, which suddenly takes on a special quality of its own, to the most unexpected archetypal manifestation. But whatever the appearance, the effect is essentially the same: they transform. The following example of a symbol is a-typical in certain respects, but completely typical in the two chief features that need to be illustrated: its non-rational character, and its effectiveness. The woman to whom the symbol came begins the story:

'I was spending a night in a chalet hotel preparatory to a mountain excursion. As the hotel was full, we slept in a loft on the hay, closely crowded together. Fairly early in the night I awoke with a violent feeling of claustrophobia. I have had this before and since, but never so acutely. The distress was so great that I was obliged to go outside and sit on the steps. Finally I went back and found a clear space near the door; where I fell into a short and uneasy sleep. I then had this dream. I could see, on an oval patch of black, shading off vaguely, a rod made of yellowish-white metal; at one end of it was a monogram of the figures 124. I was so sure that this was the order of the figures and not 214, 142, etc., that in the morning I said, not "I dreamed of a rod with figures", but "I dreamed of 124". The rod was lying on its side; there were no people, no movement, no special emotional colouring; I just saw it.'

The woman had no personal amplifications to offer, only the vague feeling that some monogram she had seen once was like it. Eventually she traced it down. The following are the relevant passages from Gibbon's *Decline and Fall of the Roman Empire*:

'But the testimony of a contemporary writer . . . bestows on the piety of the emperor a more awful and sublime character. He affirms, with the most perfect confidence, that, in the night which preceded the last battle against Maxentius, Constantine was admonished in a dream to inscribe the shields of his soldiers with the celestial sign of God, the sacred monogram of the name of Christ; that he executed the commands of heaven; and that his valour and obedience were rewarded by the decisive victory of the Milvian Bridge.'

The 'sacred monogram' consists of the Greek letters Chi (X) and Rho (P), the two first letters of the word Christ. Both in the Eastern and in the Celtic Church this monogram became one of the foremost symbols of Christianity.

'But the principal standard which displayed the triumph of the cross was styled the Labarum, an obscure though celebrated name, which has been vainly derived from almost all the languages of the world. It is described as a long pike intersected by a transversal beam. The silken veil which hung down from the beam was curiously enwrought with the images of the reigning monarch and his children. The summit of the pike supported a crown of gold which enclosed the mysterious monogram, at once expressive of the figure of the cross and the initial letters of the name of Christ . . . There is still extant a medal of the emperor Constantius, where the standard of the Labarum is accompanied with these memorable words, BY THIS SIGN THOU SHALT CONQUER.'

The story passes now to a man who was one of the party on the mountain excursion:

'For some years, as a boy and young man, I suffered from a recurrent nightmare of being buried alive. Sometimes I was caught in a narrow cleft in the earth along which I was crawling. Sometimes a great rock was closing down on me. Sometimes it was just the sensation of being buried, struggling, and unable to breathe. These nightmares were terribly real and caused in me fear far greater than any physical danger in the outside world.

During the war of 1914–18 I actually was buried alive and survived only by a fortunate chance. From that time on, the nightmares ceased for some fifteen years.

They then started again with all their old-time intensity. N. told me when we were on our way up the mountain that she had dreamt of 124 but I paid no particular attention to it until one day, months later, she showed me a drawing she had made of the sceptre-like object with the monogram of inter-laced numbers. I found it strangely attractive. It spoke to me, as it were, although I had not the slightest idea what it said.

A few days later I had one of the "buried alive" nightmares. I woke in abject terror and at the moment of waking saw, as in a vision, this 124 sceptre—not lying on its side as N. had seen it, but raised as a standard might be raised. The terror dropped from me on the instant. Previously it would be half an hour or more before I could recover sufficiently to sleep again. This time I was calm at once.

Two or three times after that the nightmare came, though with decreasing intensity. On each occasion the 124 monogram—which I now consciously and deliberately invoked—drove the fear away. After that the nightmare ceased.'

As already said, this example is typical in two respects only: the non-rational character of the symbol; and its effectiveness. For no known reason, it works. Apart from this, most of the features are a-typical. In particular, it does not at all follow that a symbol coming to one person will be effective for another. Also, in the general run of cases, the symbol does not operate quasi-automatically as it did here. On the contrary, consciousness has to seize upon it and put it to use. Unless this is done, nothing happens. As Jung says, the unconscious produces symbols as a tree produces apples. If the man has the wit to pick the apples and eat them he will be nourished. If he does not, they will fall and rot and the man will starve.

The black dog

The 124 symbol is a striking and unusual one. It may be well to counterbalance it with a more obvious type of symbol-formation, this time illustrating the most essential point: that the man must take it and put it to use if it is to operate.

'I was on a liner, returning from the East. For some reason unknown to me, I became obsessed with erotic fantasies. I tried every means to get rid of them, but to no purpose.

One night I dreamed I was in a kind of fenced-in garden which belonged to me. An ugly black dog, and one or two others with it, made their appearance at the end of the garden, creeping in where the fence was broken. I tried to drive them out by reflecting the sun's ray on them with a mirror, but they only turned into wasps. I tried to beat these off with my book, but saw they were copulating and would produce a swarm.

I awoke; and perceived at once the meaning of the dream. The black dog had turned up before and stood, I knew, for sexuality. Using my intellect, my reflective apparatus, beating at the fantasies with the book I was working on, were exactly the means I had tried—to no purpose.

I fell asleep and was again in the garden. This time a whole rabble of ugly dogs was breaking in and advancing on me. I had a stick in my hand and on either side of me were friendly, shadowy beings. I moved down on the dogs menacingly (the beings with me) saying, "Get out, you beasts." The dogs turned tail and fled.

The next day when the erotic fantasies came, I faced them and said, "Get out, you beasts." They went. They did not return.'

This is an example of an obvious symbol. The man uses it and it works. But symbols, whether appearing in dreams or elsewhere, are not by any means always obvious. Frequently, the dream presents something in the nature of a choice. For instance, the man in the 'Villains in the Villa' dream, on turning the matter over in his mind, might have said: 'Well, seeing America on a bicycle seems more my line than shooting Easterners with miniature automatics. How do I start?' In such case, it is highly probable that the symbol 'America on a bicycle' would have proved effective. This does not mean that he 'ought' to have done this. On that no one can say. The point is that the unconscious presented the possibility, the means of finding the necessary energy, if the man so elected. It is as if, in the transforming symbol, new possibilities of life were offered to us, new growing points, which we take up or let go according to our insight and character.

Broadly speaking, most dreams which are felt at the time as significant contain symbols. The symbols are not always easy to find; but, once found and applied, they bring with them the transforming energy, linking together consciousness and the unconscious, changing the total attitude.

Innumerable single instances could be given of the symbol at work. But for practical purposes what most calls for illustration is the cumulative effect. The symbolic process, typically, is a gradual one, rather than a sudden burst of insight; a slow purposeful change over time. This is not easy to demonstrate. It involves using a whole dream series; with the inevitable consequence that, if the illustration is to be kept within reasonable compass, each dream instead of being fully analysed can be given no more than a few brief words of explanation, leaving the loose ends loose.

The Friend

The dream series demonstrated here has as its common factor that the figure of the 'Friend' appears in each. The running commentary, made by the man to whom the dreams came, shows how, time and again, he failed to understand the meaning of the symbols incorporated in these dreams: and how, time and again, a later dream presented the symbols in a different form which he was able to grasp.

'These dreams of the "Friend" stretched over a period of some eight years, beginning when I was about thirty-seven years of age. Between each of them there were many other dreams, of a more ordinary kind. Those in which the "Friend" appeared were of a special quality. At that time I knew nothing of the psychology of the unconscious beyond what one picks up in general reading.

This first dream impressed me so much that, though I made no record of it, the visual impression remains with me to this day.

THE MAN FROM THE CITY

I am outside the house where I lived as a child (a busy London road). There is a street fight going on. I strike a match, raise it above my head, and run in a circle. The match becomes a torch, and I a knee-skirted Greek goddess bearing the torch.

I wonder what will happen next: and thereupon (still in the form of the Greek goddess) meet a good-looking, well-dressed man of the "City" type. I walk along with him singing (inaudibly) two or three of the most wonderful wordless songs. We meet a "man in the street", who has on a huge diver's helmet with one large glass window in front, but too thick and frosted for him to see through.

As I can see now, this was a most interesting and in some ways auspicious start. In the unconscious I am still in my childhood's setting, the old house. There is conflict, a street fight, the collective side is in a state of confusion. I "strike a match" and raise it above my head. This refers, I take it, to some work I was trying to do, which I believed to be of enormous importance to the world, and which in fact carried me away (i.e. into the unconscious) although I realized nothing of that at the time.

There I become identified with the anima in her divine form and am taken back some two thousand or more years to the classical age. The "wordless songs" I associated with Keats' *Ode to a Grecian Urn*:

> *Heard melodies are sweet, but those unheard*
> *Are sweeter; therefore, ye soft pipes, play on;*
> *Not to the sensual ear, but, more endear'd,*
> *Pipe to the spirit ditties of no tone.*

By means of these "ditties of no tone" I am able to charm the "Man from the City" into my life. Together we inspect the "man in the street"—myself, the ego, the ordinary man, dressed for diving into the unconscious, but unable to see through his observation window.

True enough, I failed completely to understand this dream. I somehow half-believed that this friendly "Man from the City" would appear in real life and help me in the task in which I was sinking all my energy at that period. What I ought to have done, no doubt, was to have recognized that this auspicious figure was constellated in the unconscious and have taken steps to get into touch with him. But, identified with the anima as I was, and with no knowledge of psychological technique, there was little chance of this idea getting through to consciousness.

The next dream showed the Friend at work.

THE DELIVERANCE

I am in prison in a blockhouse with the "Friend". Two gaolers are there. My friend and I look at each other understandingly, spring upon the gaolers and lay them out. We go outside where we meet two other gaolers. They look at us suspiciously. I talk to one of them (who is like X) in a way calculated to allay suspicion, and gently reach down to a sword that is lying between us. My Friend and I again exchange glances. I snatch at the sword but the hilt breaks away as I grasp it. I catch up the blade in my two hands and draw it across X's throat. The other gaoler dashes upon my Friend. My Friend runs him through cleanly with a great long sword.

I am exhausted and lie panting on a hillock. The gaoler like X comes at me, but before he reaches me the wound in his throat gushes with blood and he dies. I see my Friend down in the valley with his long sword glittering, looking up at me. I know that he will help me if necessary. I think, I must summon up energy to get to the blockhouse where I was imprisoned. I shall find powder and shot there.

X was a man of great force of character for whom I worked, who overpowered me (as he did everyone else) with his masterful personality. In a sense, under him I was again back in the childhood condition. The dream told me three things, two of which I grasped, while the third I misunderstood. These were: (1) That I could break loose and live my own life—which to a great extent I did with the help of this symbolic gaol-breaking: (2) That my Friend with the long sword was there—in the background, as I put it to myself, in other words, *in the unconscious.* I had got it right this time, at least in part: *I did not expect a Friend with a long sword to appear in my outer life!* Although I did not phrase it to myself in that way, I recognized him as a source of inner strength. (3) The "powder and shot" I got wrong; I thought it was munitions for my outer activity, not for the inner struggle. In other words I made the same mistake as with the "Man from the City", thinking first, last and all the time of my work in the outside world.

The next dream is on a familiar theme, the going down into the unconscious.

THE DESCENT

With the Friend I am on a broad, long and terrifyingly steep flight of steps going down into a valley so deep that I cannot see to the bottom. I am particularly afraid of the lower steps where the angle becomes fearful. My Friend makes nothing of it. I notice that to the left side, beyond a stone balustrade, there is an earth ramp. I go down it with comparative ease, a little despising myself for having been afraid of the steps.

The dream is again correcting my mistake, showing me that it is the depths, the world of the psyche not the outer world, that has to be dealt with. I doubt though whether I grasped this point at the time, it was so contrary to anything likely to occur to me. Happily I kept close to the earth, or I might have gone in headlong.

The next dream shows the strange land to which I had come.

THE LIZARDS AND THE BIG GUN

I am in a pleasant country spot. There is a tree. Round it are three man-sized lizards (like the Komodo so-called "dragons") solemnly and methodically lowering by means of a line a large white fish hanging from the tree. In a fit of bravado I throw my revolver at the nearest of the lizards, saying to myself that since I have no more ammunition it is no longer any use. The revolver hits the lizard on the back. He turns and I take to my heels. The lizard picks up the revolver and pretends to throw it at me. Instead he throws a round white stone that goes wide.

I join the Friend, who has a big gun of the most modern type (at the same time it might be an astronomical telescope). I ask him to train it on to the lizards, laughing to think how scared they will be. I suggest we might fire off a blank so as to frighten them. He agrees that we can do this as soon as the gun is dry.

This is a highly symbolical dream, most of which I completely failed to see at the time. There are these strange survivals of an earlier age, these great lizards (an interesting image for the archetypal activity), demonstrating that the fish (the thing coming out of the sea, the unconscious) is to be obtained from the tree (the impersonal growth).

None of this penetrated to me. What did penetrate, and pleased me greatly, was that in place of an empty revolver there was the "big gun". Some while before the dreams of the Friend started I had a dream, which at the time I recognized as crucial, where I had in some fashion to choose between a big gun firing far away in the mountains, and a man playing a kind of bagpipe outside the door. In the dream I chose the gun—and now, here it was.

At the same time there was the beginning of a very important change. As with the "Man from the City" and the "Deliverance" dreams, I thought this big gun meant (when it was "dry") some great increase in capacity in the outside world. But the fact that it was also an astronomical telescope left with me the impression that it was something else besides—an immense increase in insight, in understanding; a means of seeing far beyond the range of ordinary vision.

Apparently the Friend had succeeded by now in giving me an inkling that it was personal development rather than outer achievement that the dreams were concerned with. Also by this time I was beginning to acquire some elementary psychological knowledge. In any case the next three dreams proceeded to impart direct personal instruction.

THE CASTLE

I am in the courtyard of a castle full of people dressed in the Tudor fashion. I go down a staircase as if I were a ghost with no weight, able to do the most extraordinary gymnastic feats. My friend (a tall, well-made young man, rather like an American college man in Elizabethan dress) is with me. We want to get out of the castle. We make for a small gate which is closing and at the last minute slip through. As we go, my friend gives a sheathed dagger to one of the men at the gate, who receives it in a haversack. Outside my friend turns to me and says: "You see what that means, to get out of the castle you must give up the dagger."

We then go on to some modern dress-making rooms. There are very attractive-looking girls, dressed in summer frocks, lying down on couches. I bend over one of them, desirously; only to find she is nothing but hat and clothes held together by string.

In this dream I had little difficulty in understanding what was meant. Two or three other dreams coming at the time emphasized the same general theme. I am again in prison—this time the prison of two besetting faults—hyper-critical intellectualism on the one hand, sentimental romanticism on the other. In the romantic castle I can do the most marvellous things, but I have no substance, no weight. To be free I must "give up the dagger". The "dagger" I understood to be my inveterate intellectualist habit of stabbing my friends, colleagues and fellow-technicians by the "faint praise and civil leer" method. "Yes, so and so is very good, but . . ." "Yes, so and so's work is first-class, but . . ." The other point was equally well-taken: an inveterate tendency to be infatuated and make a fool of myself over mere femininity, summer frocks, hats and clothes. Once out of the romantic castle I was enabled to see these for what they were.

These two symbols—the dagger and the stylish hat and clothes held together by string—at least did something to counteract two crippling traits in my personality. Next time I was tempted to stab a colleague I remembered the dagger; and next time a summer frock dazzled me, I remembered the string.

The ensuing dream turns from the shortcomings of the outer life to the situation in the unconscious.

THE FISHERMAN

I sit with a man who is fishing in the twilight from the rocky bank of a river. He is a tall spare man with a fisherman's hat and a capacious jacket. He has an impressive face as of one of wide experience. We are by a deserted house. He points out to me that the place might be dangerous, since a shuttered window of the house commands the point where we are sitting. I agree but say that, with several of us there, a hold-up would be difficult. (In point of fact we two are alone.)

He moves to one side and I admire the very special and strange fishing-rod he uses. It is only about five feet long, made of some composition material, very broad at the butt but tapering to a point.

I look down and see that a silver fish is on the line. I start hauling in. The fish gets bigger as it approaches, and turns out to be a brilliant silver seal.

I feel uncertain what to do next, but my friend takes a gaff and strikes the seal mercifully but firmly on the right shoulder. The seal turns over and dies; and is at once transformed into a tall, roughish-looking man in soldier's uniform with corporal's stripes. The water has now risen so that it is on a level with me. I hold the man on the end of the line with the hook in his mouth.

The first part of the dream I did not understand at all until some years later, and then by the hard way. The friend was warning me that in my depths there was a shut-up and deserted house which might be dangerous. It was dangerous—the whole of the personal unconscious which later I had to face.

The second part of the dream, on the contrary, I understood. I had by now acquired the first elements of the psychology of the unconscious and took in at least some of the significance of this "corporal". I was a corporal myself in the war of 1914–18: and although this man was nothing like me, except that we were about the same height, he stood for the dark side of myself which I preferred not to see: unscrupulous, self-seeking, considering his own interests and nothing else—a shadow-figure, in short. Characteristically, in fishing the shadow out of the unconscious, the water rises—the conscious personality is in danger of being swamped. On the other hand, as I recognized progressively over a period of years, this figure was a help to me as well as a menace. He had a rashness, a capacity to fight back, a devil-may-care kind of "guts" which I had not: unassimilated, out of control, these traits were dangerous; assimilated, under control, a strength.

In the next dream the "Friend" resembles an actual, flesh-and-blood, very good friend in outer life. (It is an interesting point that in each dream the appearance of the Friend was different.) We make a long and strange journey together into the desert, the details of which are not especially relevant here, and then:

The Mothers

We come to a room, a kitchen, I look through a door to the left. There is a steep stairway going down into a cellar, and at the bottom of it something horribly evil. At the top of the stairs is a cross-eyed girl with spectacles, neatly dressed in servant's clothes. I have great difficulty in getting back into the room and in closing the door leading to the cellar.

I am offered a square-headed hammer, which I refuse. I go into another room in which there are two women and a child. One woman is elderly. The other is younger, round-faced, rather like a young peasant woman. She wears the blue mantle of the Virgin Mary. The child is a girl, about seven, shadowy. The elderly woman is the mother of the younger one, who in turn is the mother of the child. There is a feeling of tranquillity and peace. I see the hammer handed in through the slit in the partly open door. It is as though it were following me. I take it and ask whether I can keep it here. They say, No. I debate whether to throw it down the stairs, but decide not. Outside, in the kitchen, I give over the hammer, very politely.

Scene, the kitchen, the place where new contents are made assimilable. The cellar and the cross-eyed girl (by a most ingenious combination of personal amplifications, too detailed to be unravelled here) represent infantile sexuality. Happily I managed to close the door of that cellar. (Incidentally, I used active imagination afterwards to see what was down there. It was a large and particularly ugly, dead-flesh-colour octopus.)

The hammer I took to be my tendency—rather pronounced at that time—to hammer a thing through inexorably. Even in consciousness I knew this was the wrong way to go about anything worth while, but had great difficulty in believing that any other way could be effective. (As will be noticed, the dreams are still bearing upon the same two points—sex and will-to-power. But now it is infantile sexuality in place of romanticism; and the hammer instead of the dagger.)

Two things I half understood from this dream. One, that I must "give up the hammer"—which I did to some extent with the help of this symbol, becoming rather more flexible, less dogmatic, in my action in the outer world. The other, that the dream must have been a profound one since it had led to "The Mothers" (I knew the famous passage in Goethe's *Faust, Part II*), with the younger of the women wearing the blue mantle of the Virgin.

The essential point I missed: that, *in dealing with the inner world, it is necessary to "give up the hammer"—the masculine fashion—and work by way of "The Mothers", the gradual, natural process of growth and birth.*

The next dream picks up this point.

THE REBIRTH THEME

I meet a man—my friend—who guides me. He is of medium height, squarely built, with good, serious face, and steady eyes, a workman, vaguely foreign, but of no particular nationality. He says that we shall now pass where I had not understood with the dream of the Mothers. There is a sort of turnstile in the middle of the road, with a bent, witch-like figure sitting by it. The road is very wide and in some confusion as if being made up. My guide takes me to the left and I wheel my bicycle safely past.

We come to a place where we must crawl. There is a small square opening before us leading to the light. My guide tells me to give the guardian—a strange figure, half imp, half angel—two coins. I give him an American cent and some queer coloured coin out of my purse. For good measure I give him another cent, and a coin like a soldier's brass button. The guide is lying to my left slightly forward. I ask him whether he will show me the way through the narrow square. He says he will; but there the dream ends.

Of this dream I got one point only: that it dealt with rebirth—the narrow opening leading to the light. The main feature in it I missed altogether. At first everything is favourable. I get by the witch, the negative mother figure that can devour a man. The road is wide although not yet finished—my psychological studies were proceeding apace, though so far more learned than lived. I am wheeling my bicycle, not trying to drive a car or otherwise forge ahead by artificial means, not even riding the bicycle. In all these things my attitude was right, until it came to the essential operation—paying my passage. I proffer an American cent and a "queer-coloured coin". Then "for good measure"—the unconscious has its irony—another cent and a button. In other words I value rebirth at two cents, and throw in a couple of counterfeits as well. That the proceedings stopped at that point was logical enough. The money, energy, I was prepared to put into the most fundamental process in the whole of psychological development was no more than that. I remained where I was.

The next dream brings the correction.

THE OLD OPERA HOUSE

My friend and I are national soldiers, but with old rough coats on instead of tunics. We are reconnoitring in a railway truck. We pass rebel soldiers working on the road. My friend shoots at them with a rifle at close range. I fire at longer range with an old-fashioned rifle. The soldiers digging take no notice. In some inexplicable fashion we are ineffective.

We now manhandle the truck up a narrow side lane to the left where rebels are working. It ends in a cul-de-sac, but my friend finds a man he knows: a small, stocky, dark-skinned man with fine dark eyes and white teeth—a Mediterranean peasant—powerful and quietly energetic. Two rebel soldiers come and are a little suspicious, but my friend lets them understand that we are on their side. We talk with the small, dark man first in French, my friend afterwards in slow German.

The dark man leads us along a wooden paved way through the forest and we come to an old opera house, a ruin that has been excavated. People are being shown over it. The dark man takes us to see the "mirror" upstairs—a tawdry wall decoration—and a flashy, not very young or fresh, woman of whom people are making a fuss.

With the dark man leading we climb up and through narrow square holes into a sort of attic and out through the roof, my friend following and helping me to place my feet. I feel a little ashamed at having to be assisted so much. We make good progress.

For the "rebel soldiers" I had one quite definite amplification:

> *Poor soul, the centre of my sinful earth,*
> *(Foil'd by) these rebel powers that thee array.*

Against these rebel powers my friend and I shoot ineffectively. At this level, the level of the "old opera house"—the old works—we can do nothing.

My friend brings me to what is clearly a shadow figure, but a very positive one. Again we encounter the two familiar themes: the tawdry "mirror", the reflective process, intellectualism: and an immature attitude to sex (cf. the dagger and the summer frocks of the "Castle" dream, the hammer and the squint-eyed servant of the "Mothers" dream). But now they are more like exhibits in a museum. We are passing beyond them.

And this time we get through. The "climbing out" theme has both a personal and an archetypal amplification. In my personal life, a gymnastic feat of this kind, getting up through a series of square holes on to the roof, was something in which I took a peculiar pride as a youth. In some way, as I vaguely knew, it symbolized my becoming a man. In legends and folklore this process of climbing out, being pulled through the hole in a rock, crawling out of a narrow passage, is a frequently recurring image of rebirth.

This dream, I realized, marked a turning point. It had been a long journey since first I left the childhood environment with the "Man from the City"; was delivered from the "blockhouse" in which the overpowering personality of X had confined me; went down the steep earth ramp into the bottomless valley; threw away the empty revolver and first realized that it might be insight, not outer action, that was the true objective; made my way out of the romantic castle; fished the "corporal" out of the unconscious; came to the realm of the Mothers and did not understand; came to the place of rebirth and valued it at two cents; came finally to the "old opera house" and made the break-through at last. With this emergence from the "old works" I felt I had moved, as it were, to another level. This brought with it a great feeling of release. A point I did not realize was that the process of rebirth now had to be by way of the shadow. What that meant I learnt in later years.'

As already noted, the analysis made of individual dreams in this series is so brief that all except the most salient points are passed over. For this reason they do not carry much conviction to anyone but the dreamer. The aim in presenting such illustrative material, however, is not to convince in any way—only direct personal experience will ever do that—but to exemplify. These dreams, with the 'Friend' as *psychopompos*, show symbol after symbol being used to direct energy to new aims, a progressive transformation of the personality. First, that the man has to free himself from those things which hold him to ways he has outgrown: the childhood environment; the blockhouse where he is imprisoned by X; the romantic castle of intellectual stabbing and hat-and-frock sentimentality; the 'old opera house', in which he is no longer effective. Second, that it is the inner world that needs to be dealt with, when the man himself thought only of achievement in the outer world. Third, that intellectual pride and immature sexuality—his chief obstacles in psychological development—need to be seen for what they are. Fourth, that there are aspects of himself, potentialities both positive and negative (the big gun which is also an astronomical telescope, the empty house, the 'corporal', which must be realized if progress is to be made. Most important of all, that the creative process proceeds by way of 'the Mothers'—rebirth—not by way of the hammer: *and it has to be paid for*. As a result, the man who at the beginning was thinking only of outward effectiveness, at the end has come to see inward development and growth as his real need: and to this end is finding and using the transforming symbols by which such development may be achieved.

The deep centre

Rebirth, the theme of the 'Friend' series of dreams, is one aspect of the creative activity coming from the unconscious. There is another aspect, equally fundamental: the discovery of what is here called the deep centre. How the deep centre is found, and what follows from it, constitutes the principal subject-matter of the ensuing chapters. At this point all that will be attempted is to give some general impression of the manner in which the deep centre may be encountered.

William James, in *The Varieties of Religious Experience*, describes how the discovery of the deep centre takes place with those 'more developed minds' having a religious bent:

'. . . . there is a certain uniform deliverance in which religions all appear to meet. It consists of two parts:
  1. An uneasiness; and
  2. Its solution.

1. The uneasiness, reduced to its simplest terms, is a sense that there is *something wrong about us* as we naturally stand.

2. The solution is a sense that *we are saved from the wrongness* by making proper connection with the higher powers.

In those more developed minds which alone we are studying, the wrongness takes a moral character, and the salvation takes a mystical tinge. I think we shall keep well within the limits of what is common to all such minds if we formulate the essence of their religious experience in terms like these:

The individual, so far as he suffers from his wrongness and criticizes it, is to that extent consciously beyond it, and in at least possible touch with something higher, if anything higher exist. Along with the wrong part there is thus a better part of him, even though it may be but a most helpless germ. With which part he should identify his real being is by no means obvious at this stage; but when stage 2 (the stage of solution or salvation) arrives, the man identifies his real being with the germinal higher part of himself; and does so in the following way. *He becomes conscious that this higher part is conterminous and continuous with a MORE of the same quality, which is operative in the universe outside of him, and which he can keep in working touch with, and in a fashion get on board of and save himself when all his lower being has gone to pieces in the wreck.'*

This 'germinal higher part' leading to the 'MORE' has been variously experienced and variously described. In the Upanishads it is the Atman, 'smaller than small and greater than great'. In the Christian Gospels, it is the Kingdom of Heaven within a man: the mustard seed, the smallest of all seeds but the greatest of all herbs; the leaven a woman hid in three measures of meal until the whole was leavened; the pearl of great price; the treasure in a field which a man sells everything to buy. In the Pauline epistles it is the living Christ: 'I am crucified with Christ: nevertheless I live; yet not I, but Christ liveth in me.' In the Muslim faith it is the Secret, closer to a man than his jugular vein. With the alchemists and others in the secret tradition it is the philosopher's stone, the *lapis*, which can transmute base metal into gold. In Chinese wisdom it is the diamond centre, the house of the square inch in the field of the square foot (the body); or it is the small round thing, the pearl, the jewel, that the dragons guard. In the Tantric yoga it is the Kundalini serpent, twined three and a half times around the *lingam* (phallus), the serpent-power which, when aroused, can change a man utterly. Marcus Aurelius the 'pagan philosopher' knows of it also: 'Look well into thyself; there is a source of strength which will always spring up if thou wilt always look there.' With the Quakers, it is the inward light, the seed, 'that of God in every man' which can bring about the 'inward transforming experience of God'. In the chivalric tradition of the Middle Ages it is the Holy Grail which all good knights seek but few find. Plotinus calls it the soul-centre. Richard Law speaks of 'the birth of God within'. Meister Eckhart has this to say of it:

> 'There is a spirit in the soul, untouched by time and flesh, flowing from the Spirit, remaining in the Spirit, itself wholly spiritual. In this principle is God, ever verdant, ever flowering in all the joy and glory of His actual Self. Sometimes I have called this principle the Tabernacle of the soul, sometimes a spiritual Light, anon I say it is a Spark. But now I say that it is more exalted over this and that than the heavens are exalted above the earth. So now I name it in a nobler fashion . . . It is free of all names, and void of all forms. It is one and simple, as God is one and simple, and no man can in any wise behold it.'

The modes of expression differ, but behind them all is the same fundamental perception, the experience of something lying beyond the ego-consciousness but which nevertheless affects consciousness, as in the heavens a dark star cannot be seen but its existence is known from its gravitational effect. And the effect of the deep centre is to transform, integrate, re-create the human being who finds and holds to it:

> I am all at once what Christ is, since he was what I am, and
> This Jack, joke, poor potsherd, patch, matchwood, immortal diamond,
> Is immortal diamond.

In the experiment in depth the typical form in which the deep centre is encountered is the *mandala*, at its centre the jewel, the child, the flower, the gold, the flame, the seed, the citadel, the stronghold, the city built on a rock, or however else the 'germinal higher part' may be symbolized. Eliot in the *Four Quartets* speaks of it as 'the still point', 'the unknown, remembered gate', the 'timeless moment', 'the point of intersection of the timeless with time'.

> . . . *to apprehend*
> *The point of intersection of the timeless*
> *With time, is an occupation for the saint—*
> *No occupation either, but something given*
> *And taken, in a lifetime's death in love,*
> *Ardour and selflessness and self-surrender.*
> *For most of us, there is only the unattended*
> *Moment, the moment in and out of time,*
> *The distraction fit, lost in a shaft of sunlight,*
> *The wild thyme unseen, or the winter lightning*
> *Or the waterfall, or music heard so deeply*
> *That it is not heard at all, but you are the music*
> *While the music lasts.*

As Eliot suggests, in the past, experience of the deep centre has come only to the highly percipient man or woman, the mystic, the saint, the seer; or, in any case, has been vividly realized only by such unusual beings. The great possibility opened up by the constructive technique is that the discovery of this 'germinal higher part' may be made, if not by the many, at least by more than the very few. There can be little question that the deep centre is normally encountered in the experiment in depth; and, indeed, is apprehended in some form wherever and whenever men and women are dealing with life in a spirit of responsibility and devotion.

What is needed is that such men and women should know of this potentiality, not as some strange experience coming only to the saints and mystics but (so far as can be judged) as a natural fact in man. Most people in the modern world, should they come upon the deep centre, are more than likely to pass the experience by unnoticed, or see it at the time and afterwards forget. But when they come to know that the deep centre is as naturally and normally a part of the man as the ego, it can be found and held.

This does not mean that the process of going over to life lived from the deep centre is easy. To travel beyond the ego–centred condition is felt at first as equivalent to death. Such, in a fashion, it is, a continuous dying. But it is dying to be reborn, reborn in depth. And life so lived is wholly different, in nature and effect, from the ego-centred activity. It is the means by which a man most truly becomes himself, serving as channel for the creative power.

THE TRANSFORMING SYMBOL

At the moment which is not of action or inaction
You can receive this: 'on whatever sphere of being
The mind of a man may be intent
At the time of death'—that is the one action
(And the time of death is every moment)
Which shall fructify in the lives of others:
And do not think of the fruit of action.
Fare forward.

Part Three

THE CREATIVE CONTACT

VII

THE WAY
BETWEEN THE OPPOSITES

THE transforming symbols arise out of conflict. Most people who take account of life—as distinct from merely being carried by it—recognize that they are all the time torn between incompatible courses. Situations come up, calling for decision; but we cannot decide; or if we do decide, cannot hold. We feel we ought to do one thing, yet something in us wants to do another. We make good resolutions, and break them as soon as made. One day we are co-operative, altruistic, helpful, the next day petty and mean; one day, firm and self-reliant, the next weakly going with the crowd. We set out to take a strong line, and, not knowing how it happened, find ourselves going in the opposite direction to what we intended. Life is lived in a maze of opposites; a maze to which, often, there seems no clue.

Different individuals react to the opposites in different ways. Some hurtle continually from one extreme to the other, and back again. This *enantiodromia* (literally, running between the opposites) is particularly observable when entire peoples or civilizations are considered over long stretches of time. A period of Puritanism is followed by a period of licence. A classical age is succeeded by an age of romanticism. A conservative régime is followed by a radically progressive one. A century of quiescence, such as the one we have left, is followed by a century of turmoil, such as the one we are now in. The individual life shows much the same comings and goings, typically with a shorter time interval, the movement between the opposites taking place in a matter of weeks or days or minutes, rather than centuries or decades.

A no less typical reaction to the tension of the opposites follows the contrary line. The man, instead of hurtling to and fro, comes to a standstill, is stopped in his tracks, incapable of action. Like Buridan's ass between the two equally attractive bundles of hay, he starves to death in the middle. For him the conflict is inward; until it is solved he is stuck.

There is a third way of reacting to the opposites, which consists essentially in pretending they do not exist; or, if they do exist, are really very much alike. One 'finds a formula', works out a 'solution', achieves 'complete agreement', by ignoring the true problem. This is a way of escape, the dead compromise. Faces are saved, the situation 'dealt with'. Sometimes such a course is necessary, but the net accomplishment is *nil*.

There is also a true compromise, a genuine resolution of the opposites. It is the virtue of the transforming symbol that, by its means, a man lost in the maze of contraries is able to steer a course. It would seem, moreover (but necessarily any such conclusion is highly hypothetical), that this course is *his* course, the way appropriate to that man as a unique human being, living in the unique circumstances which make up his particular mode of existence. Whether or not this is true, there is no question that (at least as the man experiences it) the transforming symbol enables him to pick a path amidst the opposites which is not the dead compromise but a living middle way.

The verdict of the philosophies

Different philosophies of life have advanced different views as to where and how this resolution of the opposites should be sought. At first sight these views appear contradictory. Later they are seen as complementary one to the other, coming together to form a whole.

The Apostle Paul postulated a particular set of opposites and a particular mode of solution.

'The good that I would I do not: but the evil which I would not, that I do . . . For I delight in the law of God after the inward man: but I see another law in my members, warring against the law of my mind, and bringing me into captivity to the law of sin which is in my members. O wretched man that I am! who shall deliver me from the body of this death?'

Paul's question, the agonized cry of the man impaled upon the everlasting dilemma of the body and the spirit, rings down the ages as poignant now as ever. His answer to it is the love of God, reached through the saving power of Christ:

'If Christ be in you, the body is dead because of sin; but the spirit is life because of righteousness . . . I am persuaded, that neither death, nor life, nor angels, nor principalities, nor powers, nor things present, nor things to come, nor height, nor depth, nor any other creature, shall be able to separate us from the love of God, which is in Christ Jesus our Lord.'

Other creeds, and other philosophies, have faced and dealt with the problem of the opposites in characteristically different fashion. Indian philosophy from the earliest times has recognized the fundamental dichotomies in and around man. 'Beneath the pairs of opposites must the world suffer without ceasing.' And its answer is likewise that a power within, the Atman, can give deliverance. But, in place of the love of God, it is extinction of desire that is seen as the saving factor.

'Whosoever is free from overweening vanity and delusion and hath overcome the frailty of dependence, whoso remaineth faithful to the highest Atman, whose desires are extinguished, who remaineth untouched by the opposites of pleasure and pain—that one released from delusion shall attain that imperishable state.'

Chinese philosophy has the same vision, with a difference; and comes to much the same conclusion, again with a difference. It sees the primal opposites of Yin and Yang. Yin is the principle of rest, the unchanging, the dark, the cool, the moist, the female, the side of the mountain in the shade. Yang is the principle of movement, of change, the bright, the hot, the dry, the male, the side of the mountain in the sun. Yin is continually going over to Yang, Yang continually going over to Yin. The two are combined in the T'ai Chi. Yin has the seed of Yang in it, Yang has the seed of Yin; Yin is perpetually becoming Yang, Yang is perpetually becoming Yin; the whole harmoniously working together for the man, or the people, who can see the opposites in their deep consonance with the

ordinances of Heaven. *Wu wei*, an untranslatable expression, usually rendered as 'not-doing', a wise acceptance of life, an inaction which enables the creative activity to operate, is the essence of the Chinese view.

The peoples of the West, the heirs of the Graeco-Roman civilization, have, perhaps, never been so consciously aware of the problem of the opposites as have those of the East. On the other hand the Western philosophers have not altogether ignored it. Heraclitus observes, 'Even nature herself striveth after the opposite, bringing harmony not from like things, but from contrasts'; and arrives at the fundamental statement (which Eliot uses as epigraph to the *Four Quartets*): 'The way up and the way down are one and the same.' Aristotle has his 'Golden Mean' between the opposites, insisting upon it with such emphasis that he incurred the criticism of being excessively moderate. At the other end of the time-scale of Western civilization, there is Hegel's famous thesis-antithesis-synthesis; which, in its various applications and misapplications, has raised much stir in the world. But, in the main, action rather than philosophy has been the theme of the Western peoples. Effort, ardour, experiment, the free search for truth, is their essential contribution to the problem of the opposites. The middle way is something to be striven for with all a man's strength; and achieved.

Eliot sums up the wisdom of these four views of life in a passage already quoted:

> . . . *to apprehend*
> *The point of intersection of the timeless*
> *With time, is . . . something given*
> *And taken, in a lifetime's death in love,*
> *Ardour and selflessness and self-surrender.*

There is perhaps no more comprehensive statement. 'Love', the way Paul learnt from the Christians; 'ardour', ardour for truth, the scientific spirit; 'selflessness', freedom from ego-centred desire, non-attachment to results; and 'self-surrender', the acceptance of life, the allowing of the creative spirit to work: together these constitute the sum of man's knowledge and experience of the opposites and the middle way.

Categories of opposites

Considered psychologically, there are certain broad categories of opposites of especial importance. This does not mean that any neat classification is possible. The 'intolerable wrestle with words and meanings' rules this out from the beginning. No two men, for instance, are likely to have the same idea as to what they mean by such opposites as good and evil. Also there are no fixed criteria of judgement. According to one's experience of life, certain antagonisms seem fundamental, others of little moment. Moreover, they change. How I see the opposites this year is not how I saw them last year, is not as I may see them tomorrow. Nevertheless, it helps towards a better understanding and perspective if these fundamental oppositions working upon man can be grouped, however tentatively.

The basic opposites at work in the human being are the claims of consciousness and the claims of the unconscious. But when we say this, the meaning of what we have said fades out even as we say it. We have no clear notion of what we mean by consciousness, still less of what we mean by the unconscious. On the other hand—in a fashion—we do know that it is the task of man to find the living middle way between them. '*Il faut être soi.*' However vaguely, we are aware of something in us which responds to the demand 'To thine own self be true', something which is self-conscious in the deepest sense, which can and must hold a balance and steer a course between inner and outer necessity. 'Visible and invisible, two worlds meet in man'; and in some way these two worlds must come together and be reconciled.

Along with, and part of, this strife of the visible and the invisible, four main categories of opposites may be distinguished.

The first of these is that of attitude: the attitude of yea and the attitude of nay, the positive and negative poles between which life is lived. There is nothing clear-cut about this category. The words and concepts available limit both our understanding and our means of expression. But everyone is aware of at least some of the pairs of opposites carrying this plus-minus connotation: good-evil, love-hate, truth-untruth, beauty-ugliness, constructive-destructive, integration-disintegration, success-failure, pleasure-pain, joy-woe, optimism-pessimism, hope-fear, elation-depression, impulsiveness-indecision, superiority-inferiority, indulgence-asceticism, extravagance-stinginess, sadism-masochism, arrogance-servility, frustration-fulfilment and so on.

In the experiment in depth, attitude is fundamental. A right attitude—the attitude of wholeness—necessarily takes into account both the yea and the nay, recognizes that to fare forward effectively we need not only engine but brakes, realizes that, in the forming of character, hardship is as essential as opportunity. As Blake puts it:

> *Man was made for Joy and Woe;*
> *And when this we rightly know,*
> *Thro' the World we safely go.*

Such an attitude is well aware that success may be failure, failure success. It sees that evil is not only the enemy but possibly the anvil; the anvil on which men and societies are hammered into their true shape. But however philosophically we may look upon them in the abstract, in practice we are continually caught between the opposites of yea and nay, the urge on, the urge back, and, according to our disposition, thrown from one side to the other or brought to a standstill, incapable of decision.

The second category of opposites, permeating every aspect of human existence, is what might be called the 'split in the libido', the self-contradictory nature of the psychic energy flowing through man. On the one hand, there are the instinctual drives we share with the animals—self-preservation, sexuality, the will-to-power, the herd instinct, and so forth. On the other, there are the moral and spiritual forces which oppose these drives. It is the everlasting struggle of 'I want' and 'I ought'. The Apostle Paul with his body-spirit dualism, Nietzsche with his contrast of the Dionysiac and the Apollonian, Freud with his id and super-ego, have all in their various ways stressed this basic opposition.

Actually, this split in the libido is far more intricate than might at first be supposed. It is not merely a head-on clash between what we vaguely call 'instinct' and, no less vaguely, 'spirit'. The instincts are divided against themselves. Driven by the sex-instinct a man may risk career, good name, life itself, throwing self-preservation to the winds. Driven by the will-to-power he may step out from and defy the herd. The spirit is likewise many. There is the spirit that is militant and the spirit that is submissive, the spirit that is fire and the spirit that is water. There is the spirit that seeks its fulfilment in the 'flight of the alone to the Alone' and the spirit that sees the fulfilment of all things in the brotherhood of man. The psychic energy flowing through us is not simply but multitudinously divided; and we with it.

The third category of opposites arises from the fact that man lives in society. How are the supreme claims of the individual and the supreme claims of the collectivity to be reconciled? Aspects of this problem are innumerable. There is the voice of duty that says: 'Become what thou art' and the voice of duty that says: 'Obey the laws of the tribe.' There is the device of the Abbey of Thélème: *'Fay ce que vouldras'*, and the device invisibly written over every suburban villa: 'Do as the neighbours think you should.' There are the self-regarding claims of the ego-centred individual and the tyranny of the totalitarian state. How to find a right balance between freedom and authority, how to combine liberty with order, how to enable the individual to develop freely and at the same time achieve the greatest good of the greatest number: these are amongst the perennial questions, both of the personal and of the public life. More obviously than any other, perhaps, the individual–collectivity pair of opposites underlies every aspect of human existence.

Lastly, there is the deep-seated but (in the present age) little-regarded opposition between time and eternity as the true setting of man's estate. That this category of opposites is largely ignored does not mean that it is of no effect. On the contrary, it works invisibly upon us with the greater power. If my underlying belief is that, both for the individual and eventually for the species, life offers no more than a fitful and essentially empty awareness of existence, ending in oblivion, then, whether or not I am consciously aware of it, everything I am and do is subtly undermined and rendered meaningless. At the opposite extreme, if I have my eyes so firmly fixed on eternity that I think only of the heavenly kingdom beyond this life, I can help to bring hell on earth by the things I do and leave undone.

Western civilization, for some centuries now, in dealing with this set of opposites has tried to have it both ways. The death-bed utterances attributed to Rabelais constitute as urbane a manner of doing this as any: on the one hand, *'Tirez le rideau, la farce est jouée'*; on the other, *'Je m'en vais chercher un grand peut-être'*. This is the agnostic 'open-minded' view. So long as it is propped up by such myths as progress, peace and plenty, it may for a while suffice. But essentially it is the dead compromise. When these myths collapse, the meaning seeps out of life and the land becomes waste. Unless and until the living middle way is found between these opposites of time and eternity, life may be urbane, but for the individual it will be essentially empty, for the collectivity chaotic.

None of these categories of opposites is clear and distinct. Each cuts across all the others. But the yea and the nay, the split in the libido, the individual-collectivity and the time-eternity aspects are all so many ways of seeing the divided state in which we live. With the help of the perspective thus given, the finding of the living middle way can, perhaps, be more readily visualized. This in itself, though, is only a first step. Becoming more conscious of the problem of the opposites does not provide a way through. The unconscious, no less than consciousness, needs to take a hand.

The opposites and the constructive technique

The manner in which the symbols coming from the deep unconscious indicate a way between the various categories of opposites is best shown by taking specific examples. In this and the ensuing section two phantasies are given in some detail, illustrating the process at work.

The following is an account, as recorded at the time by the man to whom it came, of the first stage in a long exercise in active imagination, stretching over a period of years.

'Sitting at my desk, worried as I had been for months past over the gloomy political condition of the world (this was in 1935), the thought crossed my mind that at such a time a new symbol should come into existence, to canalize and direct the distracted energies of the peoples. From this I was led on to reflect upon Jung's theory of symbol formation (to such extent as I understood it), which consisted in the withdrawal of libido from the conscious functions and the turning inward of the energy thus freed; thereby floating up into consciousness the reconciling symbol already waiting in the unconscious.

I attempted to visualize and to some extent to enact what this might mean, making my mind blank, and, in imagination, turning its energy into the midst of my inmost being. At once, to my considerable surprise, I had the impression of seeing, high up on the left of the periphery of vision (not in the outside world at all, but, as it were, in a medium interpenetrating that world) a shape

in the form of a vertical line with two short horizontal lines crossing it, one towards the top, one towards the bottom. I drew it on
a piece of paper and looked at it curiously; with the vague feeling,
now when I saw it clearly, that it had been hovering around me
for the last fortnight or more.

I speculated as to what the shape might mean, and saw
suddenly that it was a sword buried in the cross, the
upright of the cross being hollowed out to take the
blade of the sword. The many-sided meaning of such a
combination struck me; that it showed the spirit of sacrifice overcoming the spirit of war; the fusion of love
and of truth; the reconciliation of feeling and of thinking;
the coalescence of the feminine and masculine principles;
and still others. I had the impression that something of a
very special nature had come to me, and although the
world problem continued to haunt me day and night I felt that
in the symbol there lay an answer, though I could not tell what.

For some weeks this shape remained unchanged, but still keeping
its importance in my mind. One night I awoke with a feeling of
preternatural clearness and, my thoughts turning to the symbol, I
saw that it was not complete. There must be a circle in the picture.
I asked myself "But of what could a circle be made?" The reply
came at once, as if spoken inside me: "Of fire." "But," I objected,
"how can one make a circle of fire?" Again the same independent
voice came: "But also of water." A circle of fire and of water per-
plexed me, but suddenly I felt that it could be made of Iceland
spar—a form of quartz with high refractive power of which I had
read, many years ago, as being used in the polarization of light,
but which I had never thought of particularly since.

The symbol had now reached the stage shown; and I gave much

thought as to how it should be fastened together in a
practical way. In some manner the circle of Iceland
spar must be linked up with the sword and the cross so
as to make a whole. In the midst of this speculation a
further feature developed. At the centre of the whole
figure a diamond-shaped stone was let in, which I
recognized at once as having to do with myself. At
first the stone was blue. Then abruptly it changed
to red. Then back to blue. For some while, whenever

I visualized the symbol, the central stone was sometimes one colour, sometimes the other.

After a day or so of this there came a decision. The stone was fixed in colour, neither red, nor blue but yellow and the same inward voice said plainly: "It is made of jasper; your name is Jaspar." I looked up jasper in the dictionary to see if it had a special meaning. I found that the breastplate of the priests was of jasper and that jasper formed one of the foundations of the walls of the New Jerusalem. This gave me a special feeling of pleasure and of importance.

The figure was now complete. The circle of Iceland spar had slots cut in it so that the upright of the cross could be passed through it. The sword fitted into the hollow upright of the cross. The jasper stone passed clean through cross and sword, both of which were pierced at that point, and this prevented the sword from falling out.

Whether or not the symbol had anything to do with it, from that time the world problem, which had affected me sufficiently acutely before, became completely obsessing. It was as if, identified with the jasper stone, I was being pulled violently between the sword and the cross. I suffered not only mentally but in my general health, my heart in particular giving me trouble such as I had never experienced.

In this condition two further changes took place. The first was that a hand (as I thought of it, it was the hand of God) grasped the sword, so that the weight of the sword was no longer on the jasper stone. This gave me some relief; but later came the second change, in which I saw the cross on fire. The feeling of anxiety and dread became intensified.

I then realized that I was making a monumental mistake. I had been given the name Jaspar, but instead of accepting it, I had identified myself with the jasper stone, as if it were I that was holding the cross and sword together: and was naturally being pulled apart.

When I came to this realization I rapidly recovered physical and psychological health. At the same time the symbol changed. It was as if the sword and the cross had been fused together in the fire, forming a sort of composite iron-wood; and the whole symbol telescoped upon its centre, forming a cross within the circle around the central jasper stone.

This new form of the symbol gave me great relief and happiness. I looked upon it as "my" symbol, a source of psychic strength and assurance, once again identi- fying myself particularly with the jasper stone in the middle.

Very soon I found myself again in the wilderness, though not so badly as before. With my experience to help me, I found that it was necessary first of all to take my name in all humility, not as a title, but simply as a mark upon me, a growing point as it were; and next, to dis-identify myself from the symbol. I realized that I was no part of that shape; that my sole connection with it was that my given name was also the name of the stone at the centre. I felt then the symbol not as part of myself or I part of it; but as a great stability and source of power at the back of me. Yet, some- how, try as I might, I could not altogether receive the name.'

This account shows a man torn by the world opposites, the com- plex issues later destined to work out their terrible course in the Second World War. In some ways his attitude is a good and respon- sible one. He is trying to face up to the tremendous problem: what can I as an individual do to prevent this collective madness? Because of this essential rightness of approach, when he applies the con- structive technique, there is immediate response from the other side of consciousness. At the same time his attitude is also a wrong one, as the later development of the vision plainly indicates. He wants to save the world. He is assuming a kind of God-like status, a *Gottähn- lichkeit* which, if it became pathological, might add him to the num- ber of lost spirits in asylums who believe themselves anything from Napoleon to a new Messiah. He lacks essential humility. He is here; the world is there. He does not see that he also is part of the world.

With the coming of the symbol, the sword sheathed by the cross, he has, so to speak, a first analysis of the problem. Before it was a shapeless worry. Now it has taken shape. The opposites have been brought into the light of consciousness, and there is the possibility of finding a living middle way between them.

The man's response to the symbol is an essentially right one. He sees something of the manifold meaning of the symbol, the cross pierced by the sword, the sword contained by the cross. Also—Jacob fashion—he holds on to what has come to him, he will not let it go until it blesses him. Whereupon, the unconscious, this time unasked, supplies a second element: a circle of fire which is also a circle of water, synthesized into the natural material for polarizing light. This, interestingly enough, he accepts quite naïvely, concerned now only with the pattern that is taking shape and hardly at all with the meaning of the new element introduced. The broad trend of this meaning is reasonably clear. The circle is an age-old symbol of deity: 'The nature of God is a circle of which the centre is everywhere and the circumference is nowhere.' Fire and water are both aspects of the spirit. The baptism with fire and the baptism with water, the refining fire in which the impurities are burnt out, the clear-flowing water by which the impurities are washed away, form a pair of opposites. As opposites they cannot go together. But the unconscious supplies its own synthesis: the polarized, directed light, a third symbol of the spirit, combining the resplendence of the fire and the clear-flowing placidity of the water.

He has now, therefore, two pairs of opposites: one, the sword and the cross, imperfectly resolved; the other, the opposites of the spirit, adequately synthesized. The next step attempts a further union. The central stone appears. Here for the first time is the discovery of the deep centre. For the moment, like the man himself, we can take it naïvely as something at the centre of the circle of spirit which holds the cross and sword together and so completes the figure. The flickering of the colour of the stone brings in the opposites again. Red normally stands for passion, the emotions, the instincts; blue for the spirit. This is the 'split in the libido' category of opposites. The final result is yellow: the holy colour in the Buddhist religion, and here clearly of a numinous nature—the jasper which is the breast-plate of the priests, the jasper which is the foundation of the New Jerusalem.

With the fitting together of the figure and the giving of the name the man makes the fundamental mistake to which, as already noted, he is unduly prone. He identifies with the stone, he it is who is holding the sword and cross together, he is God. He suffers the agony of disintegration, the regular consequence of *Gottähnlichkeit*. From harsh experience he learns that, without the hand of God, he is broken, lost, torn to pieces between the world opposites. In the refining fire the whole figure then concentrates about the jasper stone, and the *mandala* is formed. The opposites of the outer world, the cross and the sword, the opposites of the spirit, the fire and the water, are brought together around the deep centre. Again he makes the mistake of identification: but with previous experience fresh in mind, corrects the mistake. On the other hand, the essence of the experience, the fundamental change of attitude involved in the taking of the new name, that he cannot manage.

The account continues:

'I supposed that the symbol had now reached its final form but this proved not to be the case. After some months the symbol entered upon a new stage of development. Previously it had been as if hung in the air. Now it became horizontal and was embedded firmly in a rough block of basalt. Later the block of basalt became a steep conical mountain on the top of which, out of the centre of the symbol, a tree grew. This tree remained unchanged for some weeks when, looking at it one day, I saw that there were birds flying about it. Some little while later—a fortnight or month perhaps — I noticed an underlying state of excitement growing upon me for no apparent reason. When I looked again towards the tree I saw that it had come much nearer and I was seeing it no longer as a silhouette  but in the round. After that it came nearer hour by hour. During this time I suffered from something approaching panic, having the wholly irrational fear that the approaching image of the tree might pass inside me. If it did, I felt, something terrible would happen. To my immense relief, when it came to me the foliage parted letting me through into the midst of it.'

In some fashion—the account, of course, misses a great deal of relevant attitude change in the man himself—the symbol has been brought to earth. Out of it grows the tree, the symbol of the impersonal life, the new, strange, non-human yet natural state of being. When there is a prospect of this 'tree' entering into the man he becomes as scared as did the dreamer in 'The Villains in the Villa'. He is not ready to go over from the ego-centred to the impersonal life,[1] and this experience passes him by. He gratefully accepts the lesser one of being sheltered by the tree.

'I had supposed that, with the coming of the tree and my sheltering under its branches, the process had reached its natural end. Instead, a new phase began. I saw the tree—which had changed to a fir tree—upon a cliff, with a figure which I at first took to be myself at its foot.

Later water came and dashed against the foot of the cliff, undermining it; and after a while a great block of it fell away. The figure, as if aware of the danger, disappeared. The tree was now perilously near the edge, with the water still undermining the cliff. Then the next thing I saw was that reinforcements—a sort of palisade—had been built at the base of the cliff, preventing further erosion.

The scene remained substantially unchanged for some months. In imagination I explored the district, investigated the bay the other side of the cliff, but nothing material happened or was found. The picture lost its reality and I reverted once again to the tree on the cone-shaped mountain. Then, some weeks later I saw the fir tree again, and again the figure was beneath it, as if in contemplation; but this time it was no longer on a cliff but in a field through which a river flowed placidly.

This state gave me much satisfaction and had the feeling of great permanence. Sometimes the wind blew through the tree and the figure occasionally stirred, but in the main the picture was one of peacefulness and calm. The man beneath the tree was never seen in detail but gave the impression of a foreign, yet friendly and helpful, presence.'

Four things here deserve special notice. The tree has changed in kind. It has become a fir tree, the tree found in the north, in the mountains. Presumably it has receded into the unconscious. The

[1] The 'intolerable wrestle with words and meanings' becomes particularly confused and arduous when we need to describe the state of being beyond the ego-centred, personal life. To use such terms as 'super-personal' or 'super-conscious' sounds more than a little presumptuous. I have used 'impersonal' in default of anything better: but it needs to be remembered that this 'impersonal life' includes also the personal, while transcending it.

man was not ready to engage in the impersonal life and the possibility is withdrawn. There then comes trial by water. Previously, at the earlier stage of the sword and the cross, there had been trial by fire. Now the water threatens to wash away the possibility altogether; but the possibility is held. A human figure comes into the picture: and later the tree, the figure, and the water (now in its placid form) bring a feeling of peace.

What has happened? So far, rightly or wrongly, the man has missed the two central experiences offered. He did not accept the name. He did not accept the tree. He may well have been wise in both these negations. One is not necessarily ready to become either a hero or a saint; and that, in all likelihood, is what acceptance would have meant in these two cases. But this merit he has: he holds and will not let go. Now, between the tree and the stream is a human figure. This he accepts and feels at peace. A temporary resolution of the opposites has been achieved. Between the individual impersonal life, represented by the tree, and the collective stream of life where one merely flows with the situation (an aspect of the 'individual-collectivity' category of opposites), a helpful image has constellated.

The way of the snake

The odyssey continues with a wealth of detail far too elaborate to be set out *in extenso*. A summary does grave violence to the material but is all that can be given here.

From the peaceful figure between the tree and the stream, the man goes on to what he eventually discovers to be a gigantic *mandala*, with an active volcano at the centre. In this setting a series of symbolical events is enacted, in which he himself becomes increasingly involved. It is as if he were actually exposed to the danger of the volcano and, simultaneously, as if the world drama (it was in the 'Munich' period immediately preceding the Second World War) were being worked out in the same direful setting. From it all he learns one fundamental lesson. What started by being the volcano, a thing of terror, eventually becomes 'the Rock', something on which he feels he can depend, something upon which he can build. In his own way he learns the lesson of Arjuna in the *Bhagavadgita*: that the creative process is not constructive only but also has its destructive side, the nay no less than the yea; that there is the dark and terrible aspect of God, the volcano as well as the Rock; that creation comes from conflict. In this episode, as distinct from the previous two, he seems to realize the meaning of the vision; to take it to himself—in fear and trembling—instead of retreating from it as he did with the name Jaspar and with the tree.

The ensuing episode carries him over the sea to an island. He is now a medieval knight engaged in the quest. In this phase the opposites seem to be those of *logos* and *eros*. With his sword, the *logos*, he is involved in endless combats with huge spiders (*eros*, in its negative aspect, the spinner of webs), the legs of which grow as quickly as he lops them off. In the end he meets and silently faces the Lady, an anima figure, in a temple on a hill; and, while there, is webbed in by the giant spiders. He escapes with his life but the relationship with the anima, the finding of *eros* in its positive form, eludes him.

The next episode is no less than the 'great deed', the slaying of the dragon that lays waste the land. It ends in complete ignominy. He is fertile in ingenious *logos* devices for trapping the dragon, but they all come to nothing. He never so much as sets eyes on the destroyer. What he sees finally is an ancient battlefield, with a single wheel—part of a gun-carriage, perhaps, but also the *mandala*—rising out of the wreckage.[1] He knows he has failed and must go on.

There follows a whole series of encounters with a black knight—presumably the shadow—and with a horrible and fantastic anima figure. In the end, after many adventures and mutations, the man, now in his normal habit and normal form, arrives at the gate of his own home, the house where he ordinarily lives. Everything is as in actual life, except for one thing: at his feet is a green, very alive, snake: 'his snake' as he realizes.

What does all this amount to? Before attempting to penetrate the meaning of the vision, it may be well to get the total account into some perspective. This symbolic process took place over a period of some seven years. We skim it through in as many minutes. The essential effect of it is thereby lost. No one, of course, can experience the other side of consciousness at second hand. But it is possible, at least to some extent, to put oneself imaginatively into the position

---

[1] *Garlic and sapphires in the mud*
Clot the bedded axle-tree.
The trilling wire in the blood
Sings below inveterate scars
Appeasing long forgotten wars.

where, for months at a time, the newly-found jasper stone and the new name given are strange realities in a man's life. It is possible, not to share, but perhaps to conceive, his irrational terror that the ever-approaching tree will enter into his being and utterly disrupt it. Or again, to feel the threat of the active volcano, smoking as it were within the psyche, with the outside world at the point of war. As with dreams, it is necessary to some extent to get inside the experience if anything is to be made of it.

What then is its significance? Time and again a symbol arose indicating the middle way between various of the great opposites. Time and again the opportunity was lost. The man was not of sufficient calibre to accept most of what the unconscious offered. Nevertheless, his general attitude was right. The features earlier enumerated as necessary to the constructive technique—serious attention, objectivity, involvement, steadfastness—were all to some extent present. It is true that he was too often afraid and otherwise not up to the task. He could not take the name, he could not accept the tree, he could not hold *eros*, he failed at the great work. But he did give serious attention. He was, in some measure, objective in his attitude. He was committed, but he was not caught. And he had sufficient steadfastness, the necessary psychological stamina, to hold on and, to such extent as he could receive it, obtain the blessing.

This blessing was not inconsiderable: the discovery of the deep centre, the jasper stone; the forming of the *mandala*; the shelter of the tree; the experience of the volcano and the Rock; the finding of 'his snake'—his own direct contact with the unconscious. If, in Eliot's words, he could have brought to bear upon this vision '. . . a life-time's death in love, Ardour and selflessness and self-surrender' he could, no doubt, have found and held much more. He would have gone over from the ego-centred life to the deep centre and thence-forward lived life in depth. As it was, he held what he could.

His own summing up expresses this attitude:—

'What did I get out of it all? Was it just a freak experience or did it have meaning? So far as I can tell I learnt: (1) That these things are real. I was torn by the sword and the cross, afraid of that tree, worried by that smoking volcano, at least as much as by bombing or shelling or machine-gun fire. (2) That there are things I have to do and can do, if and when I measure up to them: assume the name, accept the tree, do the "great deed", insofar as I am able; above all, follow my own snake, my own life-pattern, and not merely go the collective way. You may say "But that is all meaningless: you had these phantasies, that is true, but you can't 'learn' anything from them." To which I would reply: "But that is exactly what I did do; and that is the whole meaning of it." '

In effect, what has happened is a 'displacement of the field of action', to use Toynbee's term. The process started with the man disrupted by the world opposites. It ends with his facing his own problem of the relationship between consciousness and the unconscious. The world problem has not been lost to sight: but it has been subtly transformed. Instead of aspiring—unconsciously—to play God and save the world, the man discovers he must first deal with himself. He who set out to solve the great problem learns that the first step towards the 'one world' is that he himself shall become one. When he has made the withdrawal, then, and not until then, he may be in a position to make the return.

'I gave my hide away'

The inward journey does not always turn out this way. The following account (published in *Psychiatry*, February 1949) of the phantasy of a Chippewa Indian woman of 34 living in Northern Wisconsin, furnishes an interesting comparison. It presents the contrast of a widely different background, both of personality and environment. It brings in the same characteristic symbolism. And it shows how such an experience can remain unrealized.

'The third time I went through the Midewiwin (the Chippewa Medicine Dance), I went through because I had a vision that I should do that. We were living out in the woods at that time. Everything was still and quiet there. I was lying on a bed. I got to thinking of things I'd done way back in my younger days. I thought about my relatives and my friends, my parents who were dead and gone. I had no one to call upon except for my old man. I lay still, and my mind was working all the time. Then I said out loud, so that I could be heard: "What is there that I didn't do right? Everything that I can remember I thought I did right. What is wrong with me that I have so many visions of different things and different people?" All that summer I had had visions of people and things. I said aloud again, "Maybe the Almighty has mercy on people who see all these visions." '

Here, most authentically, is the first stage: the feeling that 'there is *something wrong about us* as we naturally stand'. The way of development now lies open. As William James puts it: 'The individual, so far as he suffers from his wrongness and criticizes it, is to that extent consciously beyond it, and in at least possible touch with something higher, if anything higher exist.'

'Then I had a vision that I was walking along a narrow trail through the brush—no tall trees. It was a beautiful day. No wind. Plenty of sunshine. I walked along this trail for about an hour until I heard the sound of tinkling bells in the distance. As I came nearer to the sound, I saw four men sitting around something that was round. Above their heads was something across the sky like a rainbow. One of these men called me his grandchild. He said, "You are supposed to tell the people once in a while when you are in trouble about something you know, something that's in you. Let them know what's in you. Don't pay any attention if people laugh at you. If they do, they're not throwing jokes at you; they're throwing jokes at themselves." One real old white-haired man sat at the far end of that round thing. He pointed to his snow-white hair. He told me that my hair would be just like his some day, if I did what I was told. "We are the ones that asked you to come here, because you are in trouble and don't know which way to turn. There are four things that I want you to remember—North, East, South and West. On all of these four there sits a man who waits and wants to receive your tobacco. You have a name that you bear, which means a great deal to me. Your name means a whole lot. As you go along, you'll realize this. Your thinking power is working real hard. It will get you somewhere, if you listen to it." '

Here is the *mandala* symbolism, as in the vision of the sword and the cross—the four old men sitting around something that is round. The woman is told there is something she knows, something in her, that she should tell people. She is, at the same time, given her orientation—four things to remember, North, East, South and West. And she is reminded of her name.

'Then another real old man spoke. "It's been a long time since you thought of your grandfather. I like to receive your tobacco once in a while too. I'm the one that suggested to this man the name that you are called by. Don't be afraid of me because I'm big. I will tell you what you are supposed to do once in a while. You are supposed to put out food, like meat and corn, and put some tobacco into the fire or on the ground when I go by. You do your own speaking (i.e. to the spirits). Nobody else needs to do it. I am the one who will listen."

Then I said, "Oh, I'm the one who made a mistake. I never thought that I would ever make such a big mistake. Sometimes when I think of the things I've done, I thought I'd done them right; but I didn't." '

As later transpires, the mistake was that the woman gave no tobacco to the people she was named after, i.e. did not adequately realize the name, and consequently did not find her true being—again as in the sword and cross vision.

'He said, "Sometimes we see you in this certain kind of dance. You are holding the precious flag (the feather flag held by the person who addresses the spirits). That flag belongs to us. Before you speak or do anything, offer some tobacco. If you have no tobacco, you have to give the price for your tobacco." That's just what I do now. If I can't speak, I have somebody speak for me.

Then I went on from this place along the trail a little ways. I hear and see some more. This man has his finger up in the air. He's talking. He's from the South. This is a different man. There's a thing about four feet high—just a stick sticking in the ground. The man takes the stick and hands it to me. "If you lean on this stick," he said, "you'll use two of them later on, as you go along the road, if you do just what I tell you. (To 'walk with two sticks' is synonymous with long life). Go to your great adviser (the old priest to whom she is married) and tell him what you have seen." '

Here is good counsel. The chief difficulty in all experience the other side of consciousness is adequate realization. If the woman tells her 'great adviser', there is a better chance of holding the experience and bringing it into life.

'As I was coming back along this trail, I saw a great big snake about this big around (six inches). He raised his head about this high (four feet) from the ground. "Don't be afraid of me," he said. "Just go back and tell your adviser what you have seen. If you don't you won't be able to walk." Then he pointed and said, "Look over there." I looked and saw myself lying flat on my back. Then the snake said, "But if you do what I tell you and tell all that you know, everything will be all right. I want to come into that place (her home). I like that place. It makes no difference how it looks. I'm coming there just the same. I'll go along now." Then I walked back home along the trail. That was all. Then I made preparations for going through the Midewiwin.'

This is the encounter with the snake, the embodiment of the unconscious; and again the good counsel for realization—'tell your adviser'.

'One afternoon, after I'd made all of my preparations for joining the Midewiwin again, I was all alone at home. The door was open about four inches. I looked at the door and saw this person coming in. I felt kind of scared. He was an unexpected visitor. He came in a few feet and said, "I have come at last." He looked around, turned over on his side and made himself at home. Then he spoke to me: "If you take care of me like you should, I will do a lot of things for you, because I am the one that suggested all this to you. When you start, have the prettiest dress you've got. I know that I am welcome here. Don't be afraid of me, because I have come a long ways to see you." That's all he said. Then he became a snake and went out.'

This is the 'bringing home' of the embodiment of the unconscious, as a separate, uncanny but helpful presence. As the ensuing passage shows, it is the snake that leads to the way.

'That's just the way that thing (the hide) looked. I got a snake hide that third time I joined. He (the snake) is the one that put these things into my mind and set me to thinking. I'd wondered what was wrong, because I'd never kept thinking and seeing things like that before. He's the one that suggested I join the Midewiwin. He also asked me if I wanted a drink. I said, No, not when I entered his house (the Mide lodge).

One of the old men spoke to me when I was in the lodge, the third time I joined. He said, "When you come tomorrow, dress as nice as you can. That's how this person wanted you to enter this house." That's just what I did. He said, "When you go along this road, do the best you can. Pay attention to what is before you, not what is behind you. When you speak, watch your tongue. After you get through here and know what to do, watch your step for the next two or three years. If you do, he'll take you along this road just as he suggested. This road never comes to an end. Pay no attention to the side roads. Pay attention to the road that's in front of you. This is his (the snake's) road, and this is his home. If you take care of yourself, he will do the rest. Your thought belongs to no one but you. Don't listen to any kind of wind that's blowing about you. Just turn the other way and do the best you can. He will know, because you're the person he intended to enter his house. He has picked a person from our midst who happens to be you. He thought that you were the most wonderful thing that God has created. That's why he picked your home to be his home; he liked that place. And this little thing that I've got in my hand (a tiny blue and white shell) belongs to him." '

Here is the deep centre (the equivalent of the jasper stone in the sword and cross vision), the something from the depths which 'belongs' to the snake. The old man continues:

' "Whatever you say and do—he knows all about it. Don't think that he doesn't hear whatever you say, because he does. He has become one of the wonderful members of your household." Then this old man pointed to my head. "See how your hair is today. As you go along this road, your hair will change to a different colour. This thing (the blue and white shell) will take you along the road that we are going to teach you about." Then he touched the tip of my ear. "These things you own yourself. They belong to nobody but you. The thing that has happened to you is the most wonderful thing I have ever heard of. I have heard of that happening in olden times. Back in my days I heard that people had such a vision like that. It is the most wonderful thing that can happen to a person on this earth. Don't be afraid to give what you've got; because later on, in years to come, you will get paid for it. As you go along this road, you will be using one stick. Maybe by that time you will have grand-children, and you will be able to tell them about this wonderful thing that has happened to you. As you go along to the end of this road, you will be using two sticks. You will still be walking toward this wonderful house that you have seen. This (the shell) is the one that owns it." '

In the Midewiwin third initiation a shell is supposed to be magically 'shot' into the candidate from a snake hide, which is referred to during the ceremony as a 'gun'. Here is the authentic symbolism of the deep centre: that which takes her along the road; that which owns the wonderful house towards which she is travelling; that which enters into and transforms the personality. The old man concludes:

' "In maybe five or six years from now, you will be entitled to join again. I hope that I may still be here to see it and know what it's all about. I'm telling you this again, to impress it on your mind. Don't regret the things that you did in your younger days. You have made only one mistake. Don't let it happen again."
(The interviewer asks: What mistake was that?)
"I didn't give no tobacco to the people I was named after . . ."
When you join the Midewiwin the third time, they tell you that the snake is wrapped all around the earth. He may scare you, but he doesn't mean to. When I joined that time, they told me that if I had anything nice that grew from the earth—like black-berries—I should give a feast. But I didn't do it, because the berries were all gone by then; and three months later I gave my hide away; so there was no use in giving a feast to the snake.'

The end is failure. 'Three months later I gave my hide away.' The experience has passed her by. The woman to whom these images came saw them as she might a film. She was aware of the archetypal processes with the natural awareness of the quasi-primitive, but she had not the means of incorporating their value into consciousness. The revelation itself was admirably complete: the *mandala*; the name; the snake; the deep centre. The way she is shown is, in effect, the resolution of the fundamental opposites of consciousness and the unconscious. 'This road never comes to an end. Pay no attention to the side roads. Pay attention to the road that's in front of you.' But she could not hold the experience. All the transforming symbols were there but not the necessary realization.

NOTE ON TERMINOLOGY

Chapters IV–VII make use of three key terms: the autonomous complex; the archetype; and the transforming symbol. The attentive reader is fairly certain to find himself enquiring how exactly these different concepts stand to one another; to what extent they are similar, to what extent different. Be it said at once, as with all the phenomena coming from the other side of consciousness, there is no clear-cut definition. But this does not mean that the distinctions to be drawn are unimportant.

The autonomous complex, as already noted, consists of a twisting-together of psychic contents, having its own energy and operating in its own fashion. The human psyche contains many such autonomous complexes. Any one or combination of these, whether in the form of projection or of invasion, is liable to take over and run the man for anything from the split-second to years at a time.

The transforming symbol, unlike the autonomous complex, does not tend to take over and run the man. On the contrary, consciousness has to recognize and use it if it is to have effect: in which case it performs the invaluable function of mobilizing the combined energy of consciousness and the unconscious, in this manner making possible a fundamental change of attitude.

The autonomous complex and the transforming symbol are, accordingly, alike to this extent that in both cases a change in attitude results. But the change brought about by the autonomous complex is liable to be a compulsive change, where we are the victims rather than the doers; while the change wrought by means of the transforming symbol is, essentially, our own.

This is not to say, however, that autonomous complexes are necessarily 'bad', transforming symbols necessarily 'good'. In both cases the attitude of consciousness is crucial. Where consciousness, instead of being possessed by the autonomous complex, makes a relationship with it, such relationship is a step towards wholeness. If, for instance, a student, instead of projecting the Wise Old Man upon some great teacher, takes that teacher as an inspiring example which, *in his own way*, he does his best to follow, then the autonomous complex may become a means of development. Conversely, if consciousness misuses a transforming symbol (e.g. for purposes of power) the transforming symbol can become a grave danger. Thus, the *mandala*, rightly taken, is integrative in its influence; wrongly taken, it may lead a man to imagine himself God, and to behave as such.

So much for the distinction to be drawn between the autonomous complex and the transforming symbol. The term 'archetype' cuts across both classifications.

An autonomous complex may be predominantly personal in nature, something arising out of our life experience which has taken on this independent status; or it may be predominantly archetypal, a figure such as the Wise Old Man or the Great Mother, to be found in widely different peoples in widely different periods, part of the psychic structure of the human being. Similarly, a transforming symbol may be predominantly personal in form—a fishing rod, a rucksack, a ring—having the strange power of changing our attitude; or a transforming symbol may be predominantly archetypal in form—the Holy Grail, the hidden wisdom, the secret valley in the mountains—images actuating us from depths beyond our knowing. Every manifestation from the other side of consciousness is necessarily personal in the sense that it takes on some of the personal characteristics of the man or woman to whom it comes. But behind these personal characteristics, sometimes inconspicuous, sometimes dwarfing the personal aspect altogether, will normally be found the archetype.

In sum, there is this double distinction to be made. The autonomous complex normally tends to possess the man; but, provided a right relationship is made with it, can become a means to wholeness. The transforming symbol normally makes possible a more developed attitude: but if misused can become a means of disintegration. Autonomous complexes and transforming symbols alike may be personal in character—in the main an outcome of the living experience of that particular individual. Or they may be archetypal, part of the psychic condition of man. In practice, they are likely to be both: sometimes the personal element preponderating, sometimes the archetypal.

VIII

THE INDIVIDUATION PROCESS

INSOFAR as the transforming symbols coming from the depths are found and realized, a man is able to discover a creative middle way between the opposites, a living integration of consciousness and the unconscious. Jung calls this the individuation process. No two people encounter it in the same manner. Nevertheless, there are certain broad generalizations which hold true for most. As Reilly says in *The Cocktail Party*, all cases are unique and very similar to others.

In the first place, to put the matter paradoxically, individuation has nothing to do with psychology. It is a way of living life. The psychology of the unconscious can help a man to understand what is happening. The constructive technique is an invaluable aid. But the 'inward transforming experience' can take place in a person who has never heard of the unconscious; while psychological knowledge which stops with the intellect, or goes over to a dallying sentimentalism, is completely unavailing.

In the second place, individuation is something which is wrought upon a man, not something he can do for himself. This does not mean that the man's part is simply to sit back and wait. On the contrary, he has to put all he has—and much more than he knows he has—into the work. But the process itself, the 'inward transforming experience', is not within his power to command.

In the third place, individuation has its own methods and its own season. With some people it comes as a sudden realization and life thenceforward is a living out of that realization. More often, though, a man undertaking the experiment in depth finds he apparently makes no progress, that his course is nothing but one long series of mistakes. But such is the nature of the experience. It is by the mistakes, no less than the successes, that the change is wrought. Until one day he wakes to the fact that, imperceptibly, he has become a totally other person from what he was.

In the fourth place, individuation needs to be distinguished sharply from individualism. It is true that, in the individuation process, a man becomes a being in his own right, differentiated from the mass. But individuation is also the means by which a new and deeper relationship is made with others. Without this new and deeper relationship, there is no wholeness.

Finally, individuation is not a 'once for all' achievement but a continuing activity. A man does not attain wholeness and thereafter remain whole. It is more in the nature of a spiral process, where certain aspects are dealt with on one level only to be met again on the next; and that throughout the entire course of life.

The dark wood

Often, though not invariably, the individuation process starts with a profound inward turning of psychic energy. The former vivid interest in people and events vanishes. The meaning goes out of life and one is left stranded. This, at best, is an unpleasant experience. It may be a terrifying one. For the psychic energy is not lost. It has gone into the unconscious, is at large in the inner world. The archetypal images are awakened, and the man, unless he is aware of what is happening, is likely at times to have doubts of his sanity.

Dante, in the opening lines of his great work, describes such an experience:

> In the midway of this our mortal life,
> I found me in a gloomy wood, astray
> Gone from the path direct . . .

This is typical. It is around 'the midway of this our mortal life', about thirty-five or forty years of age, when a man passes the meridian, that the individuation process normally starts. But there is no uniformity about it. 'Ripeness is all'; and a man or woman may be ripe in the early twenties, the late fifties, or perhaps never.

Dante continues:

> And e'en to tell
> It were no easy task, how savage wild
> That forest, how robust and rough its growth,
> Which to remember only, my dismay

Renews, in bitterness not far from death . . .
How first I enter'd it I scarce can say,
Such sleepy dullness in that instant weigh'd
My senses down . . .

The description is literal and exact. The 'sleepy dullness' and the 'bitterness not far from death' are two of the most characteristic features of the regressive libido. Often physical health is affected, heart, stomach and breathing being among the more usual casualties. But heaviness of spirit, a feeling of the utter uselessness and impossibility of effort, is the dominating impression.

In past centuries, this regression of the libido went under the name of melancholy. As the poets and artists of those times recognized, it had its two sides. *L'Allegro* sees the negative side:

> *Hence, loathed Melancholy,*
> *Of Cerberus and blackest midnight born.*

Similarly, John Ford:

> *Tell us, pray, what devil*
> *This melancholy is, which can transform*
> *Men into monsters.*

Il Penseroso holds the opposite view:

> *Hail divinest Melancholy,*

and for the person who can take it rightly, thus it is.

Dürer's famous *Melencolia* embodies both aspects of this backward flow of psychic energy. The whole tone of the composition shows the leaden, weighed-down feeling of that state. But, at the same time, it reveals the other side: the guardian angel, the bearer of the keys, with the creative symbols of the unconscious ready to come to life; above all, central to the composition, the miraculous child and the 'stone that the builders rejected', apparently useless, but actually the instrument used by Dürer in his study of perspective, the means of seeing things in their right proportion.

It is a matter of individual fate whether and how this regression of the libido is experienced. With some people it comes as an unbearable feeling of guilt, a conviction of inexpiable sin. With others it may take the form of the 'insoluble problem', halting a man in his tracks. With others, again, it comes as a seeking. There is a truth they must find—which is somehow 'their truth'—if they have to follow it to the world's end and beyond. Sometimes the quest is felt as holy, sometimes as impious, sometimes both.

> *We are the Pilgrims, master; we shall go*
> *Always a little further: it may be*
> *Beyond that last blue mountain barred with snow*
> *Across that angry or that glimmering sea . . .*

> *We travel not for trafficking alone;*
> *By hotter winds our fiery hearts are fanned:*
> *For lust of knowing what should not be known,*
> *We take the Golden Road to Samarkand.*

Normally, however, the turning inward of the libido is not a time of seeking but of despair, the mood of Hamlet:

> *How weary, stale, flat, and unprofitable*
> *Seem to me all the uses of this world,*

the dark depths, the city of dreadful night.

In such circumstances a neurosis, or worse, may overcome a man. It is thus a great danger; but a still greater opportunity. It is the tide which, rightly taken, can float the man to a new level; wrongly taken, destroy him. The problem is how to take this tide rightly, how to release and realize the transforming symbols. At such a time a man feels as if he were drowning in a fathomless sea, utterly helpless, with nothing on which to hold. Jung's advice, to those strong enough to take it, is: Don't drown—dive!

The constructive technique is a means of diving. So long as a man is dealing blindly with the undifferentiated flood of psychic experience, he is little better than a piece of driftwood alternately tossed and engulfed in a whirlpool where strong currents meet. But when he makes direct contact with the powers of the depths—the shadow, and behind it the anima-animus and the archetypal figures—then he is dealing with entities with which he can come to terms. And if he avails himself of the symbols arising at such a time—above all, when he comes upon the deep centre—what seemed a hideous descent into darkness is afterwards seen as the saving reality of life, the 'darkness of God'.

This does not mean, as is sometimes supposed, that positive acceptance of the regressive condition is the best means of 'getting back to normal'. The man who dives instead of drowning may perhaps find himself rapidly at the surface again, able to take up active life anew. More likely he will find that, while the regression of the libido is no longer insufferable, he is embarked upon a period of withdrawal, where concern with the things of the inward life takes at least equal place with the outward things which formerly held his interest. Whatever the event, he will make the discovery that the individuation process is not an incident, a brief interlude, 'In the midway of this our mortal life.' It is rather, a new and perilous mode of living:

> . . . not only in the middle of the way
> But all the way, in a dark wood, in a bramble,
> On the edge of a grimpen, where is no secure foothold,
> And menaced by monsters, fancy lights,
> Risking enchantment.

It is well that this permanently dangerous character of the individuation process should be thoroughly understood.

> In order to arrive there,
> To arrive where you are, to get from where you are not,
> You must go by a way wherein there is no ecstasy.

Some people embark airily upon the adventure of the unconscious as they would upon a swimming party or a picnic. Individuation is no picnic. 'Diving' is not a way out. It is a hard but possible way through, with many relapses, misleadings, 'dark nights of the soul', disaster never far distant, no sure guide.

'To get from where you are not'

Considered analytically, individuation consists of a two-way movement: on the one hand, a process of separating, of differentiation; on the other, a process of coming together, of integration. In order to 'get from where you are not' it is necessary to separate from those things which prevent you from being yourself. In order to 'arrive where you are' it is necessary to bring together those things which enable you to become yourself.

In practice, the two processes of differentiation and integration normally go on together. Thus, a man must separate from the shadow and the personal unconscious, so as to see them for what they are; but also, as far as possible, he must integrate them, assimilate what they have for him of value. A man must likewise separate from the forces of the deep unconscious. So long as he remains subject to various forms of archetypal possession there is no possibility of individuation. But it is also necessary to come to terms with these forces, to effect a new relationship.

There are two further acts of separation of a rather different kind. The first of these has already been referred to incidentally. It now needs to be considered in some detail. This is the situation where a man presents a façade to the world and more or less identifies himself with that façade.

To some extent, of course, we all do this. 'Putting up a front' is a necessary adaptation to outer life, at least until something better is found. According to the person with whom we are dealing, according to the circumstances in which we operate, according to the rôle we ourselves are supposed to enact, we assume an appropriate demeanour, put on an act. This façade Jung calls the *persona*, the name given to the formal mask worn in the classical drama. It plays an important part in the individuation process, for this mask is much more far-reaching and insidious than at first appears.

The ordinary aspects of the *persona* we all see: more easily in others than ourselves, perhaps; but most people having a reasonable degree of awareness are fairly open-eyed in this respect. Everyone knows the professional *personae*, to which some doctors, some pastors, some lawyers succumb—the bedside manner, the pulpit delivery, the judicial air; the national *personae*, the phlegmatic Englishman, the wise-cracking American, the mercurial Latin, the smiling Oriental; the class *personae*, the snob, the woman who does not find it quite nice, the man who only does the done thing, the keepers-up-with-the-Jones', the 'class-conscious proletarian' complete with slogan, gesture and party line. There are likewise the self-imposed *personae*, the roystering student, the hearty hand-shaker, the 'funny' man who must be funny at any cost, the hostess who is going to be charming if it kills her. And there are the great *persona* institutions, the conventions, the collective pretences of society, the 'Lavinia's Aunt' of *The Cocktail Party*.

The mask so assumed can be innocent, but it can also be disastrous in its effect. If once a man starts identifying with the *persona*, believing he actually is the part he plays, then things go wrong. Such a man is cut off from the unconscious. This does not mean that

he is free of it. What it does mean is that the forces of the unconscious will work upon him surreptitiously from every side. All
around him will be bad people and a black world—for the good
reason that his shadow is projected upon them. He himself is likely
to run into one or other of two fates—or perhaps both, alternately:
to be whirled around by the forces of the unconscious, caught up in
ambivalent action, all dynamism and no direction: or to be left high
and dry, cut off from his roots, bloodless and sterile, dried up and dis-
appointed, a mere simulacrum. Where the man thus becomes little
else than a protective shell, a mummy case with a painted top, it is
a personal tragedy but no more than that. But when he is caught by
the unconscious in its demonic aspect, terrible evil may be let loose.

Two typical instances of such identification with the *persona*—one
individual, the other collective—will suffice to indicate its possible
consequences. A woman with an only son assumes the rôle of the
perfect mother. As she is never tired of telling everyone she meets,
she devotes her whole life to him, is ready to make every sacrifice
that he shall be happy. But the shadow side will also be at work.
Such a woman will hold her son with claws of iron; fight off any
other woman in his life; or, if she cannot fight her off, do her utmost
to poison the relationship. There is no evil intention. It would almost
be simpler if there were. But the woman wholly identified with the
persona of the loving mother is, on the other side, a ravening she-
wolf, the devouring mother: and unless and until she faces this other
side of herself she will secretly consume the one she loves.

On the collective scale the outstanding example is Hitler's Germany. Nazi propaganda in the years between the wars forced upon
German youth a Siegfried *persona*. No one could be that amount
heroic, day in, day out, unless there was some depository for the dark
side. That also the propaganda provided. The Jews, the polluters of
the sacred blood stream, later the encircling predatory decadent
democracies, provided the necessary hooks for a complete projection
of the shadow. A man could then be a Siegfried, ready to live hard
and die hard, fanatically devoted, inspired with the loftiest ideals;
and ready also to torture and murder in mass, to accept the horror of
the concentration camps as in no way incompatible with the great
life-bringing mission of the Aryan race.

No less pernicious than the *persona*, and far more difficult to detect, is what Jung calls the *participation mystique*. The term itself is taken from Lévy-Bruhl, who used it specifically in regard to primitive peoples. Jung applies it generally to the condition of identification with the collective situation, where a man instead of being himself is merged in the mass.

Participation mystique normally begins with the family. When the human being first comes into the world he spends the period of babyhood and early childhood in becoming increasingly conscious. The ego progressively takes shape. But this building up of the ego does not mean that he becomes a being in his own right. For many years, perhaps a whole life-time, he remains, as it were, still in the family womb. Instead of taking his own way he takes the family way; instead of exercising his own judgement he falls back upon how the family would judge the matter; instead of making his own mistakes (and possibly learning from them) he continues making the family mistakes. Little of this is done consciously. To use a vague and, to some extent, meaningless expression, the *participation mystique* links people together in the unconscious. This link may be one of liking, or it may be one of mutual detestation. But the ultimate effect is the same: instead of a man working out his own unique experiment in living there is a kind of underground collective life of the mass kind in which the individual human being is submerged.

The family *participation mystique* is only one form of a general phenomenon. The school, the class, the club, the gang, the set, the clique, the church, the cult, the clan, the tribe, the mob, the nation, the ideology are some of the many forms in which men are bound together beneath the level of consciousness and become something other, usually something less, than themselves. People thus caught, so long as they remain caught, are incapable of individuation. As part of the mass they will be carried by the mass. If, as may happen, the mass is quiescent, they pass pointless lives leading to a pointless death. If, as may also happen, the mass is turbulent, they will be hurled with it to strange heights and sudden depths, following the archetypal way to a glory or a destruction of which they are not so much the agents as the raw material.

Everyone, inevitably, is held by the *participation mystique* to some considerable extent. Those engaging in the experiment in depth will repeatedly find themselves lapsing back into a mass valuation, being enveloped by the collective atmosphere (particularly on the side of the inferior functions) and otherwise ceasing to be themselves. They are no longer individuals in their own right. If the general feeling is blue, they will be blue. If loincloths only are being worn, they will be wearing loincloths. If 'a wave of indignation sweeps the country', they will be found among the sweepings. Or possibly they will consider themselves highly original and say, wear, do, exactly the opposite to everyone else—thinking thus to demonstrate their individuality.

To be caught and carried by the situation is everyone's fate to some extent. To that extent we fail to live. But the *participation mystique* can also be directly menacing: especially when it comes to be regarded as the highest value, and as such is enforced by public opinion or by the state. The present age knows well the demonic *participation* of the ideologies: the 'marching together' of the Hitler youth—marching together, compulsively, over the precipice; the 'class-conscious solidarity' of a totalitarian communism, which must ring its people around with an Iron Curtain, for fear they might start comparing propaganda with the facts. But there is another variety of mass *participation*, less obvious because it comes under the cloak of freedom, but hardly less lethal: freedom to conform.

> *Fear death by water.*
> *I see crowds of people, walking round in a ring.*

Where this compulsion to do as everyone else does descends upon a country, freedom can be extinguished almost as effectively as in a totalitarian state.

'To arrive where you are'

There is no generally valid prescription enabling a man to make the necessary separation from the *persona* and the *participation mystique*; nor from the other enmeshments of the unconscious—early conditioning, the complexes of the personal unconscious, the shadow, and the archetypal forces. Conscious awareness of these various elements at work in the psyche can be of help. But consciousness alone can do little. Only insofar as the transforming symbols are released and realized, the deep centre discovered and held, does the necessary separation gradually take place. To put it paradoxically, differentiation becomes effective only as and when integration takes place. 'To get from where you are not' it is necessary 'To arrive where you are'.

Fundamental to this integrative process is the finding and holding of the deep centre, the discovery of the 'germinal higher part' as William James terms it. In the past this discovery has been notably made by the 'practical mystics', men and women who in one way or another lived effectively in both worlds. The manner in which they came upon the treasure of the depths varies widely. It is encountered as the light, the fire, as a voice, as a warmth. But the underlying unity of the experience is sufficiently evident. Whatever the form assumed, it bears the distinctive mark: certitude.

St. Augustine, whose *Civitas Dei* did much to create Western Civilization, came upon it as 'the light':

'I entered, and beheld with the mysterious eye of my soul the light that never changes, above the eye of my soul, above my intelligence. It was something altogether different from any earthly illumination. It was higher than my intelligence because it made me, and I was lower because made by it. He who knows the truth knows that light, and he who knows that light knows eternity. Love knows that light.'

Pascal, mathematician, scientist, inventor, whose prose is one of the great glories of France, could find only incoherent words to describe the direct intimation which came to him one memorable night. The recording of the experience, which he kept always about him, shows the rough drawing of a blazing cross. Beneath it is written:

'In the year of grace 1654, Monday 23 November, the day of St. Clement, Pope and Martyr, and others in the Martyrology; the eve of St. Chrysofonous, Martyr, and others; from about half-past ten in the evening till about half an hour after midnight

FIRE

God of Abraham, God of Isaac, God of Jacob. Not of the philosophers and the learned. Certitude. Certitude. Emotion. Joy. Peace . . . Forgetfulness of the world and of all outside of God . . . The world hath not known Thee, but I have known Thee. Joy! Joy! Joy! Tears of Joy . . . My God, wilt thou leave me? Let me not be separated from thee for ever.'

George Fox, the founder of the Quakers, tells in his Journal how, as a young man, after a long period of mental anguish, searching the Scriptures, wandering from place to place, consulting with all who might enlighten him, he suddenly found the answer to his questionings:

'And when all my hopes in them (the priests and preachers) and in all men were gone, so that I had nothing outwardly to help me, nor could tell what to do: then, oh then, I heard a voice which said, "There is one, even Christ Jesus, that can speak to thy condition", and when I heard it my heart did leap for joy.'

John Wesley, beset with doubts, afflicted by failures, records another such sudden realization. The entry in his Journal for 24 May 1738 reads:

'In the evening, I went very unwillingly to a society in Aldersgate Street where one was reading Luther's preface to the Epistle to the Romans. About a quarter before nine, while he was describing the change which God works in the heart through faith in Christ, I felt my heart strangely warmed. I felt I did trust in Christ, Christ alone, for salvation, and an assurance was given me that he had taken away *my* sins, even *mine*, and saved me from the law of sin and death.'

John Woolman, the American Quaker, had the light come to him as to St. Augustine, and the certitude as it came to Pascal, but in more tranquil fashion. He records in his Journal:

'Thirteenth of fifth month 1757.

Being in good health, and abroad with Friends visiting families, I lodged at a Friend's house in Burlington. Going to bed about the time usual with me, I awoke in the night, and my meditations as I lay, were on the goodness and mercy of the Lord, in a sense whereof my heart was contrited. After this I went to sleep again; in a short time I awoke; it was yet dark, and no appearance of day or moonshine, and as I opened mine eyes I saw a light in my chamber, at the apparent distance of five feet, about nine inches in diameter, of a clear, easy brightness, and near its centre the most radiant. As I lay still looking upon it without any surprise, words were spoken to my inward ear, which filled my whole inward man. They were not the effect of thought, nor any conclusion in relation to the appearance, but as the language of the Holy One spoken in my mind. The words were, Certain Evidence of Divine Truth. They were again repeated exactly in the same manner, and then the light disappeared.'

This realization of an inner certitude, the something which 'speaks to the condition' of a man, whether it comes as a momentary vision or as an elaborately worked out insight such as St. Teresa's *Interior Castle*, is the central religious experience. The whole testimony of the mystics is essentially to the same effect. As R. A. Knox says in his study *Enthusiasm*:

'. . . the mystics regard the faculties of the soul, its reason, will, and affections, as exterior organs through which it expresses itself; behind all these there is an inner core (as it were) which they distinguish freely from the intellect and the affections, though not so commonly from the will. Sometimes they will call it the apex of the soul, sometimes its centre, sometimes its foundation; but always it is something which possesses an inner activity of its own. And it is with this inward activity that we love God.'

Discovery of the deep centre is not confined to the mystics. Nor is it necessary to use the constructive technique to come upon it. Wherever men live life responsibly, the deep centre may be to some extent experienced. Especially is this true in times of danger or of great emotional stress, when, almost without knowing it, a man seeks strength beyond his own. In the searing years of this present century, under bombing and shell fire, in prison compounds and concentration camps, in long agonized waiting, in fear and suffering and the presence of death, some such encounter as the following may well have come to many, whether or not at the time they had the means to hold it.

'In the summer of 1916, I was moving up with my battalion to the line. We were eager and rather nervous. It was our first active experience of war. The last march before the trenches had to be made in the late afternoon and at night. We started, heavily laden, stumbling over the cobbled roads. The rain pelted down, soaking us. We went on till midnight, and came, in the black, to a half-ruined village. Everything was quiet, almost peaceful. We quartered in such barns and farm buildings as still had roof and walls; struggled out of our equipment and were asleep at once, as our bodies touched the ground.

I awoke with a start; a shrieking in my ears and a crash like the crack of doom. For a few seconds, silence, broken only by the sound of falling fragments. Again the ghastly drawn-out shriek and another, more shattering explosion. As I lay there on the floor, torn from the depths of sleep, I felt such extremity of fear as I had never known. From the waist downwards I shook in an uncontrollable trembling, horrible to experience. In the same fraction of time, the upper part of me reached out instinctively, with a deep gasping breath, to something beyond my knowledge.

I had the experience of being caught, as neatly and cleanly as a good fielder catches a ball. A sense of indescribable relief flowed through my whole being. I knew with a certainty, such as no other certainty could be, that I was secure. There was no assurance that I should not be blown to pieces in the next instant. I expected to be. But I knew that, though such might be my fate, it was not of great account. There was something in me that was indestructible. The trembling ceased and I was completely collected and calm. Another shell came and burst, but it had lost its terror.

Some weeks later, in taking over a new position in the line, I again had occasion to be terribly afraid. I remembered how I had felt under the baptism of fire and tried to recapture the contact with what it was I had then reached. I found myself breathing deeply and with this "drawing-in", as I phrased it to myself, came the same feeling of assurance. Whereas a moment before I had been shaking with fear, it became as if I had down the centre of my body a cylinder of steel.

After that I often had recourse to this means of reaching out for help. Sometimes it was difficult to break through, but if I persisted the contact was always made, and the indestructible something was there. Sometimes, for whole weeks or months, I forgot about it. But, at whatever long intervals, always I came back to it as the supreme value, as that one thing on which I could depend.'

The finding of the deep centre does not necessarily come about in some sudden burst of insight such as this. More usually it is a gradual development, so gradual that with most people it is unperceived, unrealized, in the main unused. In effect, it is the crucial point of the individuation process, the means of differentiation and of integration alike. As and when consciousness becomes aware of the 'immortal diamond' it can make the necessary separation from the 'Jack, joke, poor potsherd, patch, matchwood' of the *persona*. As and when a man holds to this 'germinal higher part' he is progressively freed from the *participation mystique*. As and when the conscious personality comes upon its inmost truth, it can stand up against the tremendous drag of earlier conditioning. As and when the man no longer operates at the ego level only but from the depths, he can recover, assimilate, the values buried in the personal unconscious and the shadow. Previously he had no means of knowing what he was or for what he stood. Now, insofar as he lives from the deep centre, he can live the shadow side also—not as a divided Jekyll-and-Hyde existence, but as part of his wholeness. In the encounter with the archetypal forces, the deep centre is likewise effective. The man who holds to it will find that, though these forces flow over and through him, he is not possessed or carried away. For the time he may be reduced to a state of chaos, to a condition of almost complete non-entity. The archetypal forces are immensely more powerful than anything consciousness can muster. But the hold on the deep centre enables him to survive and begin anew. And as and when a man, caught in the insoluble problem of the opposites, seeks not a way out but a way through, it is the deep centre, variously expressed in the transforming symbols coming to him, that enables the way through to be found.

The whole spirit

When a man first comes upon the deep centre and its power, he feels that he has found the key to the enigma of life, that his troubles are now at an end. This is not so. Only occasionally can he live at that depth; and whenever the ego-centred personality re-asserts itself, life is not easier but more difficult than before. So long as he succeeds in holding to the deep centre, the psyche, conscious and unconscious, operates as a whole. But when he fails to hold, he learns the full meaning of the saying 'the way of the transgressor is hard'. The psyche, from being an ordered unity becomes an anarchic chaos. It is at such times that a man may judge it madness that he ever undertook the experiment in depth.

But if he persists, he learns that the finding of the deep centre is not the end of the experiment. Rather is it a new beginning. The deep centre is not only the something indestructible in the depths, the certitude, the rock. It is experienced as the 'strait gate' by which a man finds his way to God, or however else he may name the creative principle. As William James put it, the 'germinal higher part' is found to be 'conterminous and continuous with a MORE of the same quality'. And the MORE so found is vital to wholeness, the development of the 'real being'.

How the creative contact is made with the MORE varies from one person to another. The process is not necessarily religious in form, although it normally follows an essentially religious course. The man who comes upon the deep centre and, insofar as he is able, goes over to it, discovers (as the mystics throughout the ages have discovered) that it affords a different approach to God from that which is afforded by the ego-centred personality. At the ego level a man can pray to God, normally a petitionary prayer, asking for something the ego wants—since it is in the nature of the ego to want. The contact so made can be of value; but usually it is more or less vitiated by the fact that, at bottom, the man is trying to make use of God. As Toynbee says: 'The prayer "*My* will be done" stands self-convicted of futility.' At the level of the deep centre it is otherwise: a man goes directly to God. The object is not petitionary but a living contact with the primal source: the discovery of the *amor et visio Dei* as immediate experience. And not to make use of it, but to be energized and guided by it.

The nature of the MORE with which contact is thus made has preoccupied man from the earliest times. Some creeds regard the MORE as wholly 'other', the contact coming solely through grace. Some regard the MORE as part of the human being; or the human being as part of the MORE. Others again see the MORE as, at one and the same time, immanent and transcendent. In the different theologies, the attributes of the MORE fill many pages, usually including omnipotence, omniscience, omnipresence and the like; with the consequence that theologians find themselves faced with thorny problems concerning free will and predestination, the origin of evil, responsibility for sin and the like. Here, controversy is unending and fruitless.

Oh, Thou, who Man of baser Earth didst make,
And who with Eden didst devise the Snake;

For all the Sin wherewith the Face of Man
Is blacken'd, Man's Forgiveness give—and take!

The fact is, we are not in a position to know whether the MORE is omnipotent, omniscient or any other of the infinitudes. Such matters are beyond our range. What we can know is this. There are certain qualities of being experienced in this mortal life which we describe as best we can with such words as truth, love, creativity, personality. It seems hardly likely that we as human beings invented these things, spun these qualities out of our bellies, so to speak, any more than we invented the universe, or our own physical frames. They came, as we should say, from somewhere. Empirically, it is a heightened experience of truth, of love, of creativity, of personality (using each of these words in its deepest sense) that comes from the direct relationship with the MORE. It would seem not unreasonable to suppose that the MORE is the source from which they originated; and, in making the creative contact with the MORE by way of the deep centre, we are now continuing consciously what has hitherto taken place at the unconscious level.

However this may be, the man who thus draws upon the MORE, upon whom this heightened experience of truth, love, creativity, personality operates, finds his hold upon the deep centre strengthened and developed in a new way. The seed grows. The leaven works. Slowly, imperceptibly almost, the whole spirit takes shape. The archetypal forces cease to be ambivalent and become constructive. The man finds himself part of a larger being, a being which is experienced as his true self and yet something other and more than himself.[1]

But if the new being thus formed is to hold, it must continuously be confirmed in action. The ego-centred personality does not easily

[1] By what name the whole spirit thus formed may best be known is one of the unresolved problems in the 'intolerable wrestle with words and meanings'. To speak of it as the Holy Ghost is, unhappily, to become lost in the labyrinth of the various Christian theologies. William James' term—a man's 'real being'—is useful in its insistence on the essentially human quality of the experience; but it misses the more than human element. Jung calls it the Self, a term some people find confusing since 'self' is often used as synonymous with the ego. But on the whole it would seem the best word available, being of ancient usage and the more appropriate since, having no strong doctrinal connotations, it is open to adoption by religions, philosophies and psychologies alike.

abdicate. Repeatedly, in place of the new energies, new values, new aims that come with the individuation process, earlier attitudes step in; and for the time the man is torn between the old way of life and the new. It is in these periods of stress that a man may come near to breaking. It is also in these periods of stress, and by no other means, that the man becomes whole.

Experience of the individuation process having been largely formulated by, or under the spiritual direction of, men, it is highly probable that the foregoing generalized description is heavily weighted on the *logos* side. Men tend to see the ultimate things in terms of truth and action; women in terms of love and relationship. Thus, when the fourteenth-century anchoress Julian of Norwich comes upon the vision of the deep centre, the understanding of it given to her sets love before all:

'In this same time that I sawe this sight of the head bleeding, our good *Lord* shewed a Ghostlie sight of his homelie loving . . . he shewed a litle thing, the quantitie of a *Hasel-Nutt*, lying in the palme of my hand, as me seemed, and it was as round as a Ball. I looked thereon with the eie of my understanding, and thought, *What may this be?* and it was answered generallie thus.
It is all that is made. I marvelled how it might last. For me thought it might sodenlie have fallen to naught for litlenes.
And I was answered in my Understanding, *It lasteth, and ever shall: For God loveth it. And so hath all thing being by the Love of God.'*

And later, when she comes to sum up the meaning of her visions, her conclusion is wholly in terms of love:

'And fro the time that it was shewed, I desired often times to wit in what was our *Lords* meaning: And fifteen Year after and more, I was answered in Ghostly understanding, saying thus: *What? wouldest thou wit thy Lords meaning in this thing? Wit it well: Love was his meaning. Who sheweth it thee? Love. Wherefore sheweth he it thee? For Love. Hold thee therein, thou shalt wit more in the same. But thou shalt never wit therein other without end.* Thus was I learned that *love* is our *Lords* meaning.'

In the forming of the Self, love and the deep centre work together: the deep centre the nucleus; undemanding love the motive power.

From myth to mandala

It would be highly appropriate at this stage to show the individuation process actually operating in a human life, better still, in a number of lives. To do this in short compass is not practicable, even if the other immense difficulties of exposition could be overcome. What can be done, however, is to show the process at work in poetic creation.

When he adopted the 'mythical method', T. S. Eliot, whether he realized it at the time or not, embarked upon the individuation process. All his early poems are of the *persona*, of the *participation mystique*, of an empty desolation engulfing modern life: and yet, behind it all, the myth. There is Mr. Prufrock, politic, cautious and meticulous, measuring out his life with coffee spoons, wearing the bottoms of his trousers rolled; nevertheless having sight of the mermaids

> *riding seaward on the waves*
> *Combing the white hair of the waves blown back.*

There is Mr. Apollinax visiting the United States, laughing like an irresponsible foetus, scandalizing the dowager Mrs. Phlaccus and Professor and Mrs. Channing Cheetah; but again

> *I heard the beat of centaur's hoofs over the hard turf*
> *As his dry and passionate talk devoured the afternoon.*

There is Gerontion, an old man in a dry month, with all the cosmopolitan *débris* of broken personalities around him; yet

> *In the juvescence of the year*
> *Came Christ the tiger.*

There is ape-neck Sweeney, with gesture of orang-outang, for whom, no less than for Agamemnon,

> *The nightingales are singing near*
> *The Convent of the Sacred Heart.*

But the mythical method is much more than a poetical device. It works back upon the man. Eliot finds himself, like his great exemplar Dante, 'Gone from the path direct.' With Dante it was the dark wood. With Eliot it is *The Waste Land*, the country fallen under a spell, where the springs have dried up and the rivers have ceased to flow. In this poem each person, each situation, merges into the other, as in a dream; but underlying the swirling images are the archetypal themes—the hanged man, the journey to Emmaus, the Chapel Perilous, the Quest of the Grail—and behind them Tiresias, age-old, hermaphroditic, the personification of the deep unconscious in its sterile form.

Because the derelict life of the years following the First World War is here directly apprehended, felt in the bones and the blood, *The Waste Land* is not only a great poem but an experience realized. With a lesser man such an experience might have taken the form of a neurosis. With Eliot it becomes a work of creative art, none the less creative because it shows no way out. The human situation is faced in all its emptiness and ugliness: and that in itself is a creative act. The insoluble problem has been stated.

In *The Hollow Men*, the poet turns to the inward desolation.

> *This is the dead land*
> *This is cactus land*
> *Here the stone images*
> *Are raised . . .*

There, naturally, he meets the shadow. With Eliot it is not the quasi-demonic shadow, as it would normally be with someone who had not the courage to face the Waste Land. It is the something which slips between a man and his achievement, the negative side.

> *Between the conception*
> *And the creation*
> *Between the emotion*
> *And the response*
> *Falls the Shadow.*

With the *Ariel Poems* comes the first faint stirring of the individuation process. Three of them—*Journey of the Magi, A Song for Simeon* and *Animula*—all deal with death and rebirth, but as a dubious, remote, ambivalent possibility, not as something direct, immediate, personally experienced. The fourth, *Marina*, is of another kind. Here is the miraculous child, bringing the possibility of new life:

What seas what shores what grey rocks and what islands
What water lapping the bow
And scent of pine and the woodthrush singing through the fog
What images return
O my daughter.

The nightmare visions of the Waste Land start to dissolve:

Those who sharpen the tooth of the dog, meaning
Death
Those who glitter with the glory of the hummingbird, meaning
Death
Those who sit in the stye of contentment, meaning
Death
Those who suffer the ecstasy of the animals, meaning
Death
Are become unsubstantial, reduced by a wind,
A breath of pine, and the woodsong fog.

The *Ariel Poems* show the direction the mythical method is taking.
Ash Wednesday is the struggle itself, the hard task, the bitter journey;
and the beginning of the break through. For many, this is the least
comprehensible of Eliot's poems. As evidence of the individuation
process working within a man it is the most expressive of all.

Here, as often happens in dreams and phantasies, in order to find
the solution to the insoluble problem of *The Waste Land* and *The
Hollow Men*, the poet has gone back in time, back to that period in
the Middle Ages when the anima emerged as the Lady, the chivalric
and mystical ideal of womanhood. In the poem she appears in all
her ambivalence, but a creative ambivalence:

Lady of silences
Calm and distressed
Torn and most whole
Rose of memory
Rose of forgetfulness
Exhausted and life-giving
Worried reposeful
The single Rose
Is now the Garden
Where all loves end.

183

Characteristically, she is dreamlike in appearance, around her the marvellous light of the deep unconscious:

> *One who moves in the time between sleep and waking, wearing*
> *White light folded, sheathed about her, folded.*

Above all, she is the one who breaks the spell of the Waste Land. The rivers flow again:

> *Who then made strong the fountains and made fresh the springs*
> *Made cool the dry rock and made firm the sand.*

Simultaneously, as the impersonal life takes shape, the ego-centred life is disintegrated, eaten by the leopards, the bones of the body scattered—and the beginning of a new unity found.

> *Under a juniper-tree the bones sang, scattered and shining*
> *We are glad to be scattered, we did little good to each other,*
> *Under a tree in the cool of the day, with the blessing of sand,*
> *Forgetting themselves and each other, united*
> *In the quiet of the desert.*

But this is not deliverance, only an oasis towards it. There is the hard mounting of the spiral stair,

> *Struggling with the devil of the stairs who wears*
> *The deceitful face of hope and of despair.*

There is, above all, in some of the most poignant lines Eliot has ever written, the longing backward glance at the things of the personal life now being left, the feeling of loss of the magical projections upon the outer world; and the finding of them again in a new form as they become integrated.

> *And the lost heart stiffens and rejoices*
> *In the lost lilac and the lost sea voices*
> *And the weak spirit quickens to rebel*
> *For the bent golden-rod and the lost sea smell*
> *Quickens to recover*
> *The cry of quail and the whirling plover*
> *And the blind eye creates*
> *The empty forms between the ivory gates*
> *And smell renews the salt savour of the sandy earth.*

Throughout *Ash Wednesday* the transition from the personal to the impersonal life is in process, but not fully made.

This is the time of tension between dying and birth
The place of solitude where three dreams cross.

At one point only, in a maze of dissonances, Eliot touches upon the deep centre:

If the lost word is lost, if the spent word is spent
If the unheard, unspoken
Word is unspoken, unheard;
Still is the unspoken word, the Word unheard,
The Word without a word, the Word within
The world and for the world;
And the light shone in darkness and
Against the World the unstilled world still whirled
About the centre of the silent Word.

This is far from the peace that passeth understanding. But, as Nietzsche says: 'A man must have chaos yet within him to give birth to a dancing star.' 'The centre of the silent Word' has been reached.

In the *Four Quartets* comes the moment of vision, the break through, the realization of the continuous intersection of the time-less with time:

Not the intense moment
Isolated, with no before and after,
But a lifetime burning in every moment
And not the lifetime of one man only
But of old stones that cannot be deciphered.

The still point, the deep centre, is found:

At the still point of the turning world. Neither flesh nor fleshless;
Neither from nor towards; at the still point, there the dance is,
But neither arrest nor movement. And do not call it fixity,
Where past and future are gathered. Neither movement from nor towards,
Neither ascent nor decline. Except for the point, the still point,
There would be no dance, and there is only the dance.

Into the pattern of the creative dance are woven the four elements of the antique world—air, earth, water, fire; the four seasons; the four ages of man; the four aspects of wisdom—philosophy and religion, inner experience and outer experience; and, above all, the four aspects of time—time present and time future, what has been and what might have been. And, at the centre of the *mandala*, perceived in that timeless present which is the only true consciousness, the love that is the rose and the love that is the fire:

> *We shall not cease from exploration*
> *And the end of all our exploring*
> *Will be to arrive where we started*
> *And know the place for the first time.*
> *Through the unknown, remembered gate*
> *When the last of earth left to discover*
> *Is that which was the beginning;*
> *At the source of the longest river*
> *The voice of the hidden waterfall*
> *And the children in the apple-tree*
> *Not known, because not looked for*
> *But heard, half-heard, in the stillness*
> *Between two waves of the sea.*
> *Quick now, here, now, always—*
> *A condition of complete simplicity*
> *(Costing not less than everything)*
> *And all shall be well and*
> *All manner of thing shall be well*
> *When the tongues of flame are in-folded*
> *Into the crowned knot of fire*
> *And the fire and the rose are one.*

Looking back, it can be seen that the elements of individuation were there already in *The Waste Land*. (It is not for nothing that the word with which the poem opens is 'April'.) There is the many-sided anima; there is the shadow, 'the young man carbuncular'; there is the hero, Ariel in attendance, 'This music crept by me upon the waters'; there is the Other, the Wayshower of the road to Emmaus; in Tiresias there is the prototype of the whole man. But Tiresias, for all his androgynous wisdom and experience, is blind, sterile and impotent, able only to foresee and to foresuffer. It is with the finding of the deep centre and the forming of the *mandala* of the *Four Quartets,*

The drawing of this Love and the voice of this Calling

that the creative contact is made and the insoluble problem of *The Waste Land* and *The Hollow Men* resolved.

In the course of it the 'mythical method' undergoes a sea-change. It is no longer mermaids and centaurs, Agamemnon and the Grail, that Eliot uses as his backcloth. Instead there are the occasions when he himself must have felt the timeless moment breaking through— 'the winter lightning', 'the wild thyme unseen', 'the kingfisher's wing', 'between two waves of the sea', 'Quick now, here, now, always—'. What started by being a method has become an experience, the 'inward transforming experience of God'.

IX

PSYCHOLOGY, SCIENCE AND RELIGION

INDIVIDUATION, wholeness, how in fear and trembling a man may come to work out his own salvation, has always been the central theme of religion. Psychology is widely looked upon as the enemy of religion. To some extent this is true. In certain of the various versions of psychology at present current, the human psyche is in the main dismissed as nothing more than a biological by-product. In the experiment in depth the psyche is not thus dismissed, but accepted as a legitimate object of experience in its own right. The question naturally arises, what is the relationship between psychology, so understood, and religion; meaning by religion no one particular cult or creed but the age-old, world-wide effort of man to make contact with a creative possibility beyond himself.

Jung's experience on this score has been widely quoted:

'Among all my patients in the second half of life—that is to say, over thirty-five—there has not been one whose problem in the last resort was not that of finding a religious outlook on life.'

Eliot, referring specifically to Christianity, sees psychology as an 'indispensable handmaid':

'Psychology has very great utility in two ways. It can revive, and has already to some extent revived, truths long since known to Christianity, but mostly forgotten and ignored, and it can put them in a form and a language understandable by modern people to whom the language of Christianity is not only dead but undecipherable. . . . But I must add that I think psychology can do more than this, in discovering more about the human soul still; for I do not pretend that there is nothing more to know; the possibilities of knowledge are practically endless. Psychology is an indispensable handmaid to theology; but I think a very poor housekeeper.'

Toynbee, from the standpoint of universal history, likewise sees religion as primal: often mistaken, often twisted to meet man's desires, inevitably adapted to the exigencies of the age, but in itself the vision of

'a Kingdom of God which is not in Time at all but is in a different spiritual dimension, and which, just by virtue of this difference of dimension, is able to penetrate our mundane life and to trans-figure it.'

From these widely different angles of approach substantially the same conclusion emerges. Religion, rightly understood, has nothing to fear from psychology. On the contrary, psychology, properly so called, is in a position to serve religion.

The manner in which this service may be rendered has already to some extent appeared. The constructive technique makes possible an experiential approach to the 'different spiritual dimension'. By enabling men and women, active and knowledgeable in the outer world, to develop their latent psycho-perceptive faculties—the in-ward eye, the inward ear, the inward understanding—it provides the means of rediscovering at first hand the reality behind religion; and not merely as a form of belief but as the meaning and purpose and mainspring of life.

To appreciate what this may mean, it is necessary, as far as possible, to stand back mentally from the present world situation and see it in broad perspective. There are at present in existence some ten or twelve major religions, variously sub-divided into some hundreds of different cults and sects. These creeds normally date back anything from fifteen hundred to three thousand years; have been handed down for the most part in quasi-legendary form; are expressed in terms of beliefs, practices, symbols appropriate to times immeasur-ably removed from the present; and, by the accretion of the ages, have become so glossed, interpreted, overlaid with extraneous matter that often the original meaning has virtually disappeared. As a consequence, in all those countries where science and modern technology have made their characteristic impact (and they are now coming to the whole world) the great majority of active and intelligent men and women have in fact renounced religion as a way of life. They may pay it lip service. Deep down, they may still be fundamentally religious. But the living God is no longer the be-all and end-all of everything they do and are.

Meanwhile, there has entered upon the scene the new dogmatic creed of totalitarianism: deliberately using psychological techniques to mobilize the archetypal forces; inspiring by this means a devotion such as few, if any, of the earlier faiths can now match; moulding science in its own image; specifically adapted to the technological way of life; promising immediate fulfilment; infiltrating into people after people; seeking to proselytize the whole world. Numerically, totalitarianism may now claim to be the foremost faith in existence. Politically, it is the greatest force mankind has ever known. That from time to time it may suffer set-backs—such, for instance, as the defeat of Hitlerism—and at other times disguise its motives and go underground, is in the nature of things. But the fact itself remains. Especially in time of trouble, men need the inspiration of a dynamic faith in which they feel they can put their trust. In one or other of its various forms, totalitarianism proffers what appears to be such a faith. It may or may not prove lasting. But it lasts long enough for power to be seized.

Such, in broad outline, is the religious situation in our present day and age. The reality behind religion is to a great extent obscured, for many people completely blotted out, by ancient forms which for them have become more or less meaningless. Simultaneously, psychological techniques are being expertly used as a means of grasping and extending absolute power.

Against these ills the experiment in depth provides no panacea. But three things it can do. It can, as Eliot suggests, revive truths now mostly forgotten and ignored, and put them in a language understandable by modern man. It can, at the same time, sharpen the 'discernment of spirits', make clear the distinction between true religion and its demonic counterpart now active in the world. Most vital of all, from the point of view of long-period and world-wide effect, the experiment in depth makes possible an empirical, scientific approach to the reality behind religion.

Christianity and the individuation process

Christianity, more than any other faith perhaps, shows how great religious truths, now largely lost or traduced, may be recovered by direct experience of the other side of consciousness. In the Synoptic Gospels, Jesus of Nazareth sets out in unmistakable terms the salient features of the individuation process; describing in detail both the dangers encountered and the means by which men and societies may become whole. The discoveries of analytical psychology do little else than repeat, in modern phraseology, and with detailed empirical backing, the principal injunctions of the Christian way. A few only of the more obvious correspondences can be touched upon here; but they are sufficiently striking.

One absolute requirement of the teaching of Jesus, repeatedly emphasized, is separation from the *persona*. Those, such as the Scribes and Pharisees, who did everything for the sake of the external appearance, made clean the outside but paid no attention to the inside, are utterly condemned.

'Woe unto you, scribes and Pharisees, hypocrites! for ye are like unto whited sepulchres, which indeed appear beautiful outward, but are within full of dead men's bones, and of all uncleanness. . . . Ye serpents, ye generation of vipers, how can ye escape the damnation of hell?'

Jesus likewise lays down, with no less emphasis, the need for separation from the *participation mystique*, particularly of the family and of the ancestors generally.

'And another of his disciples said unto him, Lord, suffer me first to go and bury my father. But Jesus said unto him, Follow me; and let the dead bury their dead.'

Still more trenchantly:

'If any man come to me, and hate not his father, and mother, and wife, and children, and brethren, and sisters, yea, and his own life also, he cannot be my disciple.'

In a gospel of love, 'hate' is a strong word to use of the family. As in the condemnation of the Pharisaical *persona*, there is here no sentimental softness but stern and unequivocal warning against deadly peril. Where a man is caught in the *participation mystique*, there can be no wholeness.

The same is true of the need to separate from the autonomous complexes which strive to possess a man. In the description given of

Jesus' ministry, there are repeated encounters with the 'unclean spirits', with those 'possessed with devils'; and reiterated warnings of how necessary and how difficult it is to recognize and deal with these psychological powers. One fundamental truth is especially stressed: that in grappling with the unclean spirits, unless the man is watchful, apparent victory can turn into defeat.

> 'When the unclean spirit is gone out of a man, he walketh through dry places, seeking rest, and findeth none. Then he saith, I will return into my house from whence I came out; and when he is come, he findeth it empty, swept, and garnished. Then goeth he, and taketh with himself seven other spirits more wicked than himself, and they enter in and dwell there: and the last state of that man is worse than the first.'

Those with direct experience of the counter-attack from the unconscious, whenever a psychological advance has been made, will have no difficulty in recognizing this recurrent peril of the individuation process.

As against the 'unclean spirits', the 'devils' that divide a man against himself, what is needed is completeness, the spirit that is whole. 'Be ye therefore perfect, even as your Father which is in heaven is perfect.' The Holy Ghost, the comforter, the advocate, is the great strength that will come to the followers of Jesus. The Holy Ghost is vital to salvation, more vital than Jesus himself. Jesus may be denied and he who denies be forgiven, but he who blasphemes against the Holy Ghost has cut himself off.

> 'Wherefore I say unto you, All manner of sin and of blasphemy shall be forgiven unto men: but the blasphemy against the Holy Ghost shall not be forgiven unto men. And whosoever speaketh a word against the Son of man, it shall be forgiven him: but whosoever speaketh against the Holy Ghost, it shall not be forgiven him, neither in this world, neither in the world to come.'

This is not the drastic and inscrutable judgement it is sometimes taken to be. It is a plain statement of fact. The man who denies the whole spirit stands of necessity self-condemned. The love of God is always there: but if its saving grace is rejected the man is lost.

Above all, throughout the Synoptic Gospels, Jesus preaches the deep centre, the Kingdom of Heaven within a man. It is the smallest

of all seeds which becomes the greatest of all herbs, a tree. It is the
leaven that works upon and transforms the lump. It is the treasure
hidden in a field, the pearl of great price, for which a man gives all.
It is the bridegroom who comes when least expected, for whom un-
remitting watch must be kept. It is the 'strait gate', the narrow way,
which few discover. It is the one thing in life that matters, to which,
once found, all else is added. 'Ask, and it shall be given you; seek,
and ye shall find; knock, and it shall be opened unto you.'

The account in the Synoptic Gospels is clear. But this detailed and
reiterated description of the finding of the deep centre and the
forming of the whole spirit was quickly obscured. In the later
Fourth Gospel, direct references to the Kingdom are few. In the
remainder of the New Testament, the Kingdom of Heaven is referred to hardly at all; and then, almost exclusively, to say what it is
not, never what it is. Within a few years of his death, this central
feature of Jesus' teaching is lost to sight.

There is no mystery as to how this came about. In place of the
deep centre, the Kingdom of Heaven as Jesus proclaimed it, is put
the figure of Jesus himself, the crucified and risen Christ. As a transforming symbol this is immensely potent. For the ordinary man or
woman there is infinitely more strength and comfort in a personality
than in any parable. The words of St. Paul 'not I but Christ crucified
within me' are, in many respects, the most expressive of all the
symbols of the deep centre. But the image of the crucified and risen
Christ led directly into a well-beaten archetypal track, back to an
ancient myth: the hero-saviour who does the great deed, Osiris,
Zagreus, Tammuz, Attis, Adonis, Balder—the dying and resurrecting Gods.

From this substitution gradually evolves a fundamental change in
doctrine. Instead of a man seeking the Kingdom of Heaven, working
out his own wholeness in fear and trembling, he is told that the work
has been done for him. He has been 'redeemed' by the 'blood'. A
'sufficient sacrifice' has been made. His sins have been 'washed away'.
All he has to do is to 'believe' and he will be 'saved'. Each of these
affirmations, be it emphasized, has its true, integrative aspect. Insofar
as the spirit that was in Christ prevails within a man, he is redeemed.
But each has also an archetypal, magical meaning. Belief is sufficient.
Unconditional acceptance is all that is required. The hero-saviour

does the rest. Where this magical meaning gains the upper hand, the way is prepared for the latter-day messiahs, the Adolf Hitlers and Josef Stalins, whose promise is likewise of salvation, whose demand is likewise unconditional belief. With the worship of the hero-saviour, the first step is taken towards the totalitarian state.

The technique of disintegration

It was sometimes said during the First World War that such a cataclysm might well give rise to a great new religion. In a sense it did. Totalitarianism, to all appearance, is an ardent political faith, with a talent for conversion. In fact, it is not so much a faith as a psychological technique. This technique has now been operated sufficiently often for its main features to become evident. As raw material it prefers a nation defeated in war, torn by dissension, suffering under real or fancied indignities; but any people delivered over to passion or fear will serve. Given this groundwork, four main lines of action are followed with the utmost ruthlessness, using every means of propaganda, persuasion, conditioning and intimidation to secure 100 per cent conformity.

(1) The people must be induced to hate. In their midst, and all around them, encircling them on every hand, there is an implac-able, insidious, despicable, sub-human enemy. Upon this enemy —Jews, foreigners, communists, capitalists—the whole of the negative side, the shadow at its blackest and most demonic, must be projected. It is the central task of the propaganda machine to secure that this be done.

(2) With their shadow side thus removed, the people must be induced to identify with some more-than-human *persona*. They are so many Siegfrieds, supermen, heirs of ancient Rome, mem-bers of the class-conscious proletariat or equally exceptional beings, possessing the ineffable blood, the historic destiny, the scientific enlightenment, the marvellous way of life, or some such other magical means of superiority. This identification with the *persona* has the effect of cutting off the individual from the deep unconscious and plunging him into a complete *participation mystique*. The man disappears into the mass.

(3) At the same time there is in their midst a Leader, a Father of his people, a more-than-human latter-day Messiah. Upon this hero-saviour the whole of the positive contents of the deep uncon-

scious must be projected. He is the giver of the True Doctrine, the Leader of the One Party, infallible, above criticism, miraculously endowed. His picture, his name, his symbols, must everywhere appear; and behind them—since freedom dies hard—his secret police, with the special task of liquidating the recalcitrant.

(4) A great creative purpose exists, ordained by the Leader and the Party, pre-ordained by history. For this purpose all must be ready to sacrifice themselves. In the achievement of this purpose all things will be fulfilled. And, since this is a total way of life, since the implacable sub-human enemy will remain dangerous so long as he has a corner left to him in which to plot and scheme, this great creative purpose in the last analysis can be nothing less than world conquest.

Leninism, Fascism, Hitlerism, Stalinism, have all been shaped to this formula. By its means immense energy can be generated: fanatical certainty, fanatical dynamism, fanatical cruelty, fanatical self-sacrifice. The forces of the deep unconscious are aroused and their tremendous power mobilized in the service of an ideological creed.

The technique itself, however, is nothing new. Time and again, throughout the ages, religion has been perverted by substantially the same means. The recipe varies in form but in essence remains invariable. Given a people suitably disposed, a cult of bigotry and persecution is preached. As a first step, the demonic shadow is projected upon unbelievers, infidels, heretics, papists and the like. Upon the faithful themselves a marvellous *persona* is set: they alone are the chosen people, the holy, the elect, the saints of God. The magical means of victory is likewise theirs: the Heaven-sent leader, the trusty smeller-out of heresy, the infallible doctrine, the infallible rite. Above all, they are dedicated to a holy war, a sacred mission, a divine destiny, in which the enemies of God will be utterly defeated and cast down. Such is the well-worn formula for splitting the human psyche and using the archetypal energy so released for purposes of power. It is this formula, applied on a world scale, with all the facilities for conditioning afforded by the modern highly-centralized state, that totalitarianism has rediscovered and shaped to its own ends.

Seen in the perspective opened out by the experiment in depth the underlying nature of this disintegrative technique becomes evident.

It is the negation of wholeness at every point. Wholeness starts with the realization (as William James expresses it) 'that there is *something wrong about us* as we naturally stand', i.e. the shadow side is faced. Totalitarianism starts with the deliberate projection of the shadow upon others. Wholeness seeks and holds the deep centre, the 'germinal higher part'. Totalitarianism proceeds to the next step in disintegration: identification with the *persona*, the superman pretence. Wholeness seeks and finds the MORE, the creative contact, the *amor et visio Dei*, the at-one-ment with God. Totalitarianism projects the highest value upon some messianic Leader, inspired Party, magical means of superiority. Wholeness works for a world fellowship, the coming of the Kingdom of Heaven, within a man and between men. Totalitarianism exalts a 'great creative purpose': the conquest of the world, the deliverance of mankind by reducing human beings to the status of animated matter.

In the present age, this formula for disintegration has unexampled potency. It is operating simultaneously on two fronts: the world and the psyche. On the world front it has behind it the immense forces of modern methods of propaganda and intimidation, directed by men conditioned to be ruthless, exercising absolute power, liable themselves to be killed if for a moment their ruthlessness falters. For men so placed, freedom is the arch-enemy. As a consequence, over the last thirty or more years, long before the term itself became current, the free peoples have found themselves involved in a 'cold war': sometimes open, sometimes disguised, but always present.

On the front that faces inward, the formula is likewise at work. Freedom, when it loses the creative contact, loses at the same time its purpose; and much more than that. As the meaning, values, vitality of the free way of life disappear, they do not merely leave a vacuum. Invisibly, the fear, cynicism, rancour, hatred characteristic of the totalitarian way of life enter in their place. Every man, woman and child becomes a battleground. It is this infiltration from within, even more than the threat from without, that is at the root of our present time of troubles.

In the conduct of this 'cold war', moreover, totalitarianism has found an effective camouflage, effective on both fronts. If tyranny appeared in its true light, there would be little danger. But, now as always, the powers of evil are quite prepared to advance the best of motives. As the history of our own time has plentifully exemplified, the totalitarian technique can be operated under a wide assortment of political disguises. But there are two above all that are successful: communism and anti-communism.

When communism is adopted as the façade, an idealistic note is sounded. Totalitarianism becomes the champion of the under-dog, the poor, the rootless, the frustrated, the despised, the disinherited. In effect—though it would never use the name—totalitarian communism sets out to be a Universal Church. Its declared aim is the brotherhood of man, a world community where, in the words of the Communist Manifesto, 'the free development of each is the condition of the free development of all'; a classless society in which the State has 'withered away'. The complete and absolute incompatibility of these professed purposes with the cynical and ruthless methods of totalitarian dictatorship is the ultimate condemnation of this way of life. Teaching men to hate is not the means by which they learn to live as brothers. Feeding a people on lies is not the means by which they learn to honour truth. Disintegrating men psychologically is not the means by which they are enabled to develop freely. Prescribing the advancement of the Party as the fundamental moral precept is not the means by which the State withers away. Between totalitarian methods and communist ideals there is no joint. Sooner or later this will become evident, to the communist no less than to the non-communist. But, in the meantime, wherever in the world men feel themselves aggrieved, totalitarianism can proffer its specious panacea. And it needs only to win once.

At the same time, the fear and hatred aroused by totalitarian communism has brought into being a totalitarian anti-communism in some ways even more sinister. That countries such as Russia and China, awaking from a somnolence of many centuries, should fall victim to the totalitarian technique is in no way surprising. The inroads of totalitarian anti-communism among the free peoples is another matter. To use totalitarian methods to root out totalitarianism, Satan to cast out Satan, is a transparent device. That free peoples should be deceived by it is a telling indication of how low freedom has fallen. We have to recognize, and give full weight to the fact, that the environmental setting of present-day existence naturally favours the totalitarian technique. The uncertainty over values, the ubiquity of propaganda, the centralization of power, the rootlessness of a technological society, are circumstances rendering the free way of life much more difficult to set up and maintain than in the past. It is not by accident that freedom is everywhere on the defensive. Conditions are adverse and likely to remain so.

Science and religion

How to win the cold war—on both fronts—is the crucial question of the age. Only in part is this a political question. Essentially, and in the main, it is religious. The struggle is for the spirit of man. And it is here that psychology can, perhaps, render unique service. It can enable science and religion to work together as never before.

What exactly this implies calls for some explanation. So much has been said and written on the 'science *versus* religion' controversy that the whole issue has become thoroughly confused. One reason for this is that science and religion have each a number of different meanings and it is necessary to be explicit as to which of the meanings is meant.

Be it said at once that, where religion is rigidly dogmatic, science has little to contribute. Of a dogma such as the virgin birth, for instance, science can say that, from a purely scientific standpoint, an event of this kind is highly improbable. It can also point out that miraculous births are repeatedly found in the mythologies of peoples all over the world; that we are, in fact, dealing with a well-authenticated archetypal theme. But that is as far as it can go. It cannot say that such an event is impossible. An absolute statement of this kind would imply that science was in possession of all the facts, past, present, and to come: which obviously it is not. All it can do is to state its empirically-based provisional conclusions and leave it at that. Broadly speaking, between dogmatic religion and science there is no means of useful co-operation. Each draws its own boundaries and, if it is wise, remains within them.

Religion based upon experience (which in no wise excludes that form of experience known as revelation) is in a totally different category. Here science can serve. But it is necessary to be explicit as to what we mean by 'science' in this context. There is science considered as the body of tested knowledge brought together by mankind. Science in this meaning has, as yet, little to contribute to the understanding of the realm dealt with by religion. And there is science considered as a method of discovering truth: a process consisting essentially in (i) systematic observation of the facts; (ii) the forming of hypotheses based upon such observation; (iii) verification of these hypotheses by more intensive and/or more extensive reference to the facts; (iv) re-shaping of the hypotheses as a result of this verification; and so on, continuously, in a progressive deepening and widening of knowledge.

Science, thus considered as a method of discovering truth, can be applied to religion wherever religion is based upon experience. As already seen, in *The Varieties of Religious Experience* William James used this method so far as was possible with the data available to him. Taking the religious experience of the 'more developed minds' of different periods, different cultures, different faiths, and comparing them with one another as best he could, he arrived at certain tentative conclusions, *viz.*: (1) the process starts with the realization that 'there is *something wrong about us* as we naturally stand'; (2) this leads to the discovery of the 'germinal higher part' in a man; (3) this germinal higher part is 'conterminous and continuous with a MORE of like quality'; (4) from the contact with the MORE by way of the germinal higher part, the 'real being' forms.

William James was able to get thus far by applying the first two stages of the scientific process. He systematically observed the facts. On the basis of this observation he worked out his hypotheses. But the ensuing stages—verification and the progressive reshaping of hypotheses—were debarred to him. He had only a limited volume of data available and no means of putting his tentative conclusions to the test.

It is at this point that Jung's constructive technique links on to the work done by James. By means of the constructive technique it is possible for normally constituted men and women to develop to some extent the psycho-perceptive faculties used by the seers and mystics, and so become aware of the processes at work the other side of consciousness. In this way, the application of scientific method to religious experience can be set on a new footing. At stage (i) (systematic observation of the facts) a potentially unlimited volume of data can now be had, wherever men and women undertake the experiment in depth and record their experience in appropriate form. On this more adequate basis, stage (ii) of the process (formulation of hypotheses) can become much more detailed, thoroughgoing and explicit. In particular, it can cover Jung's two major contributions to the understanding of the individuation process, *viz.*: that transforming symbols, indicating the living middle way between the opposites, are continually being produced by the deep unconscious; and that the otherwise highly ambivalent autonomous complexes can, under suitable circumstances, be creatively integrated into the Self. Most important of all, stages (iii) and (iv) (the process of continuous verification) can now be undertaken. Enquiry is no longer halted because the data have given out. The sole limit to investigation is the willingness of man to experiment.

For the first time in human history, science and religion have thus the possibility of working together. This is far from saying that all is clear. There are certain inherent difficulties in applying scientific method to the data coming from the other side of consciousness which can only be partially overcome. It is not necessary here to enter into these difficulties in detail, but the more formidable of them may be briefly set down.

The first lies in the nature of the experience. We are not dealing with the so-called objective world, the data coming to us by way of the senses, but with a trans-subjective world (as Jung has sometimes called it), effects apprehended by methods of inner perception of which we as yet know little. This raises a series of problems; including particularly the ineluctable fact that, while some people are psycho-perceptive, others are not—as, in the outer world, some people have keen sight and hearing while others are not so blest. The individuation process might be taking place in a man, but he be totally unable to detect it at work. Even with the highly psycho-perceptive, the information gathered is as each man sees it from his private window on to the inner world: and through this window he perceives in terms of his own symbolic imagery, which must then be interpreted into more general terms if the phenomena themselves are to be understood.

In the second place, there is the rather special situation that, in the experiment in depth, we are dealing with an *emerging* possibility, something that may be coming into existence here and there, not something that has always and everywhere existed. In much the same way, if we could go backwards down the time-stream, to the period of our remote ancestors, we would have the question before us whether a strange new development—what we now call human consciousness—was or was not taking place. And if we could go yet further back, we would find a still more puzzling enigma: whether or not another new thing was coming into being—life. Clearly, to put an emerging possibility of this kind upon a scientific basis presents special difficulties. Conceivably—in a matter such as this we have no means of knowing—not everyone can make the creative contact directly. The possibility may have emerged for some but not for others: the same as, some half-million or a million years ago, only a small handful of our remote ancestors may have shown traces of human consciousness; and, many millions of years earlier, only an occasional sample of inter-tidal scum have shown traces of life. In selecting his evidence from the 'more developed minds' (a procedure for which he was criticized at the time) William James exercised sure judgement. It is for this reason that it is especially necessary for people high above the average in ability and insight to undertake the experiment in depth.

In the third place, in a field such as this, there can be no certainty in the conclusions reached, only an increasing degree of probability. Jung once said of his life's work that, in its present form, it constitutes no more than a 'subjective confession'. Since then, the fact that some hundreds of men and women, using the psycho-perceptive methods, have substantially corroborated certain of his conclusions, gives reason to suppose that this 'subjective confession' is something more than mere personal phantasy on his part. As and when this body of corroborative experience (deepening and widening as independent investigators in increasing numbers make the experiment) is set down and funded in suitable form, our knowledge of this realm of activity can be made more sure. But it can never be made final. The type of enquirer who seeks, above all, certainty, rather than a developing truth, will find here little to his hand.

Given these conditions, what is the right course to pursue? Is scientific method to be restricted to those areas where something approaching certainty can be achieved? If so, we condemn all those pioneers of science who in the past went forward, under every disadvantage, bent on discovering what they could with such instruments as they had; and by their courage and determination built up the body of scientific knowledge we now possess. And we condemn science itself to a meagre and misleading existence, based as it would be on such fragmentary knowledge as can be acquired by the so-called 'exact' techniques; ignoring that the small segment of reality thus adventitiously explored would be just as likely to distort as to illuminate our view of the whole.

Clearly, scientific investigation cannot be thus confined. It is true that where the pursuit of science is little more than a *persona* activity, or where the feeling of certainty it brings is clutched at as a substitute for religion, there is a natural tendency to play safe and refuse to apply scientific method anywhere outside the accepted ruts. But where the scientific spirit truly moves there can be little doubt as to what should be its scope of enquiry. Scientific method is for the discovery of truth on all fronts, the psyche no less than the physical world. And since our knowledge of the psyche is far behind that of the physical world, the investigation itself far more difficult, and the issues at stake infinitely more momentous, it is on this sector that we need to concentrate.

As a first step (and in this, as in other things, we may hope to learn as we go along) we would do well to bring together, from all available sources, present and past, such experience of the creative potentialities of the human psyche as can enable us to establish certain hypotheses for general guidance: as, for instance, how men and women do in practice disentangle themselves from the *persona*, emerge from the *participation mystique*, overcome early conditioning, deal with the personal unconscious, effect a right relationship with the autonomous complexes, encounter the transforming symbols, discover the deep centre, make the creative contact, enable the Self to form, serve as channels for the MORE; together with any and every other operation relevant to the process of withdrawal-and-return.

For this to be done, it is necessary that men and women, having the requisite devotion and aptitude, should undertake the experiment in depth in their own lives; and report back on what they encounter. This does not involve embracing some religious faith, or giving up such faith if already held. What it does involve is acquiring the psycho-perceptive methods, and applying them with the greatest possible objectivity and awareness. In doing this it is for each to make his own exploration of the inner world of man. To have some knowledge of the results of previous investigation is clearly an advantage. But such knowledge needs to be considered as indicative only. The essence of the experiment is that there shall be no rigid following of doctrines laid down, but instead a dialectical process of discovery: on the one hand, a continuous formulation and reformulation of hypotheses, to serve as guide for the individual experiment; on the other, a continuous intensive verification of these hypotheses as the individual experiments proceed.

By these means it should be feasible to make at least a first beginning towards setting the experiment in depth upon a scientific basis, so far as such a thing is possible. Until this is done, we remain in virtual ignorance of those forces—demonic, ambivalent, potentially creative—at present wrecking innumerable lives, threatening to wreck the world.

How great is the need for such systematic funding of experience may be judged to some extent from the pages that follow. In the ensuing chapter, an account is ventured of the dangers and destinations of the inward journey. In the chapter following that, suggestions are made as to certain safeguards and possible further developments. But the data on which these two chapters are based are no more than one person's observation and experience, supplemented by what he can learn of the observation and experience of a few others. Given that these others have similarly enriched their observation and experience, the coverage is not so inadequate as might at first appear. But by no stretch of the imagination can it be considered as satisfactory. Only as and when a large volume of material (coming as far as possible from active and intelligent men and women making the experiment in depth as part of their normal living of life) is systematically brought together, analysed, tested and re-tested, will it be feasible to chart the inward journey with any assurance. But once this can be done, it is not unreasonable to expect that the realization of the creative contact, the direct, personal at-one-ment with the MORE, can become possible for far larger numbers than at present.

In the conditions of the present-day world, this is something more than a pious expression of hope. The totalitarian powers, and their imitators in the free countries, have come upon the secret of splitting the psyche, a discovery infinitely more fraught with peril than the splitting of the atom. The world struggle of our time is, in essence, between the means of integrating the human being and the means of disintegrating him: with the disintegrative technique, at present, far in advance. Either we learn to understand the tremendous forces operating in the human spirit, or these forces are well calculated to destroy us.

There is here an immense new field of activity for the social sciences, the sciences of man. Whether they are capable of rising to such a challenge remains to be seen. A development in methodology which involves a development of faculties latent in the scientist himself is not to everyone's taste. A development in scope and concept which relates the social sciences directly to the greatest political, social and psychological problem of the age is a widening of responsibility many would hesitate to accept. But this much seems reasonably certain. In the experiment in depth social scientists have possibilities of action-research vastly surpassing in importance anything so far undertaken by man: an unexpected universe of experience, in which all the great inventions wait to be made. They have, also, a certain direct interest in the matter. What happens to the social sciences under totalitarian control the present century has shown. In a world so dominated the social sciences are at an end.

In sum, it is time we saw the living myth in its true light: not merely as so much infantile fantasy, part of the childhood of man—though it can be that; not merely as a means by which simple-minded people may be hoodwinked and exploited—though it can be that also; not merely as a technique by which men may be disintegrated psychologically, and collectivities moulded into a fanatical mass—as is now happening in country after country; but as the greatest of all instruments of good known to us, the transforming symbol by which men and communities may become whole. As and when this understanding of the human spirit is reached, psychology, science and religion can work as one.

Part Four

MAKING THE EXPERIMENT

X

DANGERS AND DESTINATIONS

THE experiment in depth concerns everyone, but it is not for everyone to undertake. The way is dangerous. It demands of a man that he obey the injunction 'Become what thou art'; and to this end leads him to his own encounter. What he will find there, no one can know in advance. This much, though, is reasonably certain. Wholeness has to proceed against the heaviest of odds: the values, habit-patterns, attitudes, laid down by earlier conditioning in a society where the creative contact has been to a great extent lost. Individuation does not begin with a *tabula rasa*, but with a personality more or less malformed.

Beyond lies the deep unconscious. Here, all is at the hazard. As Jung has said, there are those who go digging for an artesian well and come instead upon a volcano. Cumulated upon this uncertainty is the harsh fact that our knowledge of the other side of consciousness is still, for the most part, in the earliest stage of hypothesis. Much of it may be wide of the mark, some completely mistaken. It is not only that the beaten way does not as yet exist. Such track as there is may be deceptive. A man takes it at his peril. In making the experiment in depth there are bound to be casualties, casualties that could not reasonably be foreseen. It is well to realize that one's own name may figure among them.

But there is also the positive side. The unconscious is not fundamentally a menace, a source of fear and misgiving. It is the well-spring of life, both for the individual and for the peoples of the world. At present we are cut off from it; and worse than cut off, exposed to the utmost peril. Little as we may like it, we of the present century have no choice but to live dangerously, the threat of mass destruction over all our heads. Those who have the psychological strength and stamina to undertake the withdrawal-and-return—to live dangerously to some purpose—are the fortunate ones. Whether or not a creative minority comes into existence as a result of their efforts, they live.

Such, then, are the circumstances in which the experiment in depth is to be undertaken, or not undertaken, as the case may be. In the first part of the present chapter I have attempted to set down certain of the principal dangers encountered on the way, the misconceptions and mistakes into which one naturally falls.

A description of this kind, be it emphasized, has no more than a limited usefulness. However specific the warning, the mistakes will still be made. The principal value of such an account lies in the possibility that it may help a man, caught in the toils, to become more conscious of what is happening to him. Otherwise he may continue for months or years in the same futile round of misunderstanding. To this extent, counsel can be useful; but in the end it is experience alone that counts. In making the inward journey it is by falling into the ditches, not once but many times, that one comes to know they are there. And sometimes, more especially in the later stages, the ditches can be deep. As Ibsen remarked, there is always a certain risk in being alive, and if you are more alive there is more risk. But the risk is not for nothing. It is from the checks, the failures, the catastrophes, that one learns. The dangers of the way are, in a sense, the way itself.

The second part of the chapter deals with destinations, the states of being to which the inward journey leads: the goals of the journey, in a fashion; but goals never reached, since, like the dangers, they are also and essentially the way.

The razor edge

The most obvious peril of the inward journey is of being swallowed up by the unconscious. Such swallowing up can be violent or it can be insidious. The violent form, the sudden bursting in of the depths, like a sea sweeping all before it, is a pathological situation from which most psychologically healthy men and women are likely to be immune. But there can be no certainty of this. A man who has lived a wholly extraverted life may be as completely vulnerable the other side of consciousness as he is at ease outwardly. It does not follow that he will be. But it may so happen.

The insidious form, the gradual engulfment, the almost imperceptible going over to the unconscious, is a situation much more frequently encountered. Everyone who makes the experiment is likely to feel at times, perhaps repeatedly, the subtle fascination of the inner world, drawing him to it. In the East such God-intoxicated men take to the woods, to the mountain caves, or to a shrine, living the life of the *sanyasi*, the man who has renounced the things of the outward life. In the West there is rarely such absolute divorce from concrete reality. But partial disappearance into the unconscious is by no means uncommon. Most people have met the man—or woman— with a slightly glassy look about the eyes, giving a vague impression of being otherwhere, typically a devotee of some esoteric cult, often hopelessly incapable in practical affairs. To make the withdrawal and never to make the return is a standing danger of the inward journey.

At the opposite extreme are those who start the experiment but fail to hold the reality of the inward life. A large proportion of modern, intelligent men and women probably come within this category. In their inmost being they have felt strange stirrings. They do not need to be told that life is more than appears on the surface. In time of emotional or religious stress, moments of illumination, moments of decision, inexplicable experiences come to them. But though they know there is something living in the depths, they never break through. In the end, the humdrum ordinariness of things again flows over them and they forget that it was ever otherwise. They are back once more in the provisional life; things are as they always were; day succeeds day; situation succeeds situation; they are part of the situation, and that is how life is. Unobtrusively, the unconscious has swallowed them from the other side.

In the early stages of the experiment in depth this drift back to banality is possible without great hurt. Later it becomes progressively more dangerous. As Jung says, if you are building a house and fall off the scaffolding when it is only three feet high you may get away with no more than a few bruises. If it is thirty feet high you are liable to be killed. The same is broadly true of psychological mistakes in general. At the beginning they do not matter greatly. The correction comes with relative mildness. The same is not true for the man who goes far. 'Whom the Lord loveth He chasteneth' is one of the fundamental laws of the world of the psyche. And mistakes are not forgiven because one did not know; any more than the ignorant tourist who strays on to an avalanche slope is forgiven because he is only an ignorant tourist.

Going over to the unconscious in one form or the other is the first and greatest danger of the razor edge. There is a second danger, more ordinary, less perilous, but in its way sufficiently lethal, which no one escapes: inflation, *hubris*, the state of being 'puffed up'.

Most people, quite naturally, take the first steps in the constructive technique in an attitude of mind not far removed from scepticism. To their mingled elation and alarm they begin to find that there is a strange intelligence at work the other side of consciousness, having direct bearing upon their inmost life. Intimations are coming to them in a fashion they never imagined possible. The course after that varies from one person to another but, sooner or later (perhaps so imperceptibly that they never notice it) their feet come off the ground and they are floating in a world of fantasy. They have discovered the great truth, learnt the hidden wisdom, know at last the secret of life, the philosopher's stone is theirs.

Ben Jonson, in *Volpone*, has a vivid characterization of the inflationary experience—which, needless to say, is not confined to those making the experiment in depth:

> . . . *I can feel*
> *A whimsy in my blood: I know not how,*
> *Success hath made me wanton. I could skip*
> *Out of my skin now, like a subtle snake,*
> *I am so limber.*

This condition of 'skipping out of one's skin' is characteristically depicted in dreams by an airy disregard of gravity. We find ourselves skimming lightly over the earth, flying through the upper air, perched on a cloud or in a balloon, taking haystacks at a jump, making marvellous and improbable flights in a plane. Sometimes the dreamer is naïvely delighted at this new freedom. Sometimes the dream intimates that such ignoring of gravity is perhaps not as good as it appears. In either case it is necessary to examine where in actual life this levitating act is taking place and get back to earth as expeditiously as may be. For *hubris* leads to *nemesis*, inflation ends in a crash. If a man is fortunate, this is no worse than a rueful realization that he has been making a sorry fool of himself. If unfortunate, then the assurance comes that one is Napoleon, the Moon Goddess, a modern Messiah. The 'whimsy in the blood' has become a madness.

This tendency to inflation is not confined to the early stages of the inward journey. It is a continuous risk. Particularly when a psychological experience is only partly realized we are especially liable to attribute its creative quality to our own extraordinary cleverness. Nothing does more to impair the experiment in depth than this over-weening conceit, this perpetual self-delusion. And the cure for it is usually little to our liking, more painful than the disease itself.

The only wisdom we can hope to acquire
Is the wisdom of humility: humility is endless.

At the opposite extreme to inflation is prostration, collapse. For a while a man goes about feeling semi-divine, sure of himself and sure of his way, ready to advise anybody and everybody on what they ought to do. Something comes to puncture his blown-out balloon of self-admiration; and suddenly he is nothing, less than nothing. For he is not back again where he started but deep in abysmal despair. There is reason for this. In the process of individuation the old ego-centred personality gradually disintegrates. When, after a period spent in the upper air, a man is returned to earth, he finds to his horror that the ordinary everyday person he once knew is no longer there. And he will wonder who he is and what he is doing, where he has been and where he is going, utterly lost.

Seen in retrospect, this running between the opposites of *hubris* and *nemesis* is a highly salutary discipline. From it we become aware of our limitations. Admittedly it is a drastic means of learning. A man can be jolted to pieces in the process. But for most people it is the only way of coming to a fundamental realization, absolutely necessary to wholeness, *viz.* that a man cannot create himself; he can only be created: and without the creative process is nothing.

Most people who make the experiment in depth will find themselves forever tottering between these opposites of the razor edge: one day happily drifting into the unconscious, over the pass, oblivious of the world; the next, back to banality, carried by the situation, caught by the *persona* and the *participation mystique*; one day up in the stratosphere, inflated to the eyebrows, feeling themselves the answer to prayer; the next, punctured, hopeless, collapsed. For those who follow the inward way, there is no sovereign specific for keeping one's head and keeping one's feet. It is something only to be learnt from experience; and to learn from experience it is necessary to be aware of what is happening. For this reason, at least during the early stages of the experiment in depth, there is much to be said for keeping a journal, a day-to-day record not only of the events the other side of consciousness, the dreams, visions, voices, but of one's ever-veering attitude: the inflation following what seemed at the time to be a great advance; the reading of a 'thriller' on a railway journey and the feeling afterwards that the experiment was utterly meaningless and absurd; a sudden realization of the complete emptiness of present-day existence, so that for the next few days everything except the inward reality seemed mere phantasm; a disastrous interview, in which one made a complete fool of oneself and only perceived afterwards that all touch with the outer life had been lost. For those who have the systematic persistence required, there is no better instruction in the difficult art of living the two worlds than a journal so kept.

Dangers of the constructive technique

In steering a middle way between the demands of inner and outer life, the constructive technique is an invaluable guide. The dreams, visions, voices warn of deviations from course, show new possibilities, float into consciousness the transforming symbols by which the necessary energy may be found. But the psycho-perceptive methods have their own perils, which need to be known.

The commonest error in applying the constructive technique is to accept the dreams, visions, voices as oracular: with disastrous consequences. Not only is this a total misunderstanding of their nature, but the attitude of irresponsibility on the part of consciousness falsifies the witness of the archetypal contents of the psyche. Whereas before they had wisdom, insight, knowledge beyond the reach of the conscious personality, they proceed to misinform, mislead, sap the man who has fallen into this degree of dependence. They may, indeed, assume control. It is possible to get into a condition where one is not able to turn off the vision, not able to stop the voices. It is possible to become so completely under the domination of the unconscious that no action can be taken, not even the slightest, until the omens have been consulted. This is a pathological condition, and most people do not run to such lengths once they have had a taste of what it involves. But it is by no means uncommon to remain at the stage where the multiplicity of the psyche is experienced much more vividly than its oneness: and over-dependence upon the psycho-perceptive techniques is one of the means by which this can come about.

A rather different form of misuse (but ending up in much the same quagmire) is to be found among those who, having a natural gift for the seeing of visions and the hearing of voices, simply indulge in this inward television set without taking any account of what these manifestations of the unconscious may mean. They paint pictures by the dozen, live more the other side of consciousness than this, but realize nothing. Such playing with the constructive technique has little to do with the hard way of individuation. Those giving themselves to this type of abuse are more in the nature of drug-addicts than anything else; and the eventual effect upon them is much the same. They become lost to the world and ultimately lost to themselves.

Closely linked to both these forms of irresponsibility is the tendency to drift off into a concealed or overt belief in magic. Most people when they discover that there are extraordinary forces at work in the psyche, extraordinary wisdom, uncanny prescience, wonder exactly where facts end and superstition begins. Some do not wait to wonder. The miraculous is all about them. Coincidences become proofs. Signs and omens abound. Spells and charms, the foretelling of the future, the reading of destiny, are embraced as dazzling possibilities. These and a dozen other absurdities pour in from every side. And they are rendered so much the more dangerous by the fact that they are not altogether absurd. Abutting upon the psychological is the para-psychological, the jungle of phenomena which is the field of psychical research. There are among these things fragments of a wild wisdom at present beyond our knowing. But these fragments are almost invariably mingled with the worst kind of rubbish. To discard the rubbish and keep the wisdom would be the ideal course. But few are able to follow it. They absorb both rubbish and wisdom into their system and all too easily the rubbish prevails. Magic seems to be a short cut, but it can become a short cut over the precipice into the sea.

There remain two other incidental dangers of the constructive technique, one of particular peril to women, the other to men.

In the approach to the other side of consciousness, women are far more energetic and enterprising than men. They acquire the psychological techniques with relative ease. They are unafraid, sometimes undiscriminating, in their application. It is as if, in the world invisible, they took on the rôle of explorer, adventurer, pioneer, characteristically assumed by men in the outside world. But while women are thus active, they normally lack the synthesizing, centering capacity, which can make something out of their eager forays. This capacity the man has. The natural consequence (in no way peculiar to the constructive technique but characteristic of all dealings with the world invisible) is that around suitable men, particularly those on whom the garment of the *charisma* has fallen, an esoteric circle forms. The experiment in depth becomes a cult. This is in no way to condemn the true master-student relationship, where those less gifted or experienced learn from others having special knowledge or insight. But between the teacher and the hierophant, the learner and the worshipper, there is a difference. As R. A. Knox has pointed out in his study *Enthusiasm*, the by-ways of religion are thickly strewn with such perversions, where the man invents the heresy and the women form the cult. The *eros* principle in woman which, rightly used, is a true basis of relationship, wrongly used becomes a dependence, a failure to take responsibility; and the true end of individuation—wholeness—is lost in a tangle of positive and negative projections.

The tendency of *logos* on the other hand (as also of the animus when it is in command) is to intellectualize the experiment in depth. Because he has intellectually grasped some psychological truth, a man is liable to assume that that truth is in some way accomplished in him. This is the most fatuous of self-deceptions. Intellectual grasp is valuable, but at the most it is only a beginning. Alone, it is without effect so far as psychological development is concerned.

Intellectualizing the experiment in depth is an especially insidious danger whenever (as here) communication is by the written word. In order to communicate, it is necessary, to some extent, to appeal to the intellect. Ideas, hypotheses, examples must be arranged in some kind of order, or they will never be understood. But it is all too easy for the understanding to halt at the stage of intellectual comprehension and not carry on to the point where comprehension really matters—the realization that these things actually are.

More generally, the intellect is the natural recourse of the ego against the deep unconscious out of which consciousness has fought its way. By analysing the inner experience, systematizing it, reducing it to 'nothing but' this or that, running in intellectual blinkers at all the critical points, a man can avoid any genuine realization, i.e. experiences which fundamentally affect his life. By such means he may be able to keep clear of everything that truly counts and yet talk about it with great acumen and apparent knowledge. But he will never have been shaken to the depths and by that he may know that he has never truly made the contact.

In sum, the central danger of the constructive technique is failure to be responsible. Instead of making one's own decisions, the forces of the unconscious are accepted as oracular. Instead of using the psycho-perceptive methods for the enlargement of consciousness they are treated as a built-in television set, a distraction; whereby one loses such consciousness as one had. Instead of the hard school of experience, the deceptively easy way of magic is preferred. Instead of making the experiment oneself, some charismatic person is transformed into the God-man who will do the great deed. Instead of the living acceptance of the experience, an intellectual formula is sought. As methods, these are spurious. Responsibility is the touchstone of the constructive technique.

The unclean spirits

The perils of the razor edge and the misuses of the constructive technique are general dangers. Everyone falls into them to some extent. No one is ever altogether free of them. But once a man is well engaged in the way, it is the specific encounters, the lions in the path of his own unique experiment, that are likely to occupy him most: none more than the autonomous complexes, the strange quasi-personalities in the depths.

Sufficient has been said in earlier chapters of the dangers and possibilities incidental to the encounter with the archetypal figures. Four simple maxims embody most of what is at present known: as far as possible, separate from the activity of these figures; get on to terms with them by means of the constructive technique; through the deep centre, enlist them in the service of the Self; in this service, work along with them to the fullest possible extent. It is true that enumerating these maxims is one thing, putting them into effect another. But the general line of action is evident.

In practice, however, the situation is neither so clear nor so uncomplicated as this might suggest. The archetypal figures are by no means the only autonomous complexes likely to be encountered. The 'internal society', as it has been aptly called, may well include split-off parts of the personality, earlier attitudes which from time to time seem to acquire a life of their own. Thus, the spoilt brat, the idealistic adolescent, the temporary soldier, the hard-boiled business man, are attitudes which may at times take over in a personality otherwise very differently constituted. These behaviour patterns, coming from earlier conditioning, may on occasion run the man their own way, possibly for months or years at a time. Especially is this true where life has been cut about by outer events—wars and the like—or lived in water-tight compartments.

To deal with these unassimilated parts of the personality, a rather different technique is required. As with the shadow, it is necessary first of all to become specifically aware of their existence; and then, by a process of rectification—confronting them continually with the facts—bring their habit patterns, values, outlook on life, into line with the total personality. Unless and until this is done, the 'internal society' can be a standing menace whenever a situation arises, reminiscent of earlier years, calling into renewed existence some residue of the past which for the time takes control.

Beyond this are still other figures, coming from a psychological no-man's-land where our knowledge is practically nil. The most that can be said here is that considerable evidence exists for believing that autonomous complexes, which in no way belong to an individual's wholeness, may invade the psyche. Children, for instance, sometimes appear to harbour dark presences which properly belong to their parents: and this may continue long after the stage of childhood has passed. In like manner, a family 'comes under a curse'; and for generations, perhaps, it is as if a sinister power had descended upon it. At times, entire peoples seem to be invaded by a malignant spirit. Underlying such phenomena as these there is the fundamental question of the nature of evil, the possible existence of spiritual entities deliberately working against wholeness.

For many people this aspect of inner experience is likely to savour too much of medieval superstition to be acceptable. Here, all that need be said is that, since we know nothing definitely, the best course is to keep an open mind and the maximum of conscious awareness. Then, if such phenomena are encountered they can be recognized; while if they are not encountered, nothing is lost. But it may well prove that, in the alien spirit, much that is most incomprehensible in the lives of individuals and of peoples may find its explanation.

Dangers of the return

In distinguishing certain dangers of the return, there is no intention of representing the withdrawal and return as totally distinct operations. They may be so, but with many people they are not. Under the term 'withdrawal', a variety of different kinds of action is comprised. One obvious kind is where a man goes apart by himself for some considerable period; and only when he has thus made a rather complete adjustment to the inner world attempts the return. This hermit type of withdrawal is not everyone's medicine. Another method is where the man continues in his normal way of life but gives far more attention than before to the other side of consciousness. This, probably, is the most usual type of 'withdrawal' for people of the present age. Yet another is where there is not so much a movement of 'withdrawal' followed by a movement of 'return' as a continuous process, a step in the 'withdrawal' being matched by a 'return' at that level. But however the return is made, there are certain typical difficulties and dangers of fairly general incidence.

The first comes from sheer exhaustion. Individuation is a hard journey. For a time one seems to make no progress, only the same continuous round of mistakes. The body often sickens. The old ego-centred personality is undermined. Energy fails. Lao-tse, in the *Tao te Ching*, having said in the preceding sections how marvellous, universal and life-giving is Tao, turns at the last to himself:

'All men are radiant with happiness, as if enjoying a great feast, as if mounted on a tower in spring. I alone am still, and give as yet no sign of joy. I am like an infant which has not yet smiled, forlorn as one who has nowhere to lay his head. Other men have plenty, while I alone seem to have lost all. I am a man foolish in heart, dull and confused. Other men are full of light; I alone am listless. I am unsettled as the ocean, drifting as though I had no stopping-place. All men have their usefulness; I alone am stupid and clownish. Lonely though I am and unlike other men, yet I revere the Foster-Mother, Tao.'

While some of this no doubt is in pursuance of Lao-tse's own precept ('when merit has been achieved, do not take it to yourself') much is straightforward honest description of the difficulty of the way itself, and the discordance with a world which has not found the way. In particular, there is the sense of isolation, of chilling unrelatedness, when one emerges from the *participation mystique*. Celia in *The Cocktail Party* comes to this realization:

> . . . *what has happened has made me aware*
> *That I've always been alone. That one always is alone.*
> *Not simply the ending of one relationship,*
> *Not even simply finding that it never existed—*
> *But a revelation about my relationship*
> *With everybody.*

The greatest danger of the return is that one may never find the strength and resolution to make it.

If this peril be passed, its opposite appears: the 'straight-line fallacy'. There is a tendency throughout the experiment in depth, in the withdrawal phase no less than in the return, to think that the shortest distance between two points is a straight line. Psychological development does not follow the straight line but goes by way of the snake, first this direction, then the other, indirectly. The reason for this is that individuation is a process of growth, in which the thing and its opposite must both be embodied. There is no short cut. Growth involves facing one's inferior side, living what previously one has refused to live.

Once the return phase is reached this all seems to be over. But it is not. The unconscious has now to be faced in a different form: the 'cake of custom' as Bagehot called it, the fixed ways of the tribe. Moreover, in making the return, different psychological functions and attitudes are needed from those which enabled the withdrawal to be made. The inferior side—personal and collective—has to be dealt with all over again. And for this there is no quick route.

Lying between the peril of exhaustion and the fallacy of straight-line action there is a dead middle way for which the Quakers have a fitting name: 'creaturely activity'. Once the immediate danger is past, once life appears to be proceeding normally, once the libido flows outward again, there seems no time for anything beyond the regular round. Cakes must be baked, rooms dusted, professional engagements kept, conferences attended, plays seen, books read, calls paid; God, the creative process, alone can wait.

Finally, when by one means or another a man starts the return journey in earnest, there is a double danger waiting for him, the more insidious because it appears so innocent. Almost inevitably the basic principle of non-attachment to results is lost to sight. He is back again in the 'real' world; and in the real world everything is judged by tangible performance, achievement, success. Automatically, the great value is projected upon whatever it is he is attempting to do. Without recognizing it, he is caught in an immense inflation. He alone has the secret. He alone can do the great deed and deliver the world. He is God. And, until such time as he recognizes what is happening, he will be torn to pieces in the process.

When this has happened a sufficient number of times and the man at last realizes the danger of projecting the great value upon what he is attempting to do, he is likely to go over to a deliberate non-attachment to results. But non-attachment has its own perils. All too easily it leads to what, in the ensuing account, the writer calls 'white stone alley'.

'In an especially vivid dream of the Friend, that in which the dragon-lizards appeared (cf. Chap. VI), one of these lizards threw at me a white stone—which went wide. Some ten years later I encountered that white stone again, having in the meantime completely forgotten this incident in the dream.

I was out walking in Wiltshire, indulging an amateur taste for prehistory. On the slopes of an early iron-age fort I picked up a round white stone (a kind of fossil, I believe, since I have found others elsewhere) which I thought might have been used as a sling-stone by the defenders. From that time the attraction of prehistory took on an altogether compulsive form. I wanted to do nothing else. If, as Whitehead says, religion is what a man does with his solitariness, prehistory for a while came near to being my religion. Whenever I was by myself I was working on some problem in prehistory, at the point where it impinged upon the psychological. Other, practical, issues were forgotten, set aside. And my white stone somehow symbolized it all.

Then I had a dream. I was in a country spot with the white stone, and I broke it in half, as one might a fruit. In the centre of it was a confused mass of small caterpillars. They came out by the thousand, growing in size and numbers as they came. In a minute they were all over a beautiful springing bush near by me and I felt that something bad had been let loose upon the world. But a fire came and burnt fiercely over all the bush. The bush itself was not in the least harmed. But the blight of caterpillars was burnt up.

For some reason, I did no work on this dream but simply looked at it in a spirit of detached curiosity. One day I told it to a friend. She said at once—"burning bush", have you ever heard of a burning bush before; "and the bush was not consumed". So then I came to my senses, looked up the third chapter of Exodus and realized what the dream might mean.[1] From that time "white stone alley" as I called it had no power over me. I remained interested, fascinated in a fashion, with prehistory: but it was a controlled fascination. I was not drawn off on that byway.

Some year or so later, in John Read's *Prelude to Chemistry*, I came upon this doggerel from one of the old alchemists.

> *After all this upon a day*
> *I heard my noble* Master *say,*
> *How that manie men patient and wise,*
> *Found our* White Stone *with Exercise;*
> *After that thei were trewlie tought,*
> *With great labour that Stone they Caught;*
> *But few (said he) or scarcely one,*
> *In fifteene Kingdoms had our* Red Stone.

Since then I have wondered whether the White Stone which the dragon-lizard threw at me in the dream those many years ago is not, as it were, part only of the great work, the kind that enlists the fascinating and energy-giving power of the archetypal forces but uses it simply to pursue some hobby or other distraction; while

---

[1] 'Now Moses . . . came to the mountain of God, even to Horeb. And the angel of the Lord appeared unto him in a flame of fire out of the midst of a bush: and he looked, and, behold, the bush burned with fire, and the bush was not consumed.'

it is the Red Stone, the bringing of the vision into the life of the world, that is the true *lapis philosophae*.'

'White stone alley' is, perhaps, the typical danger of the return, as seen more particularly from a man's standpoint: the *logos* seduction in its myriad forms, the solving of mysteries as against the living of the mystery. For a woman, it may be, the *eros* equivalent is where the supreme value is projected upon some relationship, real or imaginary; and this projection—upon husband, lover, children, friend, film-star, miracle-worker, prophet—assumes the place of wholeness as the meaning and purpose of life.

The life abundant

The inward journey is not made up solely of dangers. It has also its destinations, changes of attitude which transfigure the way. The experiment in depth leads to the 'life abundant' as it has sometimes been called, a different quality of being, growing out of but far removed from the ego-centred existence.

The nature of this life cannot readily be put into words. What is known of it has to be drawn from many sources—different faiths, different ages, different modes of living. But four main features may perhaps be discerned: a fundamental change in a man's attitude to outer events; a fundamental change in relationship to others; a fundamental change in the springs of action; and a fundamental change in ultimate perspective. Any attempt to describe these changes necessarily leans heavily upon the charity and understanding of the reader: but, as the counterpart of the dangers incurred, some account of them needs to be given.

The change in attitude to outer events Jung calls the experience of Tao; using, for lack of a Western equivalent, the undefinable Chinese word basic to Lao-tse's philosophy of life as expressed in the *Tao te Ching*.

Tao (as Jung conceives it) is the primal harmony, the underlying togetherness of things; perhaps what Rilke had in mind when he wrote to a young poet: 'Let life happen to you, believe me life is right.' The experience of Tao, expressed in its simplest form, is that, to the man with the right attitude, the right thing comes. It is the living perception of the 'different spiritual dimension' at work in the world. In a sense Tao is a counterpart of the Self, the whole spirit;

the Self being the harmony of the inner world of man, Tao the harmony of the outer world of phenomena. The Christian saying: 'All things work together for good to them that love God' is one expression of this experience.

The concept of Tao is obviously open to misunderstanding, to caricature, to exploitation. The idea of Kismet (as interpreted by the Western mind), the passive submission to destiny, is one of the misunderstandings. Candide's reiterated conviction that everything is for the best, in the best of all possible worlds, is one of the caricatures. The comfortable view (for those comfortably placed) that the rich are rightly rich and the poor rightly poor, God having accorded to each his appropriate station in life, is one of the many forms of exploitation of the underlying harmony. But Tao is not rendered the less real because it is readily traduced. Nietzsche makes an approximation to its true meaning, a typically dangerous and extreme approximation, in the Stoical formula *amor fati*: that a man should embrace his fate with open arms, however harsh that fate may at first appear. Dante's *'E la sua volontate è nostra pace'*, In his will is our peace, shows Tao in another, and infinitely greater, aspect: the peace that passeth understanding. The man of faith who sees the hand of God in all things and humbly seeks the guidance of God, saying, 'Though he slay me, yet will I trust in him', has a true vision of Tao. Put in the most general terms, it is the realization that when God, the creative process, and 'that of God in every man', the deep centre, work together, the right thing—the creative thing—comes to pass; outwardly no less than inwardly.

Tao, so understood, is neither resignation nor is it a facile optimism. It is the seeing of the things of this world in their eternal aspect, no less than in the form in which they outwardly appear. The man who has found his way to this insight knows that he both must and can trust the process, provided his own attitude is right. This does not mean that 'everything will work out nicely in the end'. The creative process is not necessarily comfortable. It is the right thing—which may or may not be the pleasant thing—that happens. There can be a black Tao—but nevertheless Tao. When Jesus prayed, 'O my Father, if it be possible, let this cup pass from me: nevertheless not as I will, but as thou wilt', and went to his torture and death, that also was Tao.

Closely linked to this living experience of the underlying harmony is the second main aspect of the life abundant: a fundamental change in the relationship to others, a relationship in depth.

Most contact between human beings is by way of the *persona*. We meet in masks, which means, in effect, not at all. Where relationship goes beyond the *persona*, to the ego level, it is a demanding, self-interested relationship, since the ego is by nature demanding and self-interested; while underneath, the *participation mystique* grips us, so that we are bound together as part of the situation, caught in the general flux. Or relationship may be archetypal, magical, essentially unreal, compounded of attraction and repulsion, love and hate, flickering and fluctuating as the projection waxes and wanes.

The relationship in depth is otherwise. It is to meet in the 'different spiritual dimension', in the 'things that are eternal', as well as, and no less than, in the outer world. Here the 'real being' in one person speaks to the 'real being' in the other. The Quaker phrase descriptive of the good life expresses this kind of relationship: 'to walk cheer-fully over the earth answering that of God in every man'. Instead of meeting at the *persona*, or the ego, or the archetypal level, deep answers to deep.

It is by such means, as Plato long ago perceived, that knowledge of the individuation process may be communicated. His famous answer to Dionysius, quoted by Toynbee, sets out the situation in unforgettable words. Dionysius had asked for a short statement, in writing, of the Platonic philosophy. Plato comments:

'. . . There is no written work of my own on my philosophy, and there never will be. For this philosophy cannot possibly be put into words as other sciences can. The sole way of acquiring it is by strenuous intellectual communion and intimate personal intercourse, which kindle it in the soul instantaneously like a light caught from a leaping flame; and, once alight, it feeds its own flame thenceforward.'

The 'light caught from a leaping flame' is one aspect of the rela-tionship in depth, an essentially intellectual aspect, intellectual in its best and deepest sense. When the relationship is not primarily in the realm of the intellect but of the emotions, new possibilities and new perils arise. Love between man and woman, bringing in as it does the instinctual drives, is at once the most intense and the most danger-ous of all the forms of relationship in depth. Here religion has spoken with a divided voice. The attempts made through the ages to find a formula governing this bond vary all the way from cults which prohibit to their adherents any relationship whatever between the sexes, including marriage, to cults which see in the sex act—with or without marriage—the greatest of sacraments. And there is no aspect of religion, or of life, so riddled with hypocrisy and lies.

The reason for this is not far to seek. What passes as love between man and woman can be many things. Promiscuity, possessiveness, misuse of sex for purposes of power, are all highly disintegrative. They tend to destroy the capacity for love, properly so called, and with it the chief force making for wholeness. Romantic projections, the over-valuing of sex as the great meaning of life, compulsive 'fallings in love', are all highly ambivalent. In one form or another they give over control to the archetypal forces. But love between man and woman that is the relationship in depth, the 'marriage of true minds', is a drawing to wholeness. Each calls up in the other the deep centre, the seed of the Self. It is by such love that the 'real being' grows and lives.

Seen in its wider aspect, the relationship in depth becomes the 'beloved community', the Universal Church, a fellowship in which manifoldly diverse personalities may become 'members one of another' in a manner wholly different from the *participation mystique*. In the *participation mystique* the relationship is that of the flock of sheep, or the wolf-pack, characteristically both. The fellowship in depth is different, and not merely in degree but in kind. It bears certain distinguishing marks, the marks of the 'gathered life', as the Quakers call it: the most complete individuality is maintained at the same time as a feeling of complete togetherness; long absence is not destructive of the fellowship, provided the individuals have continued in depth; there is no chasm between old and young, rich and poor, man and woman, or between those of different nationality, race, class or creed; the method of working together is contributive and cumulative, not competitive. It is the true social contract between man and man. Significantly, our present age has no word for what the New Testament attempted to express in the term *agape*. But without what that missing word stands for, individuals and societies alike disintegrate.

The relationship in depth is one especial aspect of a still more fundamental feature of the life abundant. Where the creative contact is made and held, a new kind of energy flows through the man.

Two forms of psychic energy we know well. There is the energy of the ego-centred life, self-regarding, engaging in action for the sake of the results accruing to the ego. A society so based has acquisitiveness as its central drive; money, possessions, prestige, power as its principal values. And there is the energy coming from the archetypal forces. A man so driven will not necessarily be self-regarding in his action. He may be completely disregardful of his own personal interests, a fanatic, a martyr even, for the cause. But archetypal energy is inherently ambivalent, as destructive as it is constructive, a dynamic which in the end is self-annihilating. The totalitarian ideologies—at their highest—tend to produce men and societies thus impelled.

The energy of the life abundant derives neither from the ego nor from the archetypes, as such; but from the MORE. The man who lives from the deep centre discovers a new dynamic. He is worked through, in a manner wholly different from archetypal possession. With the archetype in its primitive form all is fury, intensity, drive—the opposites in their extreme manifestation. The energy coming from the MORE is not subject to the law of the opposites. It is quiet. This is not to say that the man through whom the energy flows lives a life of placid ease. He has to strive and agonize at the conscious level, more so than before, perhaps; but he does not agonize for nothing. New and creative springs of action arise in the depths; and in the midst of his striving the man finds himself serving as a channel by which they find their way into life.

In treating of this energy and its manifestations, religion has again spoken with what sometimes appears to be a divided voice. Because the energy is quiet there has been a feeling in certain faiths against outward activity, in favour of the purely contemplative life. It is possible that for some people this may be the right course—the right mode of action, for them. They demonstrate, to the utmost of their capacity, that the world invisible is real: by living in it. But with many the life consisting of contemplation only is manifestly an escape, or not so much an escape as a seduction. They go over the pass, are swallowed up by the deep unconscious, and never come back. Their bodies remain in this world but their souls are otherwhere. In Toynbee's terminology, they make the withdrawal only, not the return.

The great religious leaders of all races and all ages have, in the main, set themselves against this world-forsaking course. They have taught that a man's personal salvation—his wholeness—is inextricably bound up with the salvation of all. As Chuang-tse says: 'The sages of old first got Tao for themselves, then got it for others.' Even the Buddha, as Toynbee points out, while preaching Nirvana as the goal of human existence, himself made the return to help others find the way. It would seem that to all those who achieve the whole spirit, by whatever means, there comes an imperative which says: 'I must be about my Father's business.'

What form this business takes necessarily varies from one man to another, from one age to another. The emphasis may be predominantly inward, or predominantly outward, predominantly practical, or predominantly in the realm of the intangible. But regularly it has this special characteristic: it brings the 'different spiritual dimension' into the space-time world. Toynbee, in his analysis of the ways in which men at various times have sought to find a new vision in their 'time of troubles', sees the process which he calls Transfiguration as the one true return among the many deceptive and false.

'The aim of Transfiguration is to give light to them that sit in darkness and to make the darkness comprehend this light that is shining in it; and this aim is pursued by seeking the Kingdom of God in order to bring its life, which is "the light of men", into action—or rather into visibility, since God is in action always and everywhere—in the field of life in This World.'

Such is the essential quality of the energy coming from the creative contact. It begins, not by reshaping society, but by reshaping the man. It bears the marks of the MORE—the enhancement of truth, of love, of creativity, of personality. It is not attached to results as such: right action is what it seeks, not success as ordinarily understood. Above all, it persists. The sound and fury typical of archetypal possession is absent. But, long after the archetypal fit has gone over to its opposite, or collapsed altogether, creative action continues.

There remains the fundamental change in ultimate perspective. Of all the destinations of the inward journey, the first and the last is the whole spirit, the man at one with the MORE. This is not to say that wholeness is achieved.

For most of us, this is the aim
Never here to be realized;
Who are only undefeated
Because we have gone on trying.

But the seeking of wholeness brings with it a new insight.

When a man makes the discovery that, beyond the subjective meanderings of the conscious mind, there is a realm of experience utterly different from anything he had previously imagined, his view of life gradually changes. He learns that the world invisible is not merely a poetical phrase, but a strange kind of fact he can no longer ignore. He finds that what he is, and what he does, depends to a great extent on what is happening in this other world. As and when he comes upon the archetypal forces, discovers the deep centre, makes the creative contact with the MORE, undergoes the 'inward transforming experience', he has borne in upon him that consciousness is but part of a greater being—the whole spirit, the Self—the bulk of which (to use words not adapted for such description) exists in another realm. To some extent, in however fragmentary a fashion, he begins to live the immortal life now.

And when this happens, death is seen in a different perspective. As he comes to realize, only his relatively insignificant ego-consciousness is bound up with the material world; and that, increasingly, only in part. When this tie with the material world is broken, it seems, on balance, far more probable that the Self survives than that this change of state in a relatively small part should wipe everything out. In other words, from sheer factual experience, those who in one form or another make the creative contact are led to conclude that continuation, immortality, survival—however it may be conceived—is not only the 'nobler hypothesis' (as it is sometimes called) but by far the more likely.

Seen in this changed perspective, the whole panorama of human existence takes on new meaning. What is now man was formerly an animal, a creature prompted solely by instinct. As animal, he maintained direct contact with the creative power—at the unconscious level. Unhesitatingly he obeyed the promptings set in him, at one with his creator. Some million or half-million years ago that direct

227

link with the creative was broken. The coming of consciousness (represented mythologically as the eating of the fruit of the tree or the knowledge of good and evil, the Fall, the Original Sin) brought man freedom: but a meaningless freedom, cut off from the primal source. Since then, by way of the great religious insights, he has been groping his way back; seeking, this time at the conscious level, to renew the at-one-ment with the creative power.

As and when this new at-one-ment comes about, an unprecedented situation arises. Formerly the creative power working upon man was a one-way process only. Now man is in a position to respond; feebly, it is true, the means of making the creative contact in its fullness yet to be learnt. But what was formerly a one-way process has become two-way. It is not only the MORE acting upon man, but man reacting to the MORE. The experiment in depth (on which, in one form or another, mankind has been engaged for, perhaps, these last five thousand years) is a first step in this two-way process. What eventually it may lead to, no one can tell. But this much, at least, seems likely. That process which, in its chequered course, has produced living matter from the dust, consciousness from living matter, has again leapt: from consciousness to the Self—a new kind of being, transforming life, transcending death.

Dangers and destinations, taken together, give some impression of the inward journey—perhaps too grim an impression. They stress, of necessity, its hard and strenuous side, the strife between the opposites rather than the calm of their resolution. In doing this they tend to omit something altogether essential: that feature of the pilgrimage which John Bunyan called the Delectable Mountains, the spirit of delight that haunts the way.

St. Francis of Assisi is the most universally loved of all the saints, largely because he encountered and communicated that spirit. And he is not the only one. The joyous insight of Julian of Norwich, for whom the words of God came 'merrily' to her mind; the 'walking cheerfully over the earth' of the early Quakers, who discovered 'the sweet loving freshness of it'; the poet's vision of 'the light that never was, on sea or land': these are as authentically part of the inward journey as any of the darker and harsher aspects.

Throughout the Christian Gospels the key word, continually recurring, is 'Behold'. The good news is not primarily of hardship

and of suffering, but of creative experience, an immense enlargement
and enrichment of life. No aspect of the experiment in depth is more
characteristic than this perceiving of everything, the inward world
and the outward world alike, with eyes that, for the first time, see.
That the way is hard is certain. But no less certain is its wonder.
'Behold I make all things new.'

XI

PROJECT FOR A WAY THROUGH

So much for the dangers and destinations of the experiment in depth. The destinations, for most of us, are distant: the dangers, unpleasantly at hand. In using the constructive technique to make the withdrawal-and-return, is there no route that the ordinary intelligent man or woman can follow with reasonable chance of coming through?

To this question the sole answer at present is that we do not know. The way opened up by Jung was evolved essentially for use by a professionally qualified analyst in the treatment of mental sickness, not for use by psychologically healthy men and women seeking a new way of life.[1] How to adapt the insights gained from the psychology of the unconscious to the difficult and dangerous art of living life whole is a problem yet to be solved. Jung, in one of his essays, looks towards a future when analytical psychology is 'freed from its clinical origins and ceases to be a mere method for treating the sick'. But, he adds, 'between the realization of this hope and the actual present there lies an abyss over which no bridge is to be found. We have yet to build it stone by stone.'

As it happens, a quarry for these stones does perhaps exist. Over the last three hundred years the Society of Friends—the Quakers, as they are more usually called—have been consistently practising their own version of the experiment in depth. Beginning in the 'time of troubles' of the Commonwealth period in England, this body of devoted men and women used the psycho-perceptive methods—dreams, visions, voices—to such good effect that they came upon

[1] This is not to say that Jung has drawn his material exclusively from cases of mental sickness. On the contrary, more than any other depth psychologist, perhaps, he has worked with people high above the normal in psychological development; and, more than any other, he has been concerned with the wider aspects of his discoveries.

most of the principal discoveries: the transforming symbols ('openings', 'leadings', 'concerns'); the deep centre (the inward light, the seed, 'that of God in every man'); the individuation process (the 'inward transforming experience of God'); the fellowship-in-depth ('meeting one another in the things that are eternal'); and the return—action in the outer world conceived as an integral part of the spiritual journey. They also came upon the shadow and the archetypal forces: but in the main saw them in their negative aspect only, as dark spirits. Occasionally (as in the tragedy of James Nayler) they suffered from archetypal inroads which came near to wrecking the Society. They learnt what it meant for a man to be 'dark and much out'. Also, from time to time, the tendency to identify with the *persona* of a 'peculiar people'—'the Harmless and Innocent People of God, called Quakers'—carried with it the natural consequence: a corresponding loss of the creative contact and consequent archetypal possession.

Broadly speaking, however, these ten generations of Quaker experience do furnish certain indicia of how responsible men and women, in good psychological health, can effectively make the experiment in depth without the help of a professional analyst. When Jung's work and Quaker practice are set side by side, it is evident that they complement one another to a remarkable degree, each being strong where the other is weak, and *vice versa*. Jung's great contribution is the discovery of the archetypal forces and, especially, the possibility of these otherwise highly ambivalent powers becoming integrated into the whole spirit, the Self. The great contribution of the Society of Friends is that of a way of life based upon inward experience. It is Jung's contribution that brings the fire, the intensity. It is the Quaker contribution that brings the steadiness, the light, the cohesion and discipline of a fellowship, a sense of vocation, an inner strength leading to action in the world free from attachment to results. By combining the two contributions, the fire of the one, the fellowship of the other, it may be that a means of making the experiment in depth can be worked out appropriate to the ordinary intelligent man or woman of today.

This is far from implying that anything in the nature of a definite method can be prescribed. We have not as yet a fraction of the knowledge necessary for the charting of the inward journey. But something in the nature of a sketch-map, a project for a way through, is perhaps feasible—at least as a series of hypotheses to be put to the test.

The Start

For men and women in good psychological health one of the greatest difficulties in the experiment in depth is to get started. The neurotic patient is pitchforked into the process, willy-nilly. The healthy do not know where or how to begin. One may record one's dreams and make spasmodic attempts at analysing them. One may try active imagination, painting and writing from the unconscious, and get puzzling and inconclusive results—or no results at all. One may read a book or so, discuss it with others, have a vague feeling that somehow, somewhere, there is something in it. But there is no break-through, the process never comes alive. As William James points out, the first stage in the process is the realization that 'there is *something wrong about us* as we naturally stand'. Without this realization, nothing happens.

In such circumstances there are three things that a man does well to try. The first is to look closely at his own attitude, to ask himself why it is that he is undertaking this adventure. If he is approaching the other side of consciousness in a casual spirit he is likely to get a casual response; if in a negative spirit, a negative response. This does not mean that the unconscious is simply a reflection of the conscious attitude. It means rather that this is a living process or it is nothing. Merely going through the motions of the constructive technique is meaningless. There must be a certain positive energy mustered. Whether this energy comes from inner or outer need, from a spirit of reverence, a spirit of discovery, a spirit of scepticism even—provided it is positive scepticism, the scepticism that seeks—is relatively unimportant. But unless the attitude is energically adequate, the process cannot start.

The second recourse consists in 'searching the scriptures'. The scriptures may be the Christian scriptures, the Buddhist scriptures, the Indian scriptures, the Chinese scriptures, or any others that genuinely deal with experience of the numinous. What is essential is that they shall be 'searched', not merely read; and searched, as George Fox put it, in the spirit in which they were written. An aid towards this is to take them in as near as can be managed to the original tongue—Greek, Latin, Hebrew, Sanskrit, Chinese. A Greek or Latin testament can throw light on the Parables of the Kingdom of Heaven, or the Sermon on the Mount, to be obtained in no other way: and if one has 'small Latin and less Greek', so much the better. Even a modern translation, if it is a good one, can renew the meaning. Significance that has disappeared from the familiar text, because we know the cadences too well, comes back when the words themselves are strange. And it is not only a deeper understanding that is gained by this means. It is the something that goes on beneath and beyond the understanding—the 'inward transforming experience', the 'intersection of the timeless with time', the realization of the 'different spiritual dimension' at work in life.

The third recourse makes rather greater demands. Certain people are so built that extraordinary circumstances—extraordinary in the highly artificial conditions of modern life—are necessary to enable them to discover their multiplicity and depths. T. E. Lawrence recounts his experience of how extreme exhaustion revealed the 'others'.

'Step by step I was yielding myself to a slow ache which conspired with my abating fever and the numb monotony of riding to close up the gate of my senses. I seemed at last approaching the insensibility which had always been beyond my reach: but a delectable land: for one born so slug-tissued that nothing this side fainting would let his spirit free. Now I found myself dividing into parts. There was one which went on riding wisely, sparing or helping every pace of the wearied camel. Another hovering above and to the right bent down curiously, and asked what the flesh was doing. The flesh gave no answer, for, indeed, it was conscious only of a ruling impulse to keep on and on; but a third garrulous one talked and wondered, critical of the body's self-inflicted labour, and contemptuous of the reason for effort. . . . Telesius, taught by some such experience, split up the soul. Had he gone on, to the furthest limit of exhaustion, he would have seen his conceived regiment of thoughts and acts and feelings ranked around him as separate creatures; eyeing, like vultures, the passing in their midst of the common thing which gave them life.'

Most people will not need to proceed to such lengths to find that the psyche is something more than the conscious ego. A solitary day in the mountains or on the moors; an all-night vigil, alone, far from human habitation, where one can look at the stars; a pilgrimage off the beaten track, to some chapel or shrine 'where prayer has been valid'; a few days' retreat in solitude: these are all means of coming to know more about oneself than can be seen or heard in the bustle of the street and the roar of the traffic.

William James, in a letter written to his wife, tells of his experience during a night passed on the slopes of Mt. Marcy:

> 'I spent a good deal of it in the woods, where the streaming moonlight lit up things in a magical checkered play, and it seemed as if the Gods of all the nature-mythologies were holding an indescribable meeting in my breast with the moral Gods of the inner life. . . . The intense significance of some sort, of the whole scene, if one could only *tell* the significance; the intense inhuman remoteness of its inner life, and yet the intense *appeal* of it; its everlasting freshness and its immemorial antiquity and decay; . . . In point of fact, I can't find a single word for all that significance, and don't know what it was significant of, so there it remains, a mere boulder of *impression*. Doubtless in more ways than one, though, things in the Edinburgh lectures [1] will be traceable to it.'

For many people this deliberate facing of the depths is the turning-point. Reading and talking and thinking about such things keeps the experiment in the sphere of the intellect. To spend a night on a hill-top, alone, is another matter.

Each of these methods has its special relevance. Taking account of one's attitude is an essential first step: for unless a man's attitude is one of high seriousness, a realization that what he is doing is not an intellectual pastime but a matter of life or death, the techniques will tell him nothing.

The searching of the scriptures has a purpose complementary to this. The men who wrote these scriptures knew whereof they wrote. It is true that their expressions are those of a pre-scientific age. Their knowledge of the nature of the physical universe is immeasurably surpassed by any modern schoolboy. But their knowledge of the psychological facts of life, and how man needs to deal with those

---

[1] Published under the title *The Varieties of Religious Experience.*

facts, has a wisdom in it we have lost. That is why it is necessary to search; not to pick upon the errors—which are many—but to rediscover the underlying truths.

The Mt. Marcy method brings to a focus some three or four predisposing factors. The unusual effort called for lowers the threshold between consciousness and the unconscious, there is an *abaissement du niveau mental*. For the while we step out of the artificiality of urban existence and come a degree nearer to the natural man, the state of being where wind and weather, heat and cold, hunger and thirst, earth and sky are closer to us. At the same time, we are less distracted by irrelevancies. Normally our attention is diverted, our libido dispersed, by the thousand-and-one things about us. Let these thousand-and-one things be withdrawn and the inner world has a chance of coming into its own. Especially is this so when, in some fashion, 'the dark backward and abysm of time' is visibly and invisibly around us: as on a mountain, in the woods, at night. But the essence of the Mt. Marcy method is that it takes a man out of the intellectual or sentimental miasma in which most of our seeking is otherwise done. It is a first earnest of the direct approach to the other side of consciousness. It is a tentative, partial, tacit recognition that the world invisible may be real.

These are all possible ways of starting the experiment. None is certain. In the end, probably, it is the 'insoluble problem' that sets the process in motion. Whether we recognize it or not, as life proceeds, every departure from the basic principle 'To thine own self be true' registers in the personal unconscious. The things we have left undone which we ought to have done, the things we have done which we ought not to have done, pile up and take tangible form in the outer world. There comes upon us the problem from which there is no way out, only a seemingly impossible way through: the kind of problem which a man has to solve himself on or go under in the struggle. It is when the forces of the unconscious thus enter palpably into life that the experiment in depth truly begins.

The working group and the deep centre

Once the disintegrative forces of the unconscious are felt pulling at a man, how is he to hold? First, foremost, and all the time, by recognizing these forces for what they are: the forces of life. Often they seem inimical, often utterly destructive; and they can easily become that. But they are not that alone. It is only by the breaking up of the established pattern that the process of individuation becomes possible. On the other hand, individuation is not likely to come of itself. From the very outset anyone undertaking the experiment in depth is well advised to do everything in his power to bring into operation two great integrative factors: the fellowship of a working group; and the contact with the deep centre.

Group relationship may take various forms, each of which has its value, all of which are to be sought. There is the working group of some half-dozen men and women who meet for discussion, research, exchange of experience, or whatever other activity enables them best to form a compact company for the inward journey. There is the 'strenuous intellectual communion' between two people— husband and wife, brother and sister, friend and friend—not necessarily always the same two, not necessarily of the same or of the other sex, in which the exchange goes far deeper than is possible in the working group. There is the wider relationship; men and women engaged in the experiment who meet only occasionally, at long intervals, and then perhaps only for a short while. Such meetings have a special quality in that they bring the realization, as nothing else can, of the process operating independently in others. And there is the relationship of the return, the banding together of like-minded people in the attempt to bring into the life of the world the vision they have found.

Needless to say, such group relationship has little virtue so long as it remains merely at the *persona* level. Everything depends upon the relationship being made in depth. In practice, if a small number of responsible men and women meet together in the attempt to exercise their eyes, ears and understanding the other side of consciousness, the result is seldom banal. One of the surprising features of a group so formed is how the members of it grow together in a special kind of fellowship. This does not mean that all is harmony. Projections, positive and negative, there will certainly be. But if these projections are brought into the open, instead of being hidden away in the normal fashion, they lead to an understanding—of oneself and of others—to be achieved by no other means. And the characteristic quality of such a group is that projections can actually be brought into the open and seen for what they are.

A fellowship of this kind is of inestimable value. By talking to others of the activity the other side of consciousness a man is able both to separate from that activity and, by so doing, realize it better. At the same time, he is able to see his own experience against experience similar to, yet different from, his own: so that the all-too-familiar pair of opposites—that he is mad or that he is God—are less likely to wreck him. The working group, moreover, gives stability. It helps to prevent the falling back into banality which threatens as soon as the first flurry of archetypal excitement is past. Still more important, it provides a firm hold on outer reality, a solid basis of human contact, against the disintegrating pull of the unconscious. Above all, the working group at its best brings with it that mysterious quality of being we inadequately call love: the love that is compassion in its literal sense, the suffering, the bearing, the sustaining, the undergoing, together. Such love is the drawing to wholeness, within a man and between men.

On the other hand, a working group cannot help a man much, or he the group, so long as he is psychologically adrift. Unless and until a man finds and holds to the deep centre he is at the mercy of the archetypal forces. There is no infallible specific for discovering the deep centre, but there are four main ways by which, in practice, it may be found.

The first is by the way of faith. The truly religious man who sets out to follow the injunction, 'Ask, and it shall be given you; seek, and ye shall find; knock, and it shall be opened unto you', knowing what it is he seeks—the 'alone' in himself by which the 'flight to the Alone' may be made—does not usually ask, seek, knock in vain. But he definitely needs to know that it is the deep centre he is seeking—the seed of the Kingdom of Heaven within a man. Otherwise he can be merely lost in a maze of projections.

A second main way is Plato's 'strenuous intellectual communion' with someone who has already made the discovery: the 'light caught from a leaping flame' which 'once alight feeds its own flame thenceforward'. This, at first, seems the simplest method of all. Actually it is not. Platos and their like are not everywhere to be found. Moreover, the one seeking must himself be ready to catch the spark: for it is no more than a spark that passes and a spark is easily quenched. It is a simple enough matter for a man to infect others with fanatical enthusiasm for some ideological creed. Archetypal projections are readily transmitted. The 'inward transforming experience' is not. Yet, in a working group which in some measure has found the fellowship-in-depth, this mutual kindling of the flame can happen, though none alone has more than a feeble glimmer.

The third main way is that of the responsible man: the man who holds to something deep in himself and is not deflected by every passing mood; the man who, ignoring his own self-interest, seeks to do what is right; the man who, faced with a task beyond his strength, feels himself inadequate and afraid, yet finds the courage to carry on. Whether he knows it or not, these things he does by means of the deep centre. Like Marcus Aurelius he has found the age-old wisdom: 'Look well into thyself; there is a source of strength which will always spring up if thou wilt always look there.' The difficulty lies in the last six words. We seldom want to look. In practice, the most direct means of coming upon the deep centre is when a man finds himself being carried away by a torrent of anger, fear, despair, petulance, desire. If at such time he seeks the deep centre, seeks with his whole strength, he will discover the something in the depths to which he can hold. The flood of emotion will not necessarily diminish in force. It may become more violent. But the man is not overwhelmed. As Julian of Norwich puts it: 'He said not, Thou shalt not be tempested, thou shalt not be travailed, thou shalt not be distressed: but he said, Thou shalt not be overcome.'

This recourse, be it admitted, is not as simple as it may appear. The man may have to struggle hard to get down to the deep centre; he may have difficulty in finding it; he may not be able to hold to it when found: but if once he truly makes the contact (and he may know it by the inner peace it brings) it will never again be altogether lost.

The fourth and most generally valid way of all is the continued anguished search which, in the end, comes upon the transforming symbol:

> But (when so sad thou canst not sadder)
> Cry:—and upon thy so sore loss
> Shall shine the traffic of Jacob's ladder
> Pitched betwixt Heaven and Charing Cross.

Characteristically, it is when a man is at the end of his strength and endurance, but nevertheless holds on, that the transforming symbol floats into consciousness. It is here that the constructive technique can be invaluable. The traffic of Jacob's ladder, if it is to exercise its effect, needs to be perceived and realized. Without the inward eye, the inward ear, the inward understanding, Charing Cross remains Charing Cross. In themselves, it is true, the psycho-perceptive methods amount to very little. Everything depends upon how they are used. A man may have the most marvellous dreams and visions, but get nowhere with them. Conversely, a man who has never looked at a dream, never had a vision, never heard a voice, may nevertheless have a firm hold upon the deep centre: and it is the hold upon the deep centre that matters, not the methods. But put to their right use, the dreams, visions, voices of the constructive technique, and the transforming symbols so channelled into consciousness, constitute the surest means of access to the 'germinal higher part' for the man or woman who persists.

It is the great strength of the Society of Friends that their Meeting for Worship to some extent brings together all four of these approaches. In form, the Meeting consists of a handful of men and women, often less than a score, rarely exceeding fifty or a hundred, who sit together for about an hour, for the most part in silence, in an ordinary room or hall. The silence is broken only if someone in the Meeting feels 'called to the ministry'. When this happens, the one so stirred normally speaks, for some few minutes perhaps, often less, of something that has come to him out of the silence. He may be followed by one or two others, equally brief, typically taking up the same thread and continuing it.

When it is successful (which, needless to say, is not always) the Quaker Meeting for Worship is indubitably a method by which the deep centre is experienced and the experience transmitted. How this comes about is at present a matter of surmise rather than knowledge. Partly, no doubt, it is due to the concerted seeking in silence. Since there is little to distract attention, the libido is free for inward exploration, for the discovery of the Kingdom. Partly it is attributable to the fact that in such Meetings there may be at least one or two present—possibly a number—who in their lives have gone over to the deep centre. These, as it were, can help to 'take the meeting down'. It is not only in speech, but also in the silence, that

Plato's 'light from a leaping flame' can pass. Partly it may derive from the fellowship-in-depth of a 'gathered' Meeting. This sense of togetherness is a characteristic feature. In a Meeting that has 'centred down' there is simultaneously the feeling of the most complete unity and the most complete individuality. Equally characteristic is the ministry itself. The call that comes to speak in the Meeting for Worship is experienced (at least by some) as wholly different in kind from ordinary speaking, being marked by a trepidation, a pounding of the heart, a feeling akin to dread, even to people thoroughly habituated to public address. At its best, as in George Fox's day, the ministry has the character of the transforming symbol, bringing to the common fund words and images which make possible a new direction of energy. The fact that, whether or not he speaks, everyone in a Quaker Meeting has responsibility for the ministry, is perhaps the most potent factor of all. In a Meeting where no word is said there is still this silent concentration of responsibilities, which in the end may be more effective than any speech.

By whatever means the deep centre is discovered, the great and abiding problem is to hold to it. Repeatedly there is a regression to the ego-centred condition. Repeatedly some earlier attitude comes up and for a while we are that attitude. It needs only a word or a thought or a situation to arise, and we are caught again in some entrenched habit of the past. By tracking down the wrong attitude something can be done towards correcting it. But in the end, the only means by which consciousness can hold to the deep centre is by the continuous discovery and re-discovery that any other way of life has become impossible. The man who passes beyond the ego-centred, archetypally-impelled life to the life lived in depth, is committed.

> These are only hints and guesses,
> Hints followed by guesses; and the rest
> Is prayer, observance, discipline, thought and action.
> The hint half guessed, the gift half understood, is Incarnation.
> Here the impossible union
> Of spheres of existence is actual,
> Here the past and future
> Are conquered, and reconciled,

PROJECT FOR A WAY THROUGH

Where action were otherwise movement
Of that which is only moved
And has in it no source of movement—
Driven by daemonic, chthonic
Powers.

The shadow and the archetypal images

The fellowship of the working group, the hold on the deep centre, are the great integrative factors in the experiment in depth. The shadow and the archetypal images—the 'daemonic, chthonic powers'—are experienced as disintegrative: the Adversary, the Villains in the Villa. Some people, it is true, welcome the archetypes with open arms, for the energy and insight they bring: but all too often it is a dubious embrace, the Faustian compact. Who sups with the archetypes needs a long spoon—especially if he thinks to use them for purposes of power. On the other hand, as already seen, provided they are dealt with rightly, the constellation of these images is in itself a great integrative feat. By this means a man is able to make contact with the unconscious on a human level, as it were. And eventually it is the shadow and the archetypal forces which help to constitute the Self. But, to repeat what has already been many times said, until a right relationship has been made with them, the archetypes are ambivalent. It is in attempting to deal with these forces—or in neglecting to deal with them—that a man is most likely to come to grief.

There is no universally valid prescription for effecting a right relationship with the shadow and the archetypal forces. It is here that each must make, as best he can, his own unique experiment in living. But there is here, also, a great possibility to be explored which, for some at least, may totally transform the situation.

Among widely different peoples, from the Greeks of the classical period to North American Indians of the present day, there is record of a helpful figure the other side of consciousness. This figure is variously named: it is Hermes, the messenger of the Gods: it is the *psychopompos*, the wayshower, the conductor of souls, as Virgil conducted Dante in the infernal regions; it is the *daimon* in which Socrates placed his trust, the figure of the *genius* known to the Romans, the 'angel of the Lord' of the Hebrew scriptures, the 'guardian angel' of Christian belief. Orpheus, Krishna, Buddha,

Jesus, have all been represented in this form, either as shepherd or some similar guiding figure. Raphael in the Apocrypha, Chidher in the Koran, are of this kind. Mithras, the god of light of the ancient Persians, later the tutelary deity of the Roman legions, originally meant 'Friend'.

This image of the Other, the Stranger, the Wayshower, the figure ahead on the path, repeatedly occurs in mythology, folk-lore, literature, dreams and visions.

> *Who is the third who walks always beside you?*
> *When I count, there are only you and I together*
> *But when I look ahead up the white road*
> *There is always another one walking beside you*
> *Gliding wrapt in a brown mantle, hooded*
> *I do not know whether a man or a woman*
> *—But who is that on the other side of you?*

Socrates had such faith in this friendly presence that, when the voice did not counsel otherwise at the time of his trial, he concluded with perfect confidence that death was not the extinction it seemed to be, but a transition. Henry Suso, the fourteenth-century mystic, found that it was a figure of this kind that impelled him to make the return. Modern men and women, particularly those engaged in some form of creative work, often encounter this figure. Normally it is of the same sex as the person, but with the sex factor unemphasized, an essentially androgynous image. The chauffeur of *The Family Reunion*, the 'guardian' of *The Cocktail Party*, are, in their different ways, of this kind. In *Birth of a Poem* (printed as an appendix to R. E. M. Harding's *An Anatomy of Inspiration*) Robert Nichols tells in detail of the lively exchange between himself and the 'Artificer' during some twenty minutes of intense creative action. Rilke's Angel is a like presence, but superhuman rather than human in its stature and power.

It is not only in creative work that this figure appears. Wherever the other side of consciouness has a chance of coming through, the Friend may be found: as with the 'one more than could be counted' that accompanied at times the Shackleton expedition to the Antarctic; and the 'friendly companion' to whom Frank Smythe, climbing alone at 28,000 feet, went so far as to offer part of his food.[1] Above all, the dreams, visions, voices reveal this figure. The 'Friend' described in the dream series given in Chapter VI is clearly of this type. So also is the 'friendly author' in the Villains in the Villa dream, he who held the second staircase; and the 'onlooking part' in The Black Madonna.

With some people, at least, the coming to terms with the archetypal world is made largely with the help of such an intermediary. It is the *entelechia*, the informing spirit, the archetype of the way. This does not mean that consciousness is justified in giving over responsibility to such a figure. To do so is to invite possession, with the usual ambivalent result. Daimonic can easily become demonic. But taken as the guide, the guardian, the one who knows the route, *consciousness always assuming the ultimate responsibility*, this figure of the Friend may prove of inestimable comfort and assurance in treading the knife-edge, labyrinthine way between the opposites:

Where you must move in measure, like a dancer.

Above all, the Wayshower the other side of consciousness can be invaluable in helping the man to get on to terms with the autonomous complexes—the shadow, the anima-animus, the Wise Old Man, the Great Mother and the rest—thereby converting the archetypal horde into a team. Moreover, as depicted in Dürer's *Melencolia*, it is the waiting angel that brings the transforming symbols, the means of individuation. For anyone undertaking the experiment in depth it may well be that the decisive moment comes when, in the quiet of the night or the newness of the morning, he makes contact with the Friend. There is perhaps no single feature of the inward journey more in need of research and clarification than the means by which this figure may be found.

The Self and the MORE

Once the shadow and the archetypal figures are enlisted in the

---

[1] 'After leaving Eric a strange feeling possessed me that I was accompanied by another. . . . This "presence" was strong and friendly. In its company I could not feel lonely, neither could I come to any harm. It was always there to sustain me on my solitary climb up the snow-covered slabs. Now, as I halted and extracted some mint cake from my pocket, it was so near and so strong that instinctively I divided the mint into two halves and turned round with one half in my hand to offer it to my "companion".'—F. S. Smythe: *Camp Six*.

service of the Self, the whole situation in the psyche changes. The powers that previously disputed with the ego for mastery are now, as it were, grouped with the ego around the deep centre, united in a common aim. As this new relationship becomes confirmed, they change in character. The shadow is still chthonic: but in the earthy rather than the evil sense, the part of the man linked to the primeval past, in whom the natural rhythm of life still moves. And the archetypal figures bring to the common fund—in such measure as the calibre of the man permits—their characteristic energy, wisdom and strength: so that a creative quality, such as he has not known before, flows through him.

This is far from meaning that the man is re-made overnight. He has to learn and relearn the fundamental conditions of this life. First, that consciousness must not seek to use the Self for its own power or prestige. If it does, the creative contact is lost. Second, that consciousness must never relinquish its right and duty to take its own decisions in all matters where consciousness is directly involved. If it does, the Self may collapse or become ambivalent. Consciousness plays its part in the forming and firming of the whole spirit not by abdicating but by using its faculties to the full. Third, that without love the Self cannot hold together. Why this should be, what exactly we mean by love even, are questions to which we have no satisfactory answer. But empirically, that is how it is. There can be knowledge, intellect, genius even: but without love there is no integration.

And the great source of love is the creative contact with the MORE. As the experiment proceeds, from his failures no less than from his successes, a man learns certain things necessary for his psychical health and well-being. In particular, once he has gone some distance on the inward journey, he will know that there is one thing above all he needs to do. On every occasion that presents itself, from facing death in the dark to waiting for the bus, from being caught in a sterile patch to being carried away by panic fear, he who makes the experiment in depth should consciously, deliberately, with all his strength, centre.

How best to do this each must find in his own way. To anyone who knows what it is for a Quaker Meeting to 'centre down', then it is to do like that, to hold a meeting of one. To anyone who has said to himself in a life-or-death emergency, 'I must pull myself together and face this', it is such a pulling together. For the man of responsibility it is, as it were, to follow that responsibility down to its ultimate roots in the depths of his physical and moral being. It is the deep convulsive breath with which, in an agony of fear, we seek and find ourselves. And the injunction that goes with this is, pray; especially that form of prayer which consists in a wordless, imageless, lifting of the soul—the 'naked intent directed unto God' as *The Cloud of Unknowing* puts it. For it is by this means that the 'different spiritual dimension' becomes manifest, interpenetrating and transcending the space-time cause-effect world in which our bodies exist.

Especially is it necessary to centre and to pray in the 'Infirm glory of the positive hour'. In disaster one naturally has recourse to these means. In success it is otherwise: and success, notoriously, can be far more dangerous than disaster. And not in a time of outward success only but also, and particularly, of inward success, is it necessary to 'give the glory to God'. Whenever we feel we have come through to something vital, made a drawing from the unconscious that is revealing, seen for the first time what we have been getting wrong, traced down what it was that has been separating us from those we love, that is the time to centre and pray. For it is then that inflation threatens; and the unclean spirit gathers his seven companions for the counter-attack.

Above all is it vital to centre and pray whenever, as from time to time will happen, the whole pattern of life breaks up: sometimes the outer life, sometimes the inner life, sometimes both at once. Then a man is in mortal peril: and the further he has gone in the experiment, the greater the danger. In such straits it is well to remember that individuation necessarily consists of such periods of flux: that for the wider integration to be made, some measure of disintegration is essential. But intellectual considerations at such a time mean relatively little. What is needed is that the integrative and consolidating process shall come into operation no less swiftly and no less powerfully than the disintegrative. And for this, centre and pray, *descendite ut ascendatis*, is the effective means.

Realization

Throughout the experiment, the hardest thing of all is to be fully aware of what is happening, to realize that action taking place the

other side of consciousness is real. For most people the forces at work
in the depths of the psyche seem somehow devoid of substance.
While they are operating they are real enough. They can make or
break our lives. But afterwards it is as if the whole thing was a
dream, something that took place in another existence, happened to
another person, perhaps never really occurred at all.

Actually, once Jung's discoveries are seen in their necessary perspective, there is nothing outlandish about them. On the contrary,
the situation they reveal is relatively simple—things we have half-
known about ourselves all the time, which now begin to fall into
place. There is, to begin with, the 'twisting together' of psychic
contents we call the ego, the complex of consciousness. Along with
this, there are a number of other 'twistings together'; not only the
complexes of the personal unconscious but the shadow, the anima-
animus and the other archetypal images. There is the saving fact of
the deep centre, the seed of the real person, around which these
scattered parts of the Self may be integrated. There is the saving fact
of the MORE, the creative process at work in the depths by which this
integration may be brought about. By becoming increasingly aware
of the situation the other side of consciousness, and working along
with it instead of at cross purposes, the whole spirit forms. But for
this to happen, there must be adequate realization. Nothing is more
necessary than to understand, not with the head only but through
and through, that happenings the other side of consciousness which
shake us to the core, reduce us to utter helplessness, lead us to act in
a manner completely unlike ourselves; experiences enabling us to
stand up against disaster, helping us to hold to a course however
hard, experiences bringing with them a flood of creative energy, are
real; and not real in some dubious or qualified sense, but real in
their very essence.

In this effort of realization, the present sophisticated age is at a
considerable disadvantage compared with earlier times. Men of the
classical period peopled the mountain tops with gods; while every
meadow, fountain, grove and stream had its attendant nymphs and
dryads, satyrs and fauns. During the Middle Ages miracles were
everywhere, angels and devils rubbed elbows with man. As methods
of realization these were far from ideal. To our modern eyes they
appear as so much childish superstition. But by concretizing the
world invisible they gave it a certain reality.

We of the so-called age of reason have no such recourse. With us, it has been well said, the gods have become neuroses: personal neuroses, national neuroses, racial neuroses, ideological neuroses. To get beyond these destructive half-gods we have need of that quality of spirit the Greeks called *pistis*, faith: not faith according to the schoolboy definition—'believing what isn't true'—but the faith that is loyalty, loyalty to the experience, intellectual integrity in its fullest sense; the refusal to throw out and forget the 'queer' thing because it does not happen to fit in with our stereotyped categories; the courage and determination to be true to the facts. Unless there is this loyalty, experience the other side of consciousness cannot be held.

And joined with *pistis* there must be decision, commitment, or, as it was formerly called, dedication. The only fully effective means of realization is the return, the creative contact carried over into the outer world. This is in no way to commend the tendency to 'cry out from the housetops' which comes upon some people the moment the forces of the deep unconscious are encountered, before anything about them is truly understood. Still less is it to advocate the false return, substituting action in the outer world for the 'inward transforming experience'. But where the withdrawal is carried through to the return, according to a man's own unique pattern of growth, then there is realization properly so called. The Self, formerly little more than a theoretical concept, becomes a being operating in its own right. The experiment in depth ceases to be an experiment and becomes life.

XII

THE RETURN

'Great truths do not take hold of the hearts of the masses. And now as all the world is in error, how shall I, though I know the true path, how shall I guide? If I know that I cannot succeed and yet try to force success, this would be but another source of error. Better then to desist and strive no more. But if I do not strive, who will?'—Chuang-tse. Fourth century B.C.

As in the time of Chuang-tse, so today, there is no prescription for making the return. By some means the reality of the world invisible has to be conveyed into the world of here and now. So much is evident. But what these means may be is far from evident. The totalitarian ideologies can prescribe categorically what is to be believed and what is to be done. It is the greatness and the anguish of the free way of life that men must forever discover and rediscover for themselves how the creative purpose at work in the depths can, in their day and age, come into being.

For this reason, both the way in which any particular man or woman should make the return, and the way in which the return as a whole is to be made, are matters on which nothing definite can be said. The creative process takes its own course. If it did otherwise it would not be creative. On the other hand, there are two basic data of which something can be said. Necessarily, we start from where we are, the time of troubles in which the world is now caught. And, although the creative process is itself inscrutable, it may be that something can already be distinguished of the vision emerging from the depths. Wherever men such as Jung, Eliot and Toynbee are engaged in making the withdrawal-and-return, the direction of their effort affords possible guidance. To this extent, accordingly, while the detailed course of the return cannot be plotted, certain of its broad lines may, nevertheless, be partially discerned; and, within this wider pattern, each man or woman see more clearly his or her own individual part.

Our present time of troubles has not come upon us by accident, nor is it a matter of the last few decades. For some centuries now the free way of life has suffered an invisible seepage: of meaning, of values, of vitality. In the circumstances it could hardly be otherwise. There is a fundamental split in the foundations of the free world. Ever since the faith of the Middle Ages fell away under the pressure of the new learning of the Renaissance, Western civilization has been divided between two versions of truth: the 'truth' of science and the 'truth' of religion; science dealing essentially with this side of consciousness; religion dealing essentially with the other side of consciousness; science essentially factual and inductive; religion essentially intuitive and deductive; each substantially right in its own sphere; each substantially wrong in the sphere it has failed to understand; each in its own way vital to the life of man; each, openly or covertly, undermining the other. *Magna est veritas et praevalebit:* but when truth is divided against itself, what then?

The answer to this question the present age has shown. So long as the institutions, habits and traditions of the free way of life remain substantially unimpaired, the free way of life continues, even though the creative spirit no longer animates it as before. But where the free way of life never had much hold, and when such hold as there was is shattered by disaster, men crave certainty. Totalitarianism supplies that certainty. Totalitarian ideology—Communist, Fascist, Nazi or other—makes its own characteristic synthesis of science and religion. With absolute assurance, backed by an imposing *mystique* which only the specially enlightened Party Member can expound and interpret, it declares itself the one true science and the one true faith. As such, it is the heir and instrument of a great historical imperative. To achieve universal well-being, total power must be given over to a Leader and a Party obeying that imperative. They alone can conduct mankind to the ideal society of the future. This is the totalitarian truth; not divided as truth is divided in the free world, but absolute in word and deed. A man has only to believe. The totalitarian technique of disintegration does the rest. And in little over thirty years it has conquered a third of mankind.

Meanwhile, science has discovered, and is now perfecting, the means of mass destruction. This discovery can be of immense service to the peoples of the world. Rightly controlled, it can eliminate war. In much the same way as, at the end of the feudal era, the King's artillery park could batter down the castles of the barons, and so made possible the King's peace, the atomic weapon can make possible the peoples' peace. But it can also be the most disastrous of inventions that ever afflicted mankind. There is no question that, against all-out atomic warfare, the only defence is attack. There is likewise no question what this is likely to mean when such war is waged on a world scale: the death of many millions of the civilian population—men, women and children—by direct obliteration, the slow agony and death of many millions more from the after-effects. If the threat were coming to us from another, enemy planet, the common danger would unite mankind. As it is, the enemy is in ourselves: and until we learn to deal with that enemy, the hydrogen bomb—or worse—hangs over all our heads.

Such, in broad outline, is the human situation in the present age: a world divided against itself, both sides piling up the means of mutual annihilation. The free peoples at present pin their faith upon the possibility of finding some basis of peaceful co-existence, an agreement to live and let live. But this is to ignore the very nature of our time of troubles. Mankind is divided not only politically but morally. There is no possibility of a valid agreement because, with a totalitarian power, no valid agreement can be made. Fascist, Nazi and Communist doctrine on this point are at one. Totalitarian morality does not provide for the keeping of agreements. On the contrary, it is totalitarian morality to make agreements whenever this seems advantageous, and to break them for the same reason. This is not duplicity. It is another kind of morality: a morality which places first not truthfulness, honour, good faith, or any of the old-fashioned virtues, but the advancement of the Party. The totalitarian who kept an agreement when it would advantage the Party better to break it, would be a bad totalitarian. To a problem such as this, there can be no effective solution on the political plane alone. The totalitarian technique has first to be combated in the realm of the spirit.

And there is a still more cogent reason why political action is not enough. What the free peoples seek above all is a world in which there are adequate safeguards against wanton aggression. These safeguards are now technically possible: but there is no will to apply them. The last thing on earth the totalitarian powers can stand is peace. For peace would mean they could no longer project the shadow. And if that came about, the totalitarian technique, together with the whole political structure built upon it, would collapse.

The way of freedom

It is becoming increasingly clear that, in totalitarianism, the world has come upon its insoluble problem, the problem on which we have to solve ourselves or go under in the struggle. Manifestly, what is needed is the true wholeness, of which totalitarianism is no more than the fraudulent pretence. For this, we have to rediscover the creative contact, find again the living source.

The free peoples, as they at present stand, are ill equipped for such an enterprise. The faith that once animated them has become, for the great majority, little more than a form. As Nietzsche put it: 'God is dead.' Nietzsche was mistaken in his diagnosis. It is not God who is dead. It is we who are only half alive. But the effect is essentially the same. We are cut off.

Looking back over the last few hundred years it is not difficult to see how the rift between science and religion brought this about. So long as man remained in a state of childlike acceptance he could, in a fashion, span the two worlds. The peoples of the Middle Ages who built the cathedrals to the glory of God, who partook of the Holy Sacrament firm in the belief that it was the body of the Saviour of mankind that they received, who knew that God spoke to men in the person of His holy saints, could make at least some approximation to the creative contact and, in their way, live life whole. But when, with the growth of science, the enquiring spirit of man took to investigating natural phenomena, the *sancta simplicitas* was shattered. Primitive myths of the creation and similar matters, which the medieval mind had taken literally, one by one were proved to be untenable. The process of enlightenment was necessary and inevitable: but the outcome was disastrous. Naïve credulity and true faith went down together. To some extent the usages of religion continued. Behind them (as men dimly recognized) there was still the life. But they were no longer effective. The myth alone no longer served. In a scientific age the creative contact needed to be set upon a scientific basis.

Already in the fourteenth century the possibility of applying the experimental method to both sides of consciousness had been perceived. It has been said of Roger Bacon:

> 'His serious theory is that all certain knowledge is experimental, but experiment is of two kinds, experiment made on external nature, the source of certainty in natural science, and experimental acquaintance with the work of the Holy Spirit within the soul, the source of the knowledge of heavenly things which culminates in the vision of God.' [1]

But this possibility was not pursued. Instead, by means of science, we came to know more and more about the outward world, and in so doing became conditioned into believing that only the outward was real. As a consequence, in this mid-twentieth century, we are, at one and the same time, well on our way towards mastering our material environment and in imminent danger of destroying ourselves. Science gives us the tools of freedom, but we have no answer to the question 'Freedom for what?' Cut off from the creative power, life becomes not only meaningless but self-destructive. It is to such a world that the return has to be made.

The men of the Middle Ages had little science and little freedom, but they had an idea of what life was about. Thomas Aquinas sums it up in a memorable phrase: 'To know the truth about God and to live in communities.' Since then, 'in an age which advances progressively backwards', the purpose of freedom has receded ever further out of sight. By the nineteenth century it had become 'progress', an optimistic belief that if each man pursued unremittingly his own self-interest he would thereby serve the common weal. But instead of leading to a utilitarian paradise, 'progress' led to the era of world wars, to the spreading virus of totalitarianism and, in the freedom-loving countries, to the waste land: the do-as-you-like decadents; the disillusioned and embittered, who just 'give up'; youth without standards; individualists turned totalitarian in their eagerness to beat totalitarianism; devotees of the bitch-goddess, success; above all, in their millions, the peaceable and apathetic,

[1] A. E. Taylor: 'Ancient and Medieval Philosophy' in *European Civilization*, edited by Edward Eyre, Vol. 3, p. 827.

> *. . . decent godless people:*
> *Their only monument the asphalt road*
> *And a thousand lost golf balls.*

We are now passing beyond that stage. The withdrawal-and-return has begun and it is already possible to see something of the course it is taking. Jung, Eliot and Toynbee reach much the same conclusion on the purpose of freedom as did Thomas Aquinas: 'To know the truth about God and to live in communities.' But the approach is different. Those now making the return bring with them an added insight, age-old in form but new in effect. They affirm that, for a man to know 'the truth about God' it is necessary for him to make the discovery of his own inmost being. To become at one with God a man must become at one with himself. Jung's constructive technique, Eliot's 'intolerable wrestle with words and meanings', Toynbee's search of history for the true return, all arrive at substantially the same conclusion: by facing inward and finding himself, a man may again find and make the creative contact; by turning outward and truly becoming himself, a man grows whole in action and the world grows whole through the creative power thus channelled into being. The truth about God becomes not a matter of belief only, but of direct, practical, concrete experience. Where this is the way of life, freedom no longer loses itself in emptiness and futility. The answer to the question 'Freedom for what?' is the coming of the Kingdom: the Kingdom of Heaven within a man, his depths, his integrity, his inmost truth; the Kingdom of Heaven between and among men, where depth answers to depth in fellowship; the Kingdom that is the different spiritual dimension, interpenetrating and renewing the life of the world; the Kingdom beyond the life of the world, transcending death. And this not as some far-off ideal, a quixotic Utopia never to be achieved, but a present Kingdom wherever men set themselves to discover it.

Such would seem to be the broad direction of the withdrawal-and-return, so far as it can be discerned at the present time. For individual men and women the way is clear. To the utmost of their capacity they seek the coming of the Kingdom, in their own lives and in the life of the world. But can this insight go beyond the individual life? Does it carry over to the formation of a creative minority? Is the experiment in depth a possible way through in our present time of troubles?

To questions such as these there is, of course, no assured answer. We have to face the fact that we are all more or less infected by the totalitarian virus. And there is the immense force of inertia, the tendency to continue as we have always done because we have always done it. But there are four notable possibilities implicit in the present situation which, together, may prove sufficient to turn the scale.

First, there is the change wrought in the outlook of the free peoples by their experience of totalitarian methods. Events of the present century—world wars, concentration camps, 'mind-washing', mass destruction—have made us aware, as nothing else could, of the reality of evil. We have learned (and may have occasion to learn yet more fully) that, taking mankind as a whole, 'there is *something wrong about us* as we naturally stand'. This is the possible beginning of the withdrawal-and-return; the realization that we are living, not with Utopia just round the corner, but in the City of Destruction, the city doomed to be destroyed by fire.

Second, there is the special character of the constructive technique. It is not the all-too-familiar latest novelty in philosophy or religion. It is a means of bringing into operation certain inherent capacities of man at present virtually unused—the inward eye, the inward ear, the inward understanding—capacities giving direct access to the realm of experience the other side of consciousness. What is more, the constructive technique is communicable. No human being can impart to another the force and reality of the creative contact. But it is possible to communicate the methods by which the creative contact can be made. And it is open to anyone to use these methods. No prior permission is required. International agreement, government action, official sanction and the like are none of them necessary. Given the will to undertake the withdrawal-and-return each of us has the means. If we are truly free men, responsible and responsive (as distinct from parasites upon the free way of life) we can do it.

Third, there is the possibility of placing this whole field of experience upon a scientific basis. In the past, science was forced to destroy the mythical concepts and terminology in which the religious insights of mankind were expressed. It has now the opportunity of rediscovering the reality behind these myths. If and when the creative contact can be set before all men in all lands as an empirically established psychological fact; a fact that it would be as absurd to ignore as it would be to ignore everything we know about health and disease; a fact going to the very root of personal well-being and, at the same time, underlying the life-or-death problem of our age: then a new situation arises. The creative contact becomes not a matter of conflicting dogmas but of scientific knowledge. In such conditions, the progressive extension of technology, instead of destroying the age-old beliefs and putting nothing adequate in their place, carries with it a developing fund of spiritual discovery, as much a part of the scientific heritage of mankind as technology itself.

Finally, there is the latent creative element in totalitarianism. As an essential part of its political action, the totalitarian technique invokes the archetypal forces. It arouses in men the religious spirit, the spirit of self-abnegation, the spirit of sacrifice. In this it goes clear beyond the ego-centred life. Admittedly, it invokes these forces in their demonic and disintegrative aspect, for purposes of domination and power. But, rightly taken, the archetypes are part of the wholeness of man, a step towards the creative contact we have lost. All un-wittingly, totalitarianism brings in the 'different spiritual dimension'.

The full consequences of this have yet to appear. So long as the ego-centred life is all the free world has to offer, totalitarianism shines in contrast wherever men are poor and oppressed. But if once the creative contact were being made by the free peoples, it is not among the free peoples only that the effect would be felt. Truth, undivided, spreads. Wherever there are human beings, the experiment in depth can be made. No frontier guard can arrest the movement of the spirit. Nor can the secret police track down the inward activity—until it is too late. Behind the Iron Curtain a creative minority could come into existence, of which there is no mention in the Marxist textbooks. And, in a fashion unforeseen by its prophets, the totalitarian state could, in truth, 'wither away'.

These, then, are the potentialities inherent in the present situation. But they are no more than potentialities. The question is whether and how they can be made effective. And here it is necessary to recognize the central difficulty. It is nobody's business to do this. When the possibility of nuclear fission first appeared above the scientific horizon, Governments could direct whole armies of special-ists and technicians to explore this new means of power. No Govern-ment can hire experts to make the experiment in depth. Either the responsible people of the world do it—on their own initiative—or it is not done. At a time when it seemed as if the individual citizen were becoming little more than a statistical unit in the modern mass state, it is upon the individual citizen that everything now depends.

The creative minority

By what means a creative minority can come into being in this present day and age is something of which we have no direct knowledge. But this much is evident. There are certain segments of the world community who, by their special position or special abilities, are capable of rendering extraordinary service: none more than the men of science.

By 'men of science' I do not mean professional scientists only, but all those devoted to the discovery of truth by objective enquiry; and not solely the physical scientists, but also, and especially, the social scientists. For the first time in human history it is feasible to apply scientific method to the data arising the other side of consciousness. The constructive technique renders possible the collection of a sufficient volume and variety of data to be significant. By applying the technique oneself it is possible to develop the understanding and discernment required to handle these data. In the hypotheses of James and of Jung there already exists a tentative analysis of the regularities and sequences observed. What is now necessary is that these hypotheses should be put to the test.

The men of science, above all, are fitted to do this. They are safeguarded against the dangers of the way by their intellectual integrity and scientific detachment. They are practised in the experimental approach, trained to patient and unbiassed observation, habituated to the sorting out of true from false, skilled in the progressive verification of hypotheses by repeated reference to the facts. In the last analysis, it rests with them whether the constructive technique remains, for many centuries, perhaps, little more than an esoteric curiosity or whether it is made available now.

This is not to say that the witness of the men of science will be perfect. In dealing with the effects coming from the other side of consciousness there can be no such thing as the controlled experiment, or any other of the usual devices by which human fallibility is kept in check. Only the comparative method is available: the collection, comparison, funding, revising of the largest possible volume of the most trustworthy experience to be had. This is the slowest and least sure of methods. But it is a matter of learning what we can, where we can, as best we can. With each increment of empirically based knowledge, to such extent we emerge from our present ignorance. That the knowledge so gained may never be complete, or completely accurate, does not prevent it from being by far the most vital knowledge in the world.

No less essential to a creative minority than the men of science is the man of faith. It is he who can help others to find the way. As it at present stands, the experiment in depth is for the few only. It is too arduous, too dangerous, too demanding, for the great majority of people to undertake. Later, when the inward journey has been better charted, it may be otherwise. But so far as the present generation is concerned, if the creative contact is to become effective on a world scale, other means must be found.

It is here that the man of faith can render inestimable service. He has relatively little need of the experiment in depth on his own account. For him the symbols and practices of the confession to which he belongs still hold the life. But by entering into the fire of the individuation process, he can make these symbols live for others also, others for whom the traditional forms of established religion are now dead. For he then speaks not from belief only but from experience. And when this happens the age-old symbols become new.

In so doing, moreover, the man of faith draws the religions of the world together. Varied as these religions are, behind them all is the same fire. And experience of the fire, though it speaks with many tongues, carries the same message. Toynbee, in his study of civilizations, looks to a Universal Church as the ultimate unifying factor in the world. So far as can be humanly perceived, it depends upon the man of faith whether the Universal Church of the future is the church of the Whole Spirit or the church of the Total State.

The men of science and the man of faith have thus their special spheres of action. But they alone cannot do the great work. The creative minority, if it is to be effective, needs to penetrate every sphere of human existence. It is not only upon the responsible men of science and the responsible men of faith that the ultimate issue depends, but upon the responsible men and women in all walks of life: the teachers, doctors, industrialists, housewives, nurses, bank-clerks, miners, drivers, seamen, farmers, civil servants, engineers and a hundred others. They alone can change the values, the practices, the institutions by which we live: and it is by deeds, much more than by words, that the great majority of the peoples of the world will be reached.

Especially is this true in one crucial sphere of action: the trans-mission of values. The totalitarian values can be, and are being, transmitted from one generation to the next. The free peoples are transmitting to their children, and to their children's children, little beyond their own bewilderment and uncertainty. In this we are failing in the most fundamental of all human responsibilities. As matters stand, the coming generations in the free countries are being thrust defenceless into the life-or-death struggle of the cold war. Their parents strive to give them the best start in life they can afford. But the thing that most counts—the creative contact—they cannot trans-mit, because they have not got it themselves.

Education, properly so called, is at the very heart of the return: and not the education of children only but, no less essential, the self-education of adults. Here, as in much else to do with the withdrawal-and-return, it is women who are in the key position. It is they who, as mothers and teachers, bear chief responsibility for the conditioning of the successive generations during the crucial years of infancy and of childhood. It is they who, with their gift of *eros*, can form and foster the working groups, the essential instrument of self-education. And it is women who hold the gates of love. Love misused is among the most destructive of forces. Love that is the drawing to wholeness is the essential motive power in the experiment in depth. This is not to say that women are free from the dangers of the deep unconscious. On the contrary, they are especially vulnerable in everything that requires discrimination, above all in the emergence from the *partici-pation mystique*. But in dealing with the other side of consciousness they have a courage, a readiness and an aptitude beyond that of men. If they can measure up to it, women have the means of renewing the world in the only way the world can be renewed—by the finding and transmitting of the inner life.

Such is the experiment in depth, as it goes over from the withdrawal to the return. Whether the present time is ripe for the emergence of a creative minority no man can prophesy. It may be that only after a Dark Age of unimaginable horror, possibly a long succession of Dark Ages, can the creative contact be found on a world scale. Or it may be that we are nearer to the break-through than we could dare hope. Whatever the event, so far as can be judged at present, these things hold. The realm of spiritual being of which the religions have spoken is reality, not myth. There are now the means of making direct contact with that realm. These means are such that they can, within limits, be set upon a scientific basis. It is open to anyone, having the necessary steadfastness, to engage in this work.

Commitment

To those who decide to undertake the experiment in depth, dangerous and uncharted as it is, can any specific advice be given? Clearly, there is no universally valid instruction. The right course for one may be utterly wrong for another. In the end, everyone has to find his or her own way. But something can perhaps be said on how, in the initial stages, the experiment may be set up.

Speaking by analogy, and in the most general terms, making the inward journey is like climbing in the high mountains. For this, one needs to rope up with others. Alone, without a working group, no one can go far. To seek to do so is to court disaster. Nor should everything be attempted at once. The newcomer needs to get into training, exercise his climbing muscles, become accustomed to the altitude. And he must not be ashamed to learn; as a man setting out to scale mountains learns all he can of routes and approaches, snow-craft and rockcraft, ice and wind and weather.

Beyond these generalities, there is a certain amount of detailed advice. It is highly desirable, though not essential, that one or two of the working group should already have gone some way in the experiment. To have the equivalent of an experienced first man on the rope can be very useful at the difficult places. It is likewise highly desirable—yet again, not essential—to have a balance of men and women in the group. But a working group which is predominantly women, or predominantly men, can still make good headway, provided the *logos* element, or the *eros* element, as the case may be, is not altogether absent.

Such a group can usefully begin by taking some book bearing

upon the experiment and discussing it thoroughly among them-selves: James' *The Varieties of Religious Experience*, Jung's *Two Essays on Analytical Psychology*, Toynbee's *A Study of History*, Eliot's *Four Quartets*, the *Journal of George Fox*, or whatever else may seem to them appropriate. The point of the discussion—and it is highly important that the discussion should have a point and not range in every direction—is what light this book throws on the experiment as a practical human undertaking. Throughout recorded time there has been the recurring evidence that it is possible to break through to a different realm of being: where the truth experienced is a deeper truth; where the love experienced is a deeper love; where the creative process is not a theory of what may be going on in the universe but an immediately experienced reality; where personality is not the scattered, fragmentary ego-consciousness we know, but a living in depth, the direct discovery of the 'different spiritual dimension'. What is to be our considered judgement on this? Is it no more than wishful thinking? Or is it, perhaps, the meaning of life?

For most people, some such initial discussion is a necessary first stage. By this means the group builds up its own inner coherence. Each individual is given the opportunity, moreover, to find out whether this is something he himself really wants to do. In making the inward journey there is no place for passengers. As part of such preliminary training the members of the group will probably find it useful to work out their psychological compass-bearings as they go along—extraversion, introversion, and the four functions: and not be too discouraged if, for some, this first attempt to distinguish psychological types proves to be more difficult than they expected.

Those who, as an outcome, feel they are ready to go further, would do well to start recording their dreams. Most people will probably discover that it is not appropriate to spend a great deal of time attempting to analyse each dream as it comes. Especially is it inadvisable to seek to make something out of a dream by more or less forcing interpretations upon it. The value of recording at this stage is twofold. First, as a consequence of the serious attention thus shown to the working of the unconscious, there will normally be an increase (qualitative as well as quantitative) in the flow of material. Second, when a sequence of some dozen, score, or fifty dreams has been built up, a quiet week-end spent in going over them carefully may reveal much of interest not previously apparent. In considering such a dream sequence, concentrate especially upon the positive elements, the helpful figures, the transforming symbols, however insignificant they may appear. By their means the first constructive contact between consciousness and the unconscious may be made.

Around this stage, a decision has sooner or later to be reached: and it is well to reach it consciously. Is one going to commit oneself to the mountain, or turn back and give up the quest? It is, of course, possible to go on circling the foot-hills interminably: but not to much point. If the decision is for commitment, then these three things may be worth trying.

First, get what hints you can from someone who has already gone some distance. Do not simply accept what he says as gospel. Everyone, even the most expert, is having to learn as he goes. He may easily be mistaken. And, in any case, his way is not necessarily yours. But to exchange notes with someone further along the road is invaluable.

Second, as and when you are ready for it, try some variety of the Mt. Marcy technique: a night vigil in some place sufficiently remote —hill, mountain, moor, forest, headland, beach; a pilgrimage through the night, over un-peopled country, to some place that has meaning for you. Or a night watch, spent in your own room, carefully prepared so that you know what you are doing, perhaps with some few objects set out before you symbolizing crucial moments or representative periods of your life, can tell you much between dark and dawn. Whether in the vigil, or pilgrimage, or watch, you are specifically seeking the next step on your way, grappling with the 'insoluble problem', striving to straighten out and bring together the scattered threads of your life, or some other aim, is for you alone to decide. Or there may be no specific aim at all, simply an opening of oneself to what comes.

Third, as and when you detect suitable figures and/or material in your dreams, it would be well to try acquiring the other psycho-perceptive methods: active imagination; painting and drawing from the unconscious; the inward conversation. Above all, use these methods whenever, in dream or active imagination, either of the two great integrative factors appears: the Friend and the deep centre. If the Friend is constellated, get in touch with him or her by whatever means you can. If the deep centre, in any of its many forms, makes its appearance, hold on to it and do not let it go. Along with the working group, the Friend and the deep centre are the great safeguards.

A man or woman who adventures thus far will almost certainly have come upon the shadow, the anima-animus and the archetypal world generally. Sooner or later these figures are likely to become constellated, i.e. appear in a state where they can be directly reached. This is the perilous encounter, where dissociation, disintegration, threatens. It is also the great possibility, the necessary step towards wholeness. What needs to be done is, by holding to the deep centre and working with the Friend, to get these otherwise ambivalent and anarchic personalities organized into a team, the prototype of the Self. How this is to come about is for each to discover in his own way. The one thing certain is that, here as throughout, everything depends upon attitude. The man who is centred, in depth, can hold. The man who has remained at the ego level will discover what it means to be disrupted: and learn from experience that the deep centre is a saving fact. What hindrances and what help are likely to be encountered, only experience can show. For some, early conditioning, the complexes of the personal unconscious, may present special difficulties which will have to be dealt with as part of the process. For others, the MORE, reached by way of the deep centre, will prove a tower of strength, 'a very present help in time of trouble'; and, in the end, come to be seen, perhaps, as the be-all and end-all of the experiment. This one thing is especially to be remembered. Throughout the encounter with the archetypal world, it is essential to bear ever in mind that these powers need to be integrated into the Self, not the ego; the Self, of which ego-consciousness is no more than a small, though responsible, part. And, as always, the peril of inflation waits at every turn.

Those who thus pass to the stage of commitment do well to bring into operation an invaluable means of realizing, and progressively integrating, what they have encountered. Experience of the phenomena coming from the other side of consciousness goes by us like the wind. We feel it at the time, but afterwards it is as if it had never been. This experience can be held, and seen for what it is, only if record is made of it. One method, already suggested, is to keep a journal consistently day by day. Another method, whether done in conjunction with the journal or by itself, is to get on to paper what might, perhaps, be called the 'life pattern'.

By this I mean an attempt to see the course of the experiment *as a whole*, a summation of experience thus far. Some such questions as these will probably give the necessary framework. What things in my past life led to my undertaking the experiment in depth? By what steps did I come to acquire the psycho-perceptive methods? What has been my experience of the autonomous complexes (especially the Friend)? What has been my experience of the transforming symbols (especially the deep centre)? What has been my experience of the Self and the MORE? In what respects has the experiment changed my values, aims and action in the world? By answering these questions, to oneself, as exactly and impersonally as possible, and from time to time adding new sheets to the different sections as the life pattern develops, a realization comes of the 'inward transforming experience' such as can be had by no other means.

Finally, I would suggest that, in undertaking the experiment, it should be seen from the start not as a process of withdrawal but as a process of withdrawal-and-return. By this means (and no other, so far as I am aware) it becomes a balanced activity—balanced as between the inner and the outer life, balanced as between the individual and the collectivity, balanced as between eternity and time. In what manner the return itself is to be made is for each to discover in his own way. But there is one vital aspect of the return, growing directly out of the process of withdrawal as above described, in which everyone can engage.

Nothing is more necessary in the years immediately to come than that the experiment should be set upon a scientific basis. To this work, everyone can make his own unique contribution. By keeping records, by setting out his life-pattern as carefully and explicitly as possible, by linking up with others likewise making the experiment in the scientific spirit, a man not only helps himself to find that 'real being' he knows he has it in him to become, but helps to furnish the basic data on which all empirical work in this field ultimately depends. Insofar as this can be done on a sufficient scale, the route need no longer be guessed at, as at present. To some extent, at least, it can be charted.

Such are some of the methods, seemingly insignificant, by which those who undertake the experiment in depth may (as William James puts it) 'set their own internal attitude in certain appropriate ways'. What matters in the end, needless to say, is not the methods but the attitude behind them. If that is right, the methods work. If the attitude is wrong, methods are meaningless. The search is for the living God, the creative ground of all we are and can become. Only 'in spirit and in truth', the whole-hearted devotion fundamental both to religion and to science, can it be undertaken.

This is the essence of the matter. What we all tend to look for, of course, is some potent word, magic formula, master plan which will suddenly enlighten us and enable us to make life what we feel it ought to be. The nature of the process is not like that. The creative contact does not transform men into supermen. What it does do is to transform a man into himself; and in so doing enable him to make the direct contact with the MORE.

To be thus re-created a man must lay himself open to and trust the process. By that and no other means the experiment is made. This is not to say that he should be gullible or otherwise uncritical in his approach. On the contrary he needs to be at his very highest stretch of conscious awareness. But he must be committed to the creative life. How else could it be found?

And the need to find is not for ourselves only, but for all men in all lands. As matters at present stand the whole world is in imminent peril from the totalitarian technique: the peril from within even greater, perhaps, than the peril from without. The free peoples, because they are still free, have the means of making the withdrawal-and-return, of rediscovering the creative contact by rediscovering themselves. There can be no assurance that they will fully realize this peril or make use of these means. But if they do, a fundamental change can come over the world. At present the challenge of the cold war remains substantially unanswered. The free peoples offer the modern equivalent of bread and circuses—mediocrity, comfort, amusement, welfare; but no hint of greatness. The free way of life is still free, but it has lost the life.

The thesis of the experiment in depth is that this life can be re-covered, that the creative reality behind religion is there for the finding: and that by this means it is possible not so much to defeat, as to transcend, the totalitarian technique. A new instrument of discovery has become available. It is for us now to use it aright. When the peoples of the world come to know the 'truth about God', not by hearsay only but by direct encounter, the cold war can be won—for both sides. And with it that greater and more ancient war of which it is the counterpart, through the ages fought and refought, the upshot ever in doubt yet beyond doubt *'that as Mansoul should in time be suffered to be lost, so as certainly it should be recovered again'*. There is in this present age a possibility of greatness exceeding all that has gone before, the possibility that our time of troubles can become the timeless moment, the moment of vision and of commitment.

BIBLIOGRAPHICAL NOTE

I N the preceding pages I have, wherever practicable, avoided overburdening the text with references to sources. As indicated at the outset, the purpose is not to produce a scientific study of the phenomena under consideration but to communicate, so far as may be, an awareness of these phenomena and their possible relevance to the human situation. The same treatment would seem appropriate in regard to bibliography. To print a long list of books bearing upon these questions would not be of much help to the reader. On the other hand, a brief note of guidance to those who wish to follow up some of the directions indicated may be of service.

In regard to Jung's work, a collected edition is now in process of publication, by Routledge & Kegan Paul Ltd., in Great Britain, and by Pantheon Books Inc., in the United States. At the same time, the Bollingen Foundation, which is sponsoring this collected edition, is also issuing (through Pantheon Books Inc.) a series of volumes by other authors, bearing upon Jung's methods and discoveries. In addition to such published works, much of the most valuable material for adequate insight into analytical psychology is contained in unpublished or privately published notes, papers and pamphlets. The bodies having access to this material most easily available to the English-speaking reader include: the C. G. Jung Institute (Gemeinde-strasse 27, Zürich 32) in Switzerland; the Society of Analytical Psychology (25 Park Crescent, London, W.1), the Analytical Psychology Club (Hon. Sec., 16 Wedderburn Road, London, N.W.3), and the Guild of Pastoral Psychology (Hon. Sec., 113 Biddulph Mansions, Elgin Avenue, London, W.9) in England; the Medical Society of Analytical Psychology (Eastern Division: Hon. Sec., 115 East 82nd Street, New York 28; Western Division: Hon. Sec., 2206 Steiner Street, San Francisco 15, California), the Analytical Psychology Club of New York (Hon. Sec., 177 East 77th Street, New York 22), the Analytical Psychology Club of California (Hon. Sec., Box 124, Ross, California) and the Analytical Psychology Club of Los Angeles (Hon. Sec., 6521 West 5th Street, Los Angeles, California) in the United States (addresses as of September 1954).

In regard to Eliot's work—quotations from which appear throughout the body of the book—the publishers in Great Britain are Faber & Faber and in the United States, Harcourt, Brace & Howe. It would be invidious to attempt to list the numerous commentaries, interpretations, bibliographies, etc., that have so far appeared; but one work may be judged of special interest (Elizabeth Drew: *T. S. Eliot, the Design of his Poetry*) in that the relationship between Eliot's poetry and Jung's psychology is tentatively and most interestingly explored.

In regard to Toynbee's writings, the first six volumes of *A Study of History* (Oxford University Press) have been abridged in masterly fashion by D. C. Somervell into a single volume. This is admirable as an introduction. But, excellent as the Somervell volume unquestionably is, there are passages of great interest in the original work (as, for instance, the section on Challenge-and-Response in Vol. I) for which room could not be found in the abridgement. The reader especially interested in the world aspect of the experiment in depth does well, accordingly, to go also to the original; the more so in view of the publication of the final four volumes in the autumn of 1954.

Any attempt to give due recognition to the innumerable other works which have been directly or indirectly drawn upon would be completely vain. In a sense, all notable literature is an exercise upon the archetypal themes. Sometimes this is immediately apparent, as for instance in *The Tempest*, in Goethe's *Faust*, or in *Seven Pillars of Wisdom*; sometimes it is hidden, or appears in chaotic form, as in much work of the present time. One of the not inconsiderable by-products of the inward journey is that all great writing, all great art, shines with a new light. In this sense, the true bibliography of the experiment in depth is the whole creative product of mankind, past, present and to come.

Finally, I should like to express my profound gratitude to those who have permitted me to use excerpts from their personal experience; as also to those who have read the manuscript and, by their encouragement and constructive criticism, enabled it eventually to appear in published form. That they are here nameless renders my debt so much the greater and so much the more deeply felt.

INDEX

active imagination (*see also* visions),
57–63, 67, 146–56, 232, 261
Adler, Alfred, 6–8
Adler, Gerhard, 113
alchemists, alchemy, 10, 98–9, 132
amplification method, 39–56 *passim*
analytical psychology (*see also* Jung,
C. G.), 43
clubs and societies, 267–8
anima, 78–84, 86, 87, 88, 92, 96–8, 100,
102, 103, 121, 154, 167, 183, 186,
243, 246, 262
animus, 84–91, 92, 97, 100, 102, 103,
107, 167, 214, 243, 246, 262
anti-communism, 197
Aquinas, Thomas, 252–3
archetype(s) (*see also* autonomous complexes, shadow, anima, animus,
Wise Old Man, Great Mother,
Miraculous Child, *puer aeternus*,
hermaphrodite, hero-saviour), 92–
114 *passim*, 124, 162–3, 171, 190,
193, 216–17, 220, 231, 237, 238,
255, 262
individual experience of, 96, 97–8,
100, 102–3, 106, 107, 161
relationship with, 93–4, 97, 114,
167–9, 212, 215, 241–3
and the individuation process, 165–
166, 172, 177, 179, 215, 223–7, 241
archetypal objects (*see also* bull, circle,
city, clock, cross, deep centre,
diamond, gold, Holy Grail, horse,
jasper, key, kitchen, *mandala*, name,

rock, seed, snake, stone, sword,
tree), 108–13
archetypal themes, 98–9, 101–2, 104–
108, 182, 198
Aristotle, 18, 95, 142
Atman, 132, 141
atomic fission, 5, 203, 250, 255
attitude (*see also* realization, responsibility, symbol(s)), 9, 36–8, 43, 44–
45, 51, 91, 93, 120, 143–4, 155,
162–3, 179–80, 207, 210, 221–2,
232–4, 240, 262–4
Augustine, St., 173–4
autonomous complexes (*see also* arche-
type(s)), 71–108 *passim*, 162–3, 191,
200, 202, 215–17, 243, 263
auxiliary function, 23–35 *passim*

Bacon, Roger, 252
Bagehot, 218
Barabudur, 112
Barrie, J. M., 101
Bénoit, 80
Blake, William, 144
Bollingen Foundation, 102, 267
Breuer, Josef, 5
Brontë, Charlotte, 85–6
Brontë, Emily, 85
Bruegel, Pieter, 81
Buddha, Buddhism, 112, 150, 226, 232,
241
bull, 105–6, 108
Bunyan, John, 84–5, 228, 265

INDEX

INDEX